MORE THAN LIKELY

MORE THAN LIKELY

A MEMOIR

Dick Clement and Ian La Frenais

Illustrations by Clive Francis

WEIDENFELD & NICOLSON

First published in Great Britain in 2019 by Weidenfeld & Nicolson
an imprint of The Orion Publishing Group Ltd
Carmelite House, 50 Victoria Embankment
London EC4Y 0DZ

An Hachette UK Company

1 3 5 7 9 10 8 6 4 2

A CIP catalogue record for this book is
available from the British Library.

ISBN (hardback) 9781474611534
ISBN (ebook) 9781474611558
ISBN (paperback) 9781474611541

Typeset by Input Data Services Ltd, Somerset

Printed and bound in Great Britain by Clays Ltd, Elcograf S.p.A.

www.weidenfeldandnicolson.co.uk

For Doris, Michael, Sam and Chris – best fans ever.
For Paul Allen – who opened our eyes
Ian

For Nancy and my wonderful family
And for Walter, without whom none of this
might have happened.
Dick

CONTENTS

We have been storytellers almost all our adult lives, ever since an evening when we first scribbled lines together for a sketch in an Earls Court pub. It began a career that, amazingly, has lasted longer than Rodgers and Hammerstein, Gilbert and Sullivan, Laurel and Hardy, Morecambe and Wise, Rolls and Royce. The first characters we created that night were Bob and Terry, factory hands from the North East. When they returned in *Whatever Happened to the Likely Lads?* a few years later, our reputations were secured. Fletch, the wily recidivist doing his *Porridge* in Slade Prison, superbly portrayed by Ronnie Barker, made us famous; and the (mostly) Geordie brickies working the German building sites in Thatcher's Britain reminded viewers that we had not disappeared into the Hollywood Hills and were still firmly on the side of the have-nots.

Lovejoy gave us a global audience and the working-class musicians from Dublin's Northside who aspired to be *The Commitments* gave us Hollywood cred. In more recent years, the ageing rockers in *Still Crazy*, the teenager members of *The Rotter's Club*, the sixties dreamers of *Across the Universe* and David Tennant's war-weary Colonel in *Spies of Warsaw* reminded our friends, fans and followers that we had no intention of leaving the stage gracefully and learning to play golf.

Many of the people we encountered between the lines suggested or inspired these characters; many more, the actors, brought them to life and gave them depth and insight. To all of them, factual and fictional, we dedicate this book with respect, affection and immense gratitude.

FAQ # 1

'How Did You Two Meet?'

Dick & Ian

We're sometimes tempted to change the narrative. Here are three versions of the truth.

Version One: Summer in Spain – Dick

The summer was unusually hot. Time to get out of London, away from the Earls Court flat with no air conditioning. Jay Maw, a civil engineer I'd met in the RAF, owned a Ford Zephyr. Was it his idea to drive through France and reach Pamplona in Spain in time for the Festival of *San Fermín*? I can't remember but that's where I ended up with him and a couple of Canadians. Peter Dyer never said a lot but girls didn't seem to mind. Vic Lotto was tall with a shaggy, unkempt beard. The locals stared at him and thought he might be Castro or a cousin of his. We were never quite sure whether this was in our favour or not.

We had very little money and slept in a tiny tent that we pitched, inexpertly, next to a pelota court, the thwack of the balls waking us every morning. We bought *botas,* wine skins that you filled with local plonk then squirted down your throat. On meeting a stranger it was considered polite to offer him your *bota.* One Pamplonan offered us his in a spirit of Anglo-Spanish hospitality. Its leather was soft and well weathered from years of use and the wine didn't burn our throats. We passed it around and offered ours in a reciprocal gesture. We had bought it from a souvenir stand that week and it smelt like a biker's glove. Our new friend sampled the rotgut it contained, spat it out, hurled the *bota* to the ground and stormed off in disgust.

We were in a bar one night when Ernest Hemingway came in with a young man. He swayed a little as he introduced him to the entire room in a gravelly voice slurred with drink.

'This is the greatest bullfighter the world has ever seen.'

I know that sounds hard to believe and I've often doubted my own memory but I looked up the records and yes, he was there that year.

The Running of the Bulls involves young men running in front of cattle that are let loose on a course through a section of the town streets. Crowds throng the balconies waiting to see who gets gored or trampled. It sounds, and is, bloody dangerous. How did I let myself be talked into it? I had always hated running at the best of times. I wasn't especially fond of cows, let alone the male variety with lethal-looking horns.

I wasn't entirely sober but nor was anyone else. I had enough sense to make sure that I was way ahead of the pack of embryonic *toreadors* who wanted to be close enough to feel bull's breath on their necks.

Even so, I tripped and went sprawling in the gutter. I could hear the thunder of hooves behind me. A hand grabbed my collar and pulled me to the side of the road. The bulls thundered past, cheered by the crowd. I got to my feet and turned to see whom I had to thank.

He was dark-haired and shorter than me, though just as drunk. Like the rest of the crowd he was in a white T-shirt with a red bandana round his neck so I assumed he was a local. I stammered thanks:

'*Muchas gracias, amigo.*'

He replied in a strange accent that was totally foreign to my ears.

'Ah'm Ian.'

'You're Armenian?'

'No, pet, I'm from Newcastle.'

'Wherever. I can't thank you enough. You saved my life.'

'Think nuthin' of it. Fancy a bevvy?'

Version Two: Winter in Berlin – Ian

I was on my last term at Oxford. I would soon have a degree in English Literature and I was fluent in French and German, which meant I could either teach or be a tour guide. Then an elderly don arranged for me to have lunch with a man from London. Two weeks later it took place under glistening chandeliers in the gothic dining room of a gentlemen's club in St James's.

My host was a rumpled, rotund sixty-year-old who looked like he'd dressed in the dark, and his jacket pockets were stuffed with pens, handkerchief, pocket diary and pipe. He ordered for both of us from what must have been the School Dinners special: potted shrimps, shepherd's pie and bakewell tart with custard. He seemed offended when the waiter suggested a salad.

We talked about the state of the world, Britain's role in it and Britain's obligations – a phrase he used more than once. Then he said casually, 'If you do get in the game' and it was then that I realised I was being solicited by the British Secret Intelligence Service. My God! Was it the languages or my Rugby Blue?

He dusted pipe ash from his trousers and raised a hand to a hovering waiter.

'Well, young Ian, should we have the Stilton, it looks awfully good.'

I spent four months training in a country house in Surrey. I learned the vocabulary of a spy's tradecraft – the dead drops, the cut outs, the Joes and the lamplighters and how to follow someone and to know when I was being followed myself; I learned how to withstand torture (all of us knew none of us would) and how to use a miniature camera, decipher code and forge a passport. I also learned how to kill a man with my thumb against his windpipe. On our final practical exam I forgot it was a simulation and almost killed the instructor who was rushed to a hospital in Haslemere. I was abject but my other teachers seemed impressed.

Three months later I was posted to the British Embassy in Bonn under the guise of Assistant Cultural Attaché. My superior told me about one of our agents who had worked, at enormous risk, under various aliases as a spy in East Berlin, operating right under the ears and eyes of the Stasi, the dreaded Security Service of the German Democratic Republic. But there had been a couple of arrests, a killing, a disappearance, everything that pointed to a mole. He only gave me his code name – 'Westcliff'. It was time to bring our Joe in from the cold.

So off I went to Berlin, tasked with meeting Westcliff and the subsequent debrief. It was February when I landed and the air was as cold as flint. The lights of Templehof were a bright relief from the granite-grey gloom that shrouded the divided city.

My contact drove me to a safe house in Wilmersdorf in the British Sector after several detours to throw off any possible surveillance. It smelled of floor polish and stale air but it was too cold to open windows. In the kitchen some kind soul had left a bottle of schnapps in a cupboard and I poured it into my silver hip flask, a present from my father when I graduated from Oxford.

At seven I was driven to Checkpoint Charlie. Westcliff was scheduled to cross with the last busy flow of traffic sometime between eight and ten. The East German controls were about a hundred metres away. A few VoPos stood by an Opel Rekord, smoking and talking. Beyond them was the wall, the top a tangle of barbed wire. Intermittently a searchlight would arc its beam from the nearest watchtower across the damp, dark night.

The last stragglers crossed; two official looking cars and municipal workers who service both sides. Another hour and the phone rang: Control, asking for news. I could picture him alone in his office above Cambridge Circus, his sallow face bathed in the glow of his desk lamp, his scrawny fingers reaching for the packet of cigarettes that would inevitably kill him.

My spirits began to sink as the minutes ticked away. I thought about the man I was there to meet, about what it took to spend so much of life living with danger and risk.

'Something's up.'

It was the Sergeant, outside with binoculars raised to his face. I stepped out into the freezing February night and he handed them to me. A figure was in the guard's box at the other side, a document check no doubt. After several agonising moments the figure re-emerged and gripped the handlebars of a parked bicycle. He set off across the rain-slicked street towards us. Within moments I recognised him from the photographs I had been shown. It was Westcliff.

He mounted the bike and pedalled slowly. Halfway across he stopped and my heart did too. Had he heard a command? Would the light arc towards him and catch him, frozen, in its beam? Would I hear the rat-tat-tat of machine-gun fire? But all he did was bend over and remove his bicycle clips, a simple act of astonishing composure.

When he reached us I actually laughed with relief. He smiled in return and said:

'That was a bit dicey. Anyone got a drink?'

I handed him my flask and he took a grateful swig of the schnapps. I told him:

'I'm Ian La Frenais, and I'm delighted to welcome you.'

He capped the flask, handed it back to me and shook my offered hand. His grip was firm, his gaze unflinching.

'And I'm Dick,' he replied. 'Dick Clement.'

Version Three: Spring in Notting Hill

Ian moved from the North East to London, where he had few friends. One of them was called Mike Burrage, who was at the London School of Economics. He took Ian for a pint in the Uxbridge Arms, a small pub behind the Coronet Cinema in Notting Hill. There was someone there he already knew. He called him over.

'Dick, this is Ian.'

The Way It Was and the Way We Were

Dick & Ian

Dick: If you picked Notting Hill over Pamplona and Berlin, go to the top of the class. Though for the record, I did drive to Spain with Jay and my Canadian friends, it was definitely Hemingway who entered that bar and I did run with the bulls – for about eight seconds.

Ian: I remember you were the tallest person in the pub and you wore a long overcoat with a *Guardian* tucked in the pocket, which seemed to establish your credentials as someone much better informed than this Geordie down from 'the North'. When we left, you mounted a scooter and as you rode away, your silhouette reminded me of Monsieur Hulot.

Dick: It was a Lambretta. I have to admit it's impossible to look cool on a scooter unless you're in Rome and you have Audrey Hepburn on the pillion. I didn't. And I wore a helmet.

Ian: You were too tall to be a Mod and about five hundred cc's short of being a Rocker.

Dick: You were the first person from the North East I'd ever met, though within a few days I'd met two more, Maurice and Brian, the blokes whose flat you were crashing in. It was only a short walk from mine in Earls Court, known at the time as Kangaroo Valley as it was filled with Commonwealth students and backpackers.

Ian: My flat was next to an Indian restaurant and after midday the smell of vindaloo seeped through the walls. Maurice and Brian were older and more sensible than me, but they'd given up their jobs in the North East to pursue different things in London, which in the sixties would become the epicentre of the universe.

Dick: 'The Sixties' hadn't really kicked in when we met, had they? I don't think they did till '63 – the year the Beatles had their first two Number Ones. Mini Mokes, miniskirts, sexual liberation and psychedelia – that all came later. Our London was smoke-filled pubs, coffee houses, Wimpy Bars and cheap Chinese restaurants. There was theatre but most of the plays were about debutantes and we couldn't afford to go anyway.

Ian: The whole aesthetic was leftover Fifties. There were still duffel coats around. And corduroy. And short back and sides haircuts. The whole country was stable, predictable, deferential and dull. It was the England the Kinks missed so much in many of their songs – Sunday roasts, football matches, allotments and racing pigeons.

Dick: The Kinks came later too. The music at the time wasn't so brilliant. Cliff Richard, the Kingston Trio, Bobby Vee. Someone called Jess Conrad had a hit called 'My Pullover'. Can you believe that? And then the Twist came in.

Ian: I bet you couldn't do it. I bet you were hopeless.

Dick: I was. But according to David Bailey, so was Rudolf Nureyev.

Ian: Remember how cheap London was? You could be young and broke and live within half a mile of Buckingham Palace. I lived in Earls Court, then Knightsbridge and Chelsea but the only work I had was a part-time cleaner for an agency that employed out-of-work actors, musicians, parolees and misfits like me.

Dick: A cleaner? I've never seen that side of you. No one noticed that you're domestically impaired?

Ian: I got away with it for a while. Some of my clients were annoyed to find I wasn't an actor so I told them I was writing songs for Adam Faith. That seemed to mollify them. The first really famous person I met was Sir Francis Chichester, the first man to sail single-handed round the globe.

Dick: You kept his place shipshape, did you?

Ian: I must have done, Lady Chichester gave me a jar of paprika. And an elderly widow in St John's Wood always gave me a generous tip and a piece of cake because she thought I was a nice Jewish boy.

Dick: So you forgot to mention you were C of E?

Ian: I did, yes. It was a far cry from 'Swinging London'.

Dick: It all happened so fast. Within a couple of years there were a dozen or so Brits who were considered to be the most glamorous and interesting people on the planet: Shrimpton, Bailey, Twiggy, Vidal Sassoon, Mick and Marianne, Caine, Stamp and any given Beatle.

Ian: We read about them, glimpsed them, envied them and probably hated them. The Swinging Sixties was a very exclusive party for a handful of gifted and beautiful people.

Dick: You and I were definitely not on the guest list. We lived in a parallel universe and I was still riding that scooter.

Ian: At least you were riding it to the BBC. I was very impressed when I found out you worked there. I couldn't imagine how you got a job like that. I remember the first time I went to your office. You had a road map of Nigeria on the wall.

Dick: I was in the African section – a continent I'd never set foot in. It was part of the Overseas Service at Bush House. It gave me an excuse to interview Count Basie and Duke Ellington when they came to London. I didn't know if they were big in Ghana, Sierra Leone and Somalia but I wanted to meet them.

Ian: It was an amazing place, Bush House – all those different nationalities under one roof. You told me the Albanian broadcasters were reputed to be bandits. You could always spot them because they came downstairs taking advantage of the natural cover.

Dick: Their daily broadcast was preceded by a scratchy orchestral version of the Albanian national anthem. A habit developed among some of us studio managers over drinks in the bar. One of us would suddenly command: 'Gentlemen – the National Anthem!' We'd leap to our feet, stand to attention and sing it. Not the words of course, but we knew the tune by heart. Then years later we worked with a director called Stan Dragoti.

Ian: In St Tropez. We thought from his name he was Italian but he said, 'No, I'm Albanian.'

Dick: That's right. So I told him I could sing their national anthem. He didn't believe me. If I could he promised to buy me dinner at a restaurant of my choosing. I stood up and sang it lustily, startling waiters and guests and astounding Stan.

Ian: You were on shift work, which meant you were often free during the day, so you used to come round to my place, play cards and try to get used to the smell of curry. In all the time we lived there we never once ate at that restaurant. In fact we didn't eat at restaurants at all. We went to pubs. I didn't like the Earls Court pubs much, although they had one cool one, the Coleherne in the Old Brompton Road, which had jazz on Sunday mornings. It was a gay pub, the first I'd ever been in.

Dick: Weren't there any gay people in the North East?

Ian: It was rumoured but when I left there had been no official sightings.

Dick: Your mates Maurice and Brian used to have a regular spot on Tyne Tees Television where they sang satirical songs and topical calypsos. I was very impressed that they had been in 'Show Business'. I had some ambition of being an actor myself and was in the BBC's Ariel Players. They put on cabaret from time to time and a Christmas revue, so I asked them to do a number.

Ian: I had no performing talent to offer so I felt 'left out'. All of us had seen *Beyond the Fringe* and I knew that kind of content would be part of your show. I remember I went off to a bench in the square and scribbled down a sketch, a monologue about being an Angry Young Man. I was almost too embarrassed to submit it – but you picked it.

Dick: Then we wrote something for it together – a sketch crosscutting between two boys called Bob and Terry and the girls they'd just had a date with, having a post-mortem on the evening they'd spent together. We were inspired by *Saturday Night and Sunday Morning* and my performance was a strangulated impersonation of Albert Finney. So James Bolam did not originate the role of Terry Collier in *The Likely Lads*. I did.

Ian: The sketch got a lot of laughs and so did you. I just loved the whole thing. I'd never done amateur dramatics except for school productions of Gilbert and Sullivan. I was one of those paintings that come to life in *Ruddigore* and a Japanese maiden in *The Mikado*. I remember singing 'Braid the Raven Hair' with thick makeup trying to cover the black eye I'd received that day in the schoolyard.

Dick: If only we had the video.

Ian: It wouldn't have made any difference. Any time I was on a stage I always hid behind someone else. My mother always complained: 'We never saw you!'

Dick: I got engaged in '62 to Jenny Sheppard. Jenny was at the BBC too, working at Broadcasting House for intellectual poets like Louis MacNeice. Then the Cuban Missile Crisis happened. I remember overhearing some very posh people in a restaurant saying, 'Do you think this is "It"?' and another one saying, 'Yes, I think it very probably is.' And I thought, 'Do you mind, I'm about to get married.'

Ian: Which you did. And I wasn't your best man.

Dick: No but you were an usher. We moved out of Earls Court to a house on the other side of the park with a baby on the way.

Ian: I had to schlep all the way to Kentish Town in the coldest winter on record because we'd made a commitment to write at least one night a week.

Dick: At least it made a change from painting the nursery.

Ian: We wrote a play for television and called it *The One Most Likely*. It got turned down – but very nicely. I remember Peter Willes, the head of Yorkshire Television, said we had a natural ear for dialogue. But our big break came when you got on to a directing course.

Dick: Huw Weldon gave a brilliant lecture. He told us that it's impossible to teach anyone how to direct in three weeks, or longer for that matter. It is like theorising on how to ride a bicycle. Sooner or later you have to get up on the saddle and pedal. So at the end we were given a studio for a day, a small budget and encouraged to 'make something'. And I remembered the sketch we'd written for that revue two years before.

Ian: We expanded it to twenty minutes or so and you had the money to make it with real actors in real sets and even go on location – a pub in Holloway. While we were there, the Beatles were on TV at the Royal Command Performance and John Lennon told the audience in the posh seats to 'rattle your jewellery'.

Dick: Nobody saw the recording for quite a while. We thought it had sunk without trace until Dennis Main Wilson took an interest in it. Dennis had produced *The Goon Show* on radio and *Till Death Us Do Part* on television. He was a great enthusiast, always on the lookout for new talent. Marty Feldman walked into his office while he was screening my tape. He turned to Dennis and said: 'These are good writers. Have them put down.'

Ian: We couldn't believe it when it was commissioned as a series. We celebrated in a pub called The Shakespeare. It seemed appropriate. He was a writer too.

Dick: You would leave your day job and come over to my office in Television Centre. For the first few days we stared at each other waiting for the tea lady to show up with PG Tips and doughnuts. But somehow we got six scripts written.

Ian: We agreed later that we owed a debt to Richmal Crompton because we had both been avid readers of *William* books as kids. She was great with plots and one of the lessons we learned from her was that William didn't always have to win; a satisfying ending could go either way.

Dick: We stole from her shamelessly. I remember one of our early plots featured a mobile medical unit checking people for tuberculosis. Terry was trying to pull the radiologist but as he left the house he had a row with his sister Audrey and said: 'You won't half be sorry if I've got a spot on the lung!' That was pure *Just William*.

Ian: We wrote the last script of the series in two days. We've always found it's a good sign if a script comes quickly. If we struggle with one it's usually because there's something not quite right with it.

Dick: Once the scripts were written a director was assigned. And then the poor guy died! Several other names were put forward until Duncan Wood, responsible for *Steptoe and Son,* suggested they got the bloke who did the original pilot – not that I knew it was a 'pilot' at the time. I had zero experience, but how can you turn down an offer like that? What got me through was that I didn't know what I didn't know.

Ian: I remember sitting behind you in the gallery for the taping of the first episode of *The Likely Lads*.

Dick: When we got the first laugh, I looked around for your re-action and missed five shots. Fortunately the vision mixer kept doing his job. I might as well have gone home for all the use I was the rest of the evening, my brain frozen by every reaction of the studio audience.

Ian: I was so wound up I had a panic attack and had to be taken to the nurse.

Dick: Was she cute?

Ian: You're not allowed to ask things like that these days. She pre-scribed a glass of red wine.

Dick: And you've been following her advice ever since.

Ian: Much to our amazement, and the BBC's surprise, the series was a success. The funny thing is, I still clung to the day job until we'd written three series and a feature film.

Dick: That's because your mother's words still resonated in your head. You told me what she said when you announced that you wanted to be a writer: 'Writing's all very well, Ian, but it's what you do once you've settled into something worthwhile.'

'Do You See It as a Series?' – Dick
The Likely Lads

My early ambition to be an actor has not entirely gone away. I'm open to offers. My only professional performance to date was playing a BBC newsreader – not a big reach – on an episode of *Tracey Takes On* about the end of the world. I'm glad there were no cell phones in the Fifties: someone might have a record of my portrayal of Gloria Clandon in Shaw's *You Never Can Tell*. It astounds me that I can still remember the scene where she priggishly fends off advances from her suitor:

'That seems to be an attempt at a pretty speech, Mr Valentine. Let me say at once that pretty speeches make very sickly conversation. Pray let us be friends, if we are to be friends, in a sensible and wholesome way . . .'

I promise I didn't look it up. The words are lodged somewhere in what Clive James used to call my 'cauliflower-shaped tape-recorder'. My next role was Young Marlow in *She Stoops to Conquer*, still wearing a wig but at least this time without a frock. My moments in the school Dramatic Society were far more important than my A-levels in terms of the career I ended up pursuing. I did some more amateur acting during National Service in the RAF and afterwards when I joined the BBC as a studio manager.

I only remembered some years later that my even earlier ambition was to write. At the age of something like eight I scribbled down an episode of my favourite radio serial, *Paul Temple*. It was probably a bit short as it was only four pages long. I was fascinated by the spoken word, not prose. I'm in awe of people who write novels. I tried to put myself in the shoes of other people, especially the ones who are overlooked, like a soldier on guard or a footman standing motionless by the door while his 'betters' discussed their love lives or the future of Western civilisation. What were they thinking and who would they discuss it with when they got home? What a pity I didn't think of *Downton Abbey* first.

When I finally got into television I felt as if I'd come home. The timing was in my favour. BBC2 was about to be launched and slots needed filling. Michael Peacock, head of the new channel, saw my test piece and we were summoned to a meeting. After the opening exchanges he asked us the key question:

'Do you see it as a series?'

The thought had never crossed our minds but without hesitation we said, 'Absolutely'. I used the same word when I was asked if I wanted to direct the shows. Up to that point I had directed twenty-two minutes on five-camera tape – and I knew no professional actors at all.

I started poring through *Spotlight*. I was guided by nothing more than a gut instinct that told me that some actors looked as if they might be funny. I eliminated those who looked as if they could only be serious, romantic or menacing. I was also impressed if an actor had been in a movie. This brought me to James Bolam, who had been in *The Loneliness of the Long Distance Runner* and *A Kind of Loving* and to Rodney Bewes, who had played Arthur Crabtree in *Billy Liar*. We wanted to capture the gritty reality of those movies and transfer it to the small screen. We wanted the factory floor and houses with outside lavatories. These actors checked those boxes: Rodney was from Bingley in Yorkshire, Jimmy from Sunderland.

I sweated slightly more over the casting of Rodney because Brian Miller, who had played the part of Bob in my original test

piece, was extremely good. On the other hand, I must have done something right because the chemistry between Jimmy, as the more acerbic, working-class-and-proud-of-it Terry and Rodney, as the more reflective Bob with dreams-above-his-station, seemed to work right away when rehearsals began.

Jimmy treated his work with great seriousness. He had a great respect for 'the text', a word I'd previously only heard applied to Shakespeare. As a fledgling writer I found this flattering. He was fiercely self-critical, especially of anything too obvious, which he dismissed derisively as 'face-acting'. His relationship with Rodney in that first series was totally professional. I enjoyed the creative process of directing what we had written. If something sounded off-key or a piece of business fell flat, I didn't have to ask anyone's permission to change it.

On the other hand I knew nothing about lenses, lighting or anything technical. I was helped enormously by Syd Lotterby, who was given the job of my production assistant. Syd was far more experienced than me and might well have played the old soldier, folded his arms and watched me self-destruct. Instead he gave me a nudge here, a suggestion there and steered me away from the rocks. He even gave us our first 'script-notes', pointing out that we had missed some opportunities in an episode called 'The Other Side of the Fence'. He wasn't wrong and we improved it.

No one else was giving us notes, we were totally left to our own devices. None of the BBC brass came to any of the recordings. I was faintly hurt at the time. In hindsight I realise how lucky we were. Nowadays, 'notes from the Network' from a whole raft of executives can drive anyone crazy.

When the first episode was transmitted only a handful of households had BBC2. What pushed us into orbit was when we were asked to write a sketch for inclusion in *Christmas Night with the Stars*, seen by nineteen million as they digested their turkey and mince pies. They liked it and the series was repeated on BBC1.

Suddenly, Jimmy and Rodney were recognised on the street. Rodney enjoyed this taste of fame. Jimmy did not. He didn't want to be thought of as a 'Likely Lad'. This was a typical exchange if a friendly fan called out to him:

'Hey, Terry, where's your mate?'

'He's dead!'

We did another two series and decided that enough was enough. We wrote an episode called 'Goodbye to All That' in which Bob decides to broaden his horizons and join the army, much to Terry's scorn. After two weeks Terry realises he misses his mate and signs on himself. Do you need a Spoiler Alert? When he gets off the train to report for duty, he finds Bob is going home because of flat feet. Jimmy and Rodney loved the way we had written them out of our lives. We said goodbye to each other and went our separate ways.

Six years went by. Ian and I came back from separate summer

holidays and found that similar thoughts had been bubbling through our brains: what had happened to Bob and Terry? After all, the changes in a young man's life between nineteen and twenty-five are profound, more often than not including marriage. Moreover, Terry was due to come out of the army. What would he find in his hometown when he returned? After all, he'd been stationed overseas, out of the loop. He felt it bitterly:

'I missed it all. Swinging Britain was just hearsay to me. The death of censorship. The new morality. *Oh! Calcutta!* Topless waitresses. See-through knickers.'

Bob was happy to be his guide, explaining that hair was longer, trousers flared and it was now Zeppelin on the stereo, not the Beatles.

In the intervening years Rodney had written, created and starred in a show called *Dear Mother . . . Love, Albert*. He had four series behind him already and to play Bob Ferris again he would have to turn his back on another. The effect of all this was that he now regarded himself as a star. He's not the only actor who has gone through a silly period like that and he won't be the last. He was in a play a few years later with Brigit Forsyth and she told me he was so exasperating that one night she tried to strangle him.

'*It wasn't the thought of going to prison that stopped me, it was simply that I didn't have the strength to finish him off.*'

We were fairly sure that we could talk Rodney round. Jimmy was another matter. We took him to an Italian restaurant on the Kings Road. After the preamble we put our proposal on the table. His mouth tightened.

'Not with Rodney Bewes, no.'

It wasn't a promising beginning. We poured more red wine and started to tell him what had happened to Terry Collier since we had last seen him. We told him about coming home just in time for Bob's wedding to Thelma Chambers and his own failed marriage to a German girl, not to be revealed until Episode Three. He started to laugh. He might not have seen 'the text' yet, but Jimmy knew a good plot when he heard one. By the time we got to the sambuca, he was hooked.

They had very different personalities. Rodney could be gullible. Jimmy was wary, ever looking for ulterior motives. Tears came easily to Rodney. Jimmy didn't have an ounce of sentimentality. Unsurprisingly they had flare-ups. The general view about the new series, *Whatever Happened to the Likely Lads?*, was that it was better than the old one. After all, we were now more experienced writers and we could dig a little deeper into the Lads' issues and attitudes. The series also reflected the social changes that Britain was going through at the time. So the critics said anyway. Our primary concern was still making people laugh.

I just rewatched two of these shows and it reminded me that whatever their rocky moments, there was a wonderful chemistry between Jimmy and Rodney. I remember standing on the studio floor during a scene in the second series – I think the episode was 'Heart to Heart'. I held my breath because it was like watching a perfect gymnastic routine. Every line was timed to perfection. Every pause was the right length. Every laugh came exactly where it should. When it was over, Jimmy said quietly:

'Well done, Rod.'

They may not have complimented each other all that often but they certainly complemented each other. They were a perfect duo. This, I suppose, was precisely what terrified Jimmy. I understood this in the early years but not when he had gone on to have such a long and varied career.

Rodney's recent death triggered an affectionate outpouring from the press.

Mark Lawson in the *Guardian* recalled how his performance as Bob Ferris 'radiated optimism and had a natural tenor register that, under stress, could rise to a soprano of alarm'.

Ian and I look back on those first shows in black and white with affection and gratitude. How could we not? Together they gave us our first taste of success. We thought we'd found a formula: write a series, cast it and wait for the accolades. If only it would always be that easy.

Almost The Likely Lads – Ian

Ted and Dickie

When I was eighteen I had no idea who I was or who I was supposed to be. You could call it my first identity crisis. I didn't have one. In truth I felt pretty much the same ten years later even though I was by then a credited screenwriter and living with a stunning actress slash model called Fiona. At eighteen, however I was still at a minor public school, Dame Allan's. (When Dick found this out he asked if the principal was Danny La Rue.) I lived in a seaside town, which was exciting in the summer with a flood of visitors and daily coach trips and empty and melancholy in the bleak, windswept, cold winter months.

Life was stable and safe. I lived a mile from the beach and we had a large garden. My parents were loving and nurturing. Dick enjoyed a similar life in another seaside town much further south. My father was the first person I ever saw sign an autograph. He had been an exceptional athlete in his day, a sprint champion and local hero who was only denied a place in the Amsterdam Olympics by a torn Achilles. My mother, like most of her generation, was a homemaker; an excellent cook and much loved woman. She placed great store in teaching me correct table manners.

'*Always place your knife and fork on the plate between mouthfuls, Ian, and never, ever invert the fork, even for peas.*'

My best friends were – and still are – David Hallwood, Vin Welsh and Horace Jeffcock – a name we couldn't resist using a few times over the years. Malcolm and Judy Brown provide great evenings when I'm in the North East. Webby and Mike are playing eighteen holes on some celestial golf course and a special aunt has passed too. She was the object of my anguished teenage lust the peak of which, literally, was when she taught me to foxtrot in her front living room.

Vin had the largest house so that's where we took girls. David's house was the nearest thing to Bohemia in Whitley Bay. His mother was a true free spirit, his father was a cartoonist and his sister was delectably pretty. He had a younger brother who was homosexual before we knew what that meant, and a stepbrother in the Navy who explained to the rest of us how oral sex worked. None of us believed him.

At school my main accomplishments were on the sports field, especially track and field, urged on by my father of course. I also played for the first team at rugby, which was the most prestigious of all school activities. My social life revolved around my friends, my parents and their friends. I drank in pubs with my pals and with my dad; I played poker with my pals and whist with my parents. I drank beer with people of my age but went to sherry parties with the oldies, usually on Sunday mornings where the drinks were accompanied with finger food: dates wrapped in bacon, cheese cubes on cocktail sticks stuck, for no apparent reason, in a grapefruit.

Not that the oldies (people over forty) stuck to sherry for long, quickly eschewing it and its pious connotations for gin, with a token splash of tonic water. The war was a not too distant memory. I could not know it at the time but there were many scarred people to whom gin was a solace, and small talk and social niceties a diversion against the awful realities of what they had seen. I saw very little, though at the age of three a bomb fell in our street and my mother and I were dug out of the rubble by air raid wardens. We moved to a large house near the Lake District and when I returned my town, with its bombed buildings, gun emplacements and pillboxes was a kid's fantasy playground.

As a teenager I was ill at ease with Rugby Club dances, bored with the social niceties of sherry parties, coffee mornings and weekend tennis, played on threadbare courts with an adjacent putting green and a resident paedophile, whom we were constantly told by our parents to avoid, although they never told us why. What excited me most was the seafront and the fairground and the penny arcades with the constant parade of Teddy boys and their (sometimes) girlfriends. It was the seafront that fascinated me and became for a short teenage while the epicentre of my social world.

The Teds turned the front into a catwalk as they paraded the latest fashions: the narrow, cuffed drainpipe pants, the fingertip drape jackets, some with velvet collars, the brocade waistcoats and thick-soled brothel-creeper shoes. The girls wore pencil skirts and black mascara, chewed gum and drank beer from the bottle. Deadly. There was never, surprisingly, much aggro, although I do recall one memorable occasion when a gang from Wallsend desecrated the floral clock.

My mother, bless her heart, allowed her dressmaker to narrow some of my boring, grey school trousers to a fourteen-inch bottom, with the provision that my father never got a glimpse of them. And so I wore them on my forays into Tedland, always on a Saturday when I was supposed to be at the Rugby Club or a well-mannered dance in Gosforth. And that's where I met Dickie and Ted.

Ted lived in a local council estate, Dickie in a gloomy terrace above the docks in North Shields. They worked together at Parsons, a massive electrical manufacturer in Byker but they always wore the latest cool clothes, had money in their pockets and drove around in Ted's three-wheel Morgan sports car. By then, of course, all teenagers outside the public and grammar school systems had money, working as they did since the age of fifteen in factories and foundries and ship yards. The 'teenager' was a new social species, an economic force pursued by the advertisers as they created teenage clothes, magazines, cosmetics and, of course, teenage records. They were assertive and cocky and sowing the seeds of the social revolution that would explode in the Swinging Sixties. They seemed to be saying:

'We are here, we belong, and we are not going away.'

I think I met them at a party for a local Ted who was off to do National Service. All of us were faced with that problem although I, like many others, chose to do it before, not after, university. This was in the forlorn hope that the Services would make men of us and we'd have sex. Anyway, for some reason, Ted and Dickie took me under their wing. I walked, or should I say strutted the seafront in their company now; borrowed their clothes, rode on the back of the Morgan, drank in pubs and went to dances at halls where a rope divided the room with a sign swinging on it – *'Jivers – This Side'*. My new mentors were brilliant jivers. Dickie, I believe, won first prize at a Butlin's holiday camp contest. I, after many hours of practice in front of a bedroom mirror, became passably good.

I'll never forget the sights and sound and smells of those ballrooms – the Plaza, the Empress, the Memorial Hall, and the mecca of all of them, the Oxford Galleries in Newcastle: big bands, smoke, sweat and cheap perfume.

Ted was a body builder. He had qualified for the finals of the Mister Universe contest. He may even have won it. Either way he was a local celebrity, which made his company even more appealing. He had the broadest shoulders I had ever seen and his drape jackets had to be custom made. His hair was short and wasn't combed into a 'duck's arse' that all the others favoured. Dickie was brown skinned, muscular and wiry with a kind of Sinatra thing going for him. Ted had a regular girlfriend. Dickie had whomever he wanted. I had a sort of girlfriend but I'd never touched her breasts under any of her several angora sweaters. But that was okay, I had my A-levels to pass.

While waiting for those results I took a summer job in the local fairground, which was called the Spanish City. It saved my friendship with the lads, which had definitely cooled after I asked them to my house and they seemed slightly put out by the fact it had four bedrooms and a large back garden. I think Dickie's home had an outside loo. And I think they thought I was something of a fake. Well, of course I was. I was fake hanging with Teddy boys, I was a fake at the Rugby Club or the tennis dance, or the whist evenings and even in the prefects' room at school where I wore gold braid on my black blazer and was allowed the dubious privilege of beating frightened small boys with a size-twelve gym shoe.

Working in the Spanish City restored my cred. Ted and Dickie would drop by a couple of times a night for a chat and a smoke. Music blasted out from the PA system – Gene Vincent, Marty Wilde, Connie Francis. I wanted to work on the Dodgem cars, of course. What could be cooler than hanging on to the pole of a moving car, managing to give change, chew gum, chat girls and smoke a ciggie all at the same time? Never happened. The owner did not think I was roustabout material and I was assigned to the Scenic Railway, driving four dozen excitable infants around fairy grottoes, marooned pirate galleons and Aladdin's cave at ten miles an hour.

To my astonishment Ted and Dickie asked if I would like to go on holiday with them to Torquay in two Morgans; one was Ted's, the other belonged to a lad named Terry whose part-time job was a 'smudger', photographing tourists on the seafront, a great way to pull girls. I've no idea how I sold this idea to my parents. Passing all my exams obviously helped. I have never before or since looked forward to a trip so much.

With our bags strapped on the back of the cars we set off down the A1 to London. Ted had an uncle who managed a pub in Notting Hill where we would spend two nights before the drive to Devon. Somewhere near Newark Terry's car packed in. An AA man dropped by, arranged a tow to a local garage but major surgery was required and the car would never make it to London, never mind Torquay. We decided to soldier on, picking up our bags and sticking out our thumbs. Incredibly, before twenty minutes had passed, a sporty Jag pulled up and we were offered a ride. The driver was obviously upper crust; double-breasted navy blazer, a club tie and cavalry twill trousers. He drove with panache, lighting cigarettes from his Dunhill lighter, with one hand.

We stopped at one of those ancient coaching house hotels, somewhere near Stamford, where he decided to spend the night. But he asked us for dinner, and we sat in the timbered room with its horse brasses and seductive red table lights, and silver serving carts preparing dishes that burst into flame as the black-coated waiter served another steak Diane. And we drank red wine and wondered if other hitchhikers had ever got this lucky. I have never remembered the name of our driver and host but he is a prince among men. He offered to pick us up the next morning. He went to bed and we slept in a ditch opposite the hotel with the faint sound of dance music in our ears. Maybe it was the unaccustomed red wine but we woke late and missed our lift. Never mind, two lorry rides later we were in London and on the tube to Notting Hill.

Ted's uncle's pub was on Ledbury Road, home these days to a much-praised restaurant, chic boutiques and houses that are worth north of ten million. In those days Notting Hill was for the most part a no-go area; home to Jamaican immigrants packed into converted mansions owned by slum landlords. There were music clubs, drug dealers and petty gangsters. We didn't linger in the bar, however; we were off to the West End.

Ted, Dickie, Terry and Ian. Four Northern innocents loose in Soho. We ate in a Wimpy bar, trawled pubs, bought drinks for an actor we recognised from British 'B' movies and were refused admittance to a louche bohemian club called the Mandrake. We went to a strip club. The strippers were rather old and overweight. One of them wore a large Elastoplast on her left thigh. And in between we ogled the streetwalkers. Some of them stood at corners or leaned against lamp posts, some stood in doorways, a few floors beneath a red lamp in a window. Some of them offered us a good time and brought blushes to our cheeks. Some were old slappers who'd seen it all; others were young and awkward with regional accents like our own. Eventually it came down to a dare. Who had the nerve to do it, and would the others agree to pay? It would also involve recounting the episode later in meticulous detail to the other three who would masturbate in the large bed we all shared above the snug bar.

I did console myself in the morning that I was no longer a virgin.

We drove, amazingly, to Devon in the one good Morgan; Ted behind the wheel, Dickie riding shotgun, Terry and I on the back clinging to the strapped-in luggage with our feet on the tail pipes at either side. We were never stopped by the police and the car never broke down.

In Torquay we camped in a field in a tent. We hung our clothes on hangers on tree branches, bathed in a stream and set off every night to the town's most happening bars. Teddy loaned me a drape jacket. It was almost knee-length and sky-blue. It was also, if you remember, custom made for Mister Universe so I looked like I was yoked to a plough. Years later I remember seeing Jonathan Demme's movie on Talking Heads and David Byrne was wearing a white jacket with absurdly broad shoulders. I immediately thought of my younger self, in my borrowed Teddy boy gear, heading from a campsite to the glamorous bars of Torquay. Later I walked a girl home. She was called Edwina. I kissed her by the Odeon cinema, which was showing *Ocean's Eleven* – the one with Sinatra and Dean Martin, not Clooney and Pitt.

We drove the length of England when we went home, Terry and I still clinging on to the luggage with our feet on the tail pipes. Exhausted, Ted stopped somewhere near Swindon. It was dark and there were no street lights. We climbed over a drystone wall and fell asleep on soft earth. We woke to find we were in a graveyard.

Over the years Dick and I have been asked repeatedly if Bob and Terry were based on real-life Likely Lads. I was asked the question most because the series was set in the North East. The answer is, not really. But in the original sixties series we did have the lads working in an electrical plant which, in my mind, was based on Parsons in Newcastle. Where Ted and Dickie worked. And yes, they drank with me in pubs that were later referenced in the series. But no, they weren't Bob and Terry as much as I'd like to think they were. They were Ted and Dickie, and they were great jivers.

The Casting Vote – Dick

Walter Strachan

The seaside town where I grew up is just over three hundred miles south of Whitley Bay. What would we do without Google? Westcliff-on-Sea was directly on the Luftwaffe's flight path to London so we were evacuated for a while, first to Lampeter in Wales and then Worcester. My dad, who had miraculously survived the whole of the First World War as a dispatch rider, was left behind in the Home Guard. Why didn't I turn that into a TV series?

When we returned home, most of my memories are coloured khaki. Sandbags covered the windows of a downstairs room. A piece of shrapnel embedded in one of them was traded at school for cigarette cards. Inside was a big steel table shelter with wire mesh sides. Air raids were fun. I enjoyed being carried downstairs, half-awake. My teenage sister Pat brought home a succession of boyfriends: Poles, Czechs, Canadians. I trailed after Americans. 'Got any gum, chum?' They often had.

I also had two older brothers. A third, Freddie, died of peritonitis when I was two. I don't remember him. All through growing up I heard the phrase 'Before the War'. Clearly it had been an Eden I could only imagine. Before the War had been a time of plenty, without sweet coupons, clothing coupons, bread units. My brother John swore that Before the War there had been a thing called 'white chocolate', but I never believed that one – there was a limit to my gullibility.

My schooling was initially unorthodox. Years later I discovered that Ian's girlfriend Fiona Lewis had attended the same school as me, St Bernard's Convent. So too did Helen Mirren. Naturally this would never have happened Before the War. A nun went through roll call every morning. When your name was called you were supposed to reply, 'Present, Madam'. I misheard this and for a whole term sang out *'Press Button!'*, somehow anticipating the age of automation. When I related this to my family over dinner I got the first really good laugh of my life. A career in comedy was inevitable.

My mother was born in the Isle of Dogs in London's East End. It's only about thirty miles from Westcliff but after she married my father she never went back until years later when Ray Cooper lent me his flat in Wapping. I drove her round the streets she used to know. Some of them had not survived the bombs but she looked at the house where she'd lived as a girl and said:

'We had better curtains in my day.'

Ian still has his roots in the North East. I have none in Westcliff. My whole family moved away and the Borough of Southend has never offered to name a street after me so I've had no reason to pay a visit. Another reason is that I went to boarding school at Bishops Stortford College at the age of thirteen. One of the teachers there was Walter Strachan. He taught me French and German and much else besides. It is no exaggeration to say that he directly affected the entire course of my life.

It was two years before I found myself in Walter's class. A lot of boys found him a figure of fun. He was a somewhat rarefied figure with an aura of aesthetic sensibility. Quite rightly they kept him away from the grubbier reaches of the school. You were ready for Walter at the age of fifteen. Some were never ready. He instinctively knew this but trusted that every year would produce enough kindred spirits he could reach and inspire.

It was only in later years that I learned to appreciate Walter's very real talents. He was in every sense a Renaissance man. Two collections of his poetry had been published. He translated French poets into English. He had a lifelong passion for architecture and was a great friend of the sculptor Henry Moore, who lived locally. He was a dedicated art collector to the point where his modest home was devoid of modern household appliances. Every time his wife was about to buy a washing machine Walter bought another picture instead.

Some teachers are only evaluated by their ability to get through a curriculum. Walter managed to teach me enough to pass my O-levels but what I remember with affection are his diversions. In the middle of a class he would write out an English poem he especially admired, or digress on Henry Moore's sculpture or a letter from a former pupil. As a sideline he taught italic handwriting. One effect of this is that my own writing is more legible than Ian's so when we started collaborating I was the one who put pen to paper.

One morning he arrived without his usual energy and enthusiasm, his expression sombre. I can pinpoint the date precisely: 10 November 1953. Dylan Thomas had died the day before in America. French could wait. Walter wanted each of us to understand that a great poet had gone from our midst. He succeeded.

He was not impartial, reaching out selectively to the more responsive students. I was not one of them. I spent my most creative energy trying to make my friend Terry Taylor collapse with helpless laughter in the middle of reading aloud a poem by Rimbaud or Verlaine. I was expert at this.

'Don't laugh, Terry' – this in a hoarse whisper from my seat behind him, chosen especially for this purpose. 'Whatever you do, don't laugh.'

It never failed. Terry's head would collapse onto his folded arms, his shoulders silently heaving. Walter would gaze at him with infinite disappointment then hand the cultural baton to someone else. After some weeks he observed that we seemed entirely different characters in his German classes. Well, yes, of course, there were only eight of us taking German and I was out in the open, not skulking behind Terry at the back.

I was not, then, one of his favourites, merely plodding along in the main stream, doing enough to get by. It was easy to parody him and we did, making fun of his enthusiasms and impersonating his catchphrases, most notably the long, drawn-out 'Go-osh!' he emitted whenever he encountered an especially brutal act of Philistinism. All the more surprising then that he saved my world from crashing around me.

We had an American exchange student in my final year. His name was as American as his crew cut: H. Calvin Cook Jr., from Steubenville, Ohio. Cal and I became friends, which inspired me to apply to the English Speaking Union (ESU) for the equivalent scholarship in reverse. To the surprise of parents and headmaster alike, I was chosen. I was especially pleased by the response of my father. He was battling cancer, a word I never heard uttered until after he died three years later. I felt I had done something that made him proud of me.

Eighteen of us set sail on the *Queen Mary* in September 1955. Although we were assigned to the bowels of the ship we quickly discovered how to sneak into Cabin and First Class and pretend we belonged there. To prepare myself culturally I read *The Grapes of Wrath* and *The Sun Also Rises*.

The Statue of Liberty loomed out of the fog on the morning of our arrival, followed by a host of golden taxicabs on the streets of Manhattan. On my very first day in America I saw the Brooklyn Dodgers play at Ebbets Field accompanied by the wicked witch from *The Wizard of Oz*. Margaret Hamilton was my hostess because her son had been an exchange student that year and in return she offered her generous hospitality for the few days before term began at Westminster School in Connecticut.

No one in my family had ever been to America. Nor were English tourists thick on the ground. When Americans heard my accent they tended to say, *'Pip-pip, Old Bean'*, which puzzled me because I had never read P. G. Wodehouse. I quickly became accustomed to questions like:

'You're English, do you happen to know Stephen Pryce-Ambleforth? He lives in Derbyshire, or is it Dorset?'

It hit me fairly quickly that they assumed I was posh. I was not posh. I tried to explain that Southend was the equivalent of Coney Island. Then again, Cal came from Steubenville, mostly famous as the birthplace of Dean Martin. When I visited him in the spring vacation, Southend seemed like St Tropez by comparison.

I had to field weighty questions like:

'Why did you people kick Churchill out after he won the war for you?'

It was illuminating to see one's own country from afar and re-alise how small it seemed from an American perspective. It also struck me that as an ambassador I was a novice. I made mistakes, for example in the Debating Society. In England we emulated the bawdy cut and thrust of the House of Commons by lampooning and ridiculing our opponents. I tried this in Connecticut and was met with appalled silence.

Another major difference distinguished me from my fellow students. They had money. I had been given one hundred dollars to last me for the entire year. I would look at the Coke machine in the hall and wonder whether I could afford to blow a nickel. Maybe tomorrow.

The ESU made no provision for school holidays in the assump-tion that students would receive invitations. They were right. I celebrated Christmas at a mansion in Newport, Rhode Island. My hosts, the Rutherfurd family, gave me a stocking with a silver dollar in the toe, one per cent of my annual stipend. I discovered years later that Lucy Rutherfurd had been President Roosevelt's mistress for many years, though most of my schoolmates' parents regarded FDR as only one remove from the Prince of Darkness himself.

I spent time with my friend Tony Barnes in an eighteenth-century house on the Main Line outside Philadelphia. We went to debutante dances and drank free champagne; on one occasion far too much. I fell briefly in love with a girl, visited twenty of the forty-eight states, mostly by Greyhound bus, and returned home on the *Queen Elizabeth* after eleven months in America, ready to face National Service.

Without Walter Strachan it would never have happened. In order to explain this, let's flashback to my final term at school in England. I'd taken all my exams and was bored and restless. One Saturday morning I skipped two pointless study periods and hitchhiked to London. The motive for my minor act of rebellion was to go to the pictures, an activity I can defend in hindsight as being essential to the development of the career I eventually pursued, though I can't for the life of me remember what the movie was.

When I got back I learned that a geriatric teacher had spotted me slipping away and I was summoned to see the headmaster. I viewed him as a remote, austere man with no noticeable sense of humour but I was stoically prepared to face the music: misplaced trust, loss of privileges, et cetera. Then he said the words that made my blood run cold:

'I'm not sure we can allow someone with your lack of character to go to America.'

I sweated, numb with panic for a week or so before hearing of my reprieve. It was months later before I learned how it had come about. My source was a school friend who was 'going out' with the English teacher's daughter. (We didn't date in the Fifties.) She told him of a staff meeting where my case had been discussed. The headmaster felt my scholarship should be revoked if they were unanimous. One lone hand was raised in my defence: Walter's.

I still shudder to think about what would have happened if he hadn't done so. Instead of experiencing the most memorable, character-forming year of my life I would have had to face my father's bitter disappointment and a shattering blow to my self-esteem.

About twenty years ago I wrote to thank him for that vote. I wanted him to feel that he hadn't been wrong. Walter never referred to the matter in his reply. It was written in his distinctive italic hand with rambling diversions on every subject under the sun. This had nothing to do with his increasing age. Walter always had too many enthusiasms to fit into one forty-five minute German period or on one piece of writing paper.

He died at the ripe old age of 91. I'm still in his debt.

Two Imposters – Ian

Harry H. Corbett

With the success of *The Likely Lads* we suddenly began to believe we were part of the culture of 'the Sixties'. Had we actually gate-crashed the party? Fashions seemed to change every month and the clothes and the music became more psychedelic and trippy. The Beatles had long hair and beards and wore kaftans and beads. I started buying my clothes in Chelsea and had my hair blow-dried twice a week. I spotted Jimi Hendrix in an Afghan coat so naturally I bought one myself. The Kings Road was full of them. There can't have been any left in Afghanistan. Shepherds must have been freezing their nuts off. Dick thought I looked like a yak and when it rained I smelled like one.

One day we got a call to meet Harry H. Corbett. He was already a household name from *Steptoe and Son*. He wanted us to write a series he'd devised called *Mister Aitch*. He was also the producer so it was the first time that we worked for a star who was in control. Harry had worked for Joan Littlewood's company at Stratford – the one in the East End – and played leading Shakespearean roles like Richard II. Now his audiences could only think of him as Harold Steptoe, which must have been very galling, perhaps the very problem that Jimmy Bolam was so afraid of.

Harry had added the 'H' to his name to distinguish himself from another Harry Corbett who worked with a puppet called Sooty. What did the 'H' stand for? His standard reply was 'Hennything you like.' He was up for an OBE one year but a Palace scribe goofed and left out the 'H', so the award went to the puppeteer instead. I'm sure he was delighted. Did he take Sooty to the Palace with him? Red-faced officials realised their mistake and Harry H. got his royal handshake sometime later.

We got a decent deal, a nice office at ATV's building on Kingsway and things looked good. Dick felt slightly disloyal not being at the BBC, a bit like a lapsed Catholic, but I was happy because ATV made *Ready Steady Go!*, so once a week the building was full of pop stars. Harry had clout because of *Steptoe* and he'd made some sort of independent deal, which was unusual in those days when almost every production was 'in house'.

The premise was that Harry owned a parking lot in the middle of Soho, a gold mine in property terms. He had two sidekicks, one played by an actor called Norman Chappell, whose speciality was playing dim. It's hard to write 'dim' on a weekly basis. Gordon Gostelow, a Shakespearean actor, played the other one, a tramp who hung out there.

I can't remember a single plot. We thought our writing was as sharp as ever and no one complained but the truth was, nothing gelled. Even in rehearsals we hardly ever laughed. Harry made arbitrary changes and had a very strange way of delivering lines with the emphasis in all the wrong places. Christopher Walken does this too but he's brilliant and Harry was just infuriating.

When things started to go wrong Dick talked to Duncan Wood, who had produced and directed *Steptoe*. He said Harry came to him with about fifty ideas for every episode, but only one or two of them were ever any good. But on this show he was the guvnor, so what he said went.

Week after week we dragged our arses all the way to Wembley to tape the shows. Even after retakes – and there were many – the live audience became less and less responsive and we became more and more depressed as we drove home. I used to go to

Gerry's Club, an actors' hangout in Soho. Most people went there to drink – and I really needed one.

After about seven shows, the producers asked Ray Galton and Alan Simpson to write a couple of scripts. They were gods to us, having created *Hancock* and *Steptoe*, but it felt like being fired. I remember we read the first script, looked at each other and had to admit that it was very good. Then we went to the taping, and the show was just as flat and disappointing as any of ours. For us it was an enormous relief because we'd started to doubt our own talent, wondering if we were just a flash in the pan.

Harry had a producing partner, a boxing promoter called John Arrow. Bolstered by the knowledge that we might not disappear into obscurity, I bought his E-Type Jag. I paid eight hundred quid for it and had it sprayed black as I thought red was a bit flash. The first time I drove it to Dick's house in Ham, I got a ticket for speeding in Richmond Park.

It may seem odd to pair Harry H. Corbett with Will Smith – and I doubt if it's been done before – but we had a similar experience with the Hollywood star forty years later on a project called *Amulet,* adapted from a graphic novel. Warner Brothers gave us the deal but Will Smith's company was totally in control because the idea was that it would star his two children. Our first meeting with him was in his trailer – the biggest one we'd ever seen. Will was charming and accessible, keen to put us at ease as he lined up golf balls on his Astroturf putting green. He liked our ideas, we liked his and we went away, all fired up.

The story involved two kids going through a portal into another world. The writer of the graphic novel had not actually finished it. We hoped he would soon, because we didn't have an ending. But we finished a draft and had another meeting with Will at his mansion in the Malibu Hills.

He had many new ideas, the most startling of which was that he thought there should be seven portals, not one. We looked around the table. Did everyone feel like this? Everyone did – it was Will's idea. We did rapid calculations. Did this mean seven times more work? More words? By the time we left, we'd negotiated a compromise. There would now be *three* portals.

It wasn't the last meeting by any means. At the next one more ideas were thrown at us. Some were very good, but it would have been nice to have debated them before we had started writing, not after finishing two drafts. Dick said, as tactfully as possible:

'This might mean a lot of unravelling.' Will smiled: 'We're very good at unravelling.'

So we ravelled, unravelled, and ravelled again and finished another draft. Then silence. No one picked up the phone or sent an email. It was as if they'd all disappeared. Perhaps they'd all gone through a portal – a word we never wanted to hear again.

There was no second series of *Mister Aitch* and we never saw Harry again. It was a chastening experience at the time – and quite humbling. It's said that you learn just as much from failure as you do from success. As Kipling put it:

'If you can meet with Triumph and Disaster and treat those two imposters just the same.'

Well yes, Rudyard, very wise, but Triumph was definitely a lot more fun. We didn't write anything else for television for five years.

'My Film's Got F**king Battles!' – Dick

Michael Winner

Michael Winner was the first movie producer we ever met. We were summoned to his office where he said something like:

'I've asked you here because I've heard you're very clever writers and I can get you cheap. I'm going to pay you the minimum amount allowed but in return I guarantee that if the film gets made it will be your names on the screen and not some other bugger's.'

He told us a story he'd come up with about two brothers who decide to steal the Crown Jewels for a lark. Their defence would be that they made it clear before the robbery that they had no intention to 'permanently deprive' the Crown of its property. Theft is apparently not committed when there is no intention to keep what was taken, a nicety of British law that appealed to him. He asked us to write a treatment.

When we left his Mayfair office we realised that we had no idea what a 'treatment' was. We've written plenty of them since: documents that outline the characters and plot of a movie and the way it unfolds, preferably in three acts. What we wrote was almost a novella. Michael looked at it impatiently and had it revised into something resembling screenplay format.

He was under thirty, only two years older than us, curly-haired, cigar smoking and abrasive – no, rude is the word. He was especially nasty to his secretary, who frequently dissolved into tears, which made him furious. As she sobbed one day he took us into his inner office, closed the door and said:

'Look at this panelling. I had it installed especially so I wouldn't be able to hear her caterwauling. It cost me a great deal of money and I can still bloody hear her!'

For some reason we escaped the lash of his tongue, perhaps because we outnumbered him. He expected us to work in his office where he could keep an eye on us. This was a problem because at the time Ian was working in market research and I had started to direct commercials. This meant that Ian had to show his face in his office from time to time, fortunately not too far away, and I was often in a casting session. We covered for each other. Michael would enter, expect to see two of us and be disconcerted. We had a standard explanation: 'Oh, Ian [or Dick] has just popped over to Fortnum's for coffee.'

Michael had already directed two or three moderately successful films including *Play It Cool* with Billy Fury and *The System* with Oliver Reed. He had an implacable self-assurance, perhaps because he had never been short of money – his family owned extensive property in the Holland Park area.

Before long we had written another draft and *The Jokers* had a start date. We were so naive at the time. We thought this was the way it would always be: write a screenplay, make some fixes, the movie gets made and you go to the premiere. Michael kept his promise: our names were up there on the screen.

He quickly gave us another film to write, a war story called *Hannibal Brooks*. We couldn't understand why he was so anxious for us to finish it as he was preparing to shoot *William the Conqueror* with Oliver Reed. We asked if he was worried about a rival film in pre-production, *Alfred the Great* starring David Hemmings.

'Alfred the Great? All he did was burn some cakes. He was a literary man – that was his thing. My film's got fucking battles!'

In spite of this his film got cancelled. Michael got sympathetic calls from people in the business. He wasn't fazed at all. He instantly switched the entire production crew and Oliver Reed onto *Hannibal Brooks*. He'd seen the writing on the wall and we now realised why he had pushed us so hard to finish the script. He may not have been a great director but he was a very canny producer.

We flew with him to Munich and drove around looking for locations. Our driver was German. There was no question of Michael muttering 'Don't mention the war', like Basil Fawlty. He never missed an opportunity to denigrate every aspect of our European ally. He bought cigars on one occasion and came out of the store, puffing one and complaining:

'I told them I wanted a decent cigar. They said, "Ja, ja, ja" and sold me this fucking rubbish.'

Hannibal Brooks is an odd film in many ways, astonishingly based on a true story. Oliver Reed plays the sensitive British prisoner of war who is assigned to the Munich zoo and makes friends with the elephant. Tiny Michael J. Pollard, fresh from his eye-catching role in *Bonnie and Clyde*, plays the macho shoot-'em-up action man. 'Shum mishtake, shurely', as Lunchtime O'Booze would have said in *Private Eye*. Some of Oliver's line readings sounded like a stumbling read-through with his fellow actors on the first day of rehearsal. But Michael never claimed to be subtle. An actor once asked him what his motivation was in a scene and got the reply:

'My voice!'

The moment a film got the green light he had only one thought in mind: roll camera, speed, action, cut, print and move on. He was always thinking about the next movie and the one after that. He found me reading a book one day – I can't remember what but I remember his comment:

'No point reading that, it's already been filmed!'

His abrasiveness came to its peak on a film set where there was never any shortage of people to shout at. On one movie he couldn't see his lighting cameraman on the set and yelled at his assistant to go and find him. Bob Paynter was in the Portaloo. When told that Michael wanted to see him right away his reply went into legend:

'Tell him I can only deal with one shit at a time.'

Given his caustic reputation it's remarkable that so many great movie stars agreed to work with him, including Marlon Brando, Burt Lancaster and Robert Mitchum. Presumably they were allowed to take their time over their ablutions.

Michael Crawford told us the following story about *The Games*, in which he played a marathon runner at the Rome Olympics. The climactic shot came as the athletes pounded through the streets of Rome past cheering crowds. It was crucial that the driver of the main camera car kept pace with Crawford. But he blew it and this was a very expensive shot to set up for Take Two. Winner gave the driver both barrels. I've modified the language for those with a sensitive disposition but you can use your imagination.

'You are an arsehole. I have known many arseholes in my life but it's possible that you are the biggest. If they gave out medals for arseholes, you would be up for a gold one . . .'

Crawford tapped Winner on the shoulder, trying to tell him something.

'Don't interrupt me, Michael, I'm telling this arsehole that he's an arsehole.'

Winner went on for a few more choice phrases before Crawford finally got his attention.

'He wasn't the driver, it was him!'

He pointed to another man standing nearby. Winner never broke stride.

'I'm very sorry, you are not an arsehole.'

He swivelled forty-five degrees and repeated the identical tirade to the guilty party.

Some years later we wrote a TV series for the BBC, *The Further Adventures of Lucky Jim*, based on Kingsley Amis's novel. When we came to write the final episode we did something that we had never done before – or since, for that matter – we decided to base a character unabashedly on a real person. So we had Jim Dixon, the hero, get a job as an assistant to a film producer who smoked cigars, made his secretary cry and was brusque and insensitive when a young actress auditioning tried to show him her résumé:

'Yes, yes, my dear, what this part does not require is a diploma from RADA and a glowing review for your Ophelia in the Surrey Comet. *What is does require is a great pair of tits. Let's have a look at 'em then.'*

We called him Maurice Victor. Antony Sher, a really great actor, played him to perfection and the episode is one of our all-time favourites. Michael allegedly saw it and said dismissively:

'Nothing like me.'

In his later years he became famous for being Michael Winner, writing restaurant reviews for the *Sunday Times*, notable for him revelling in his ostentatious lifestyle. Ironically, food almost killed him, a bad oyster in Barbados. Ian and I met him for the last time in California and took him to lunch in Beverly Hills. He was walking with great difficulty and was far less abrasive than his old self, not surprising considering how near death he had been after surviving a series of operations.

We thought it only fitting that we picked up the check. After all, we owed our entire movie careers to him, as he never failed to remind us. But we noticed that he made notes about every dish and wondered if he was going to write a review and claim the expenses.

The Odd Couple – Ian

Tom Courtenay

For some reason, either because I was between flats or girlfriends, I moved in as a house guest with Tom Courtenay. We were very much like the odd couple, looked after by a lovely housekeeper called Mrs Greenlands. We watched *Match of the Day*, ate in Chelsea bistros, walked Tom's dog in the park and played football on Sunday mornings, first for the Television Writers XI and then, inexplicably, for the *Melody Maker* alongside Ray and Dave Davies from the Kinks.

Just two ordinary pals, right, except at the time Tom was an international movie star and his latest film was *Doctor Zhivago* alongside Julie Christie, Alec Guinness, Omar Sharif and Rod Steiger It was hard to realise this as Tom did not act like a star and disliked parties, premieres and press junkets, preferring to be much more low key, modest and unassuming. Although I did take phone messages at times and when two of them were from Natalie Wood and Candice Bergen it was a reminder that he was not just some bloke down from the North.

We were both domestically impaired, living in dread that there would be a fuse or a plumbing problem. One by one light bulbs expired but we were incapable of replacing them. As the house grew dimmer we agreed that when the last one popped Tom would sell the house and buy another.

I had met him first when Rodney Bewes brought him to a recording of *The Likely Lads*. They had become friends after filming

Billy Liar. Dick and I loved that film, just as we had loved the book by Keith Waterhouse on which it was based. It made overnight stars of Tom and Julie Christie and he became part of that exciting and innovative period of sixties British cinema where, almost overnight, actors with regional accents could become leading men and throw off the restraints of the posh voices they had acquired at compulsory elocution lessons at Drama School. So in the mid-sixties, Tom Courtenay, Albert Finney, Michael Caine, Terence Stamp and Alan Bates became the faces of what was then referred to as the new wave or Neo Realism.

These were the films that excited Dick and me and inspired the audacity to write a television comedy about two northern lads who work in a factory, drink beer and chase birds.

Tom's first film, and the one that spelled out that here was a newcomer to watch, was Tony Richardson's *The Loneliness of the Long Distance Runner,* a memorable expression of working-class rage against the system. Tom's own roots were working class. His father had worked on the docks in the city of Hull. He was proud of his upbringing and the values it instilled in him. Years later he would write a lovely memoir as a tribute to his parents called *Dear Tom: Letters from Home.* It had great critical acclaim.

His connections to his home town have strengthened over the years: an Honorary doctorate at the University, Honorary Freeman of the City and President of the Hull City Supporters Club, this last award being the one, I'm sure, he values most. Staying at Tom's place it was almost mandatory that I became a Hull City fan too. I even went with him and Rodney Bewes to see them play at Carlisle, in a ramshackle ground with sheep grazing in an adjacent field. Fish and chips on the way back to Newcastle where we spent the night with my mother. *Lifestyles of the Rich and Famous,* indeed.

Tom and I turned out for a kind of show business football team, which included the young Python Eric Idle, Leonard Rossiter and two pop stars from a band called Marmalade. When we played at Ford Open Prison on the south coast we also included three 'ringers', two of whom were professional players from Hull. The third was Dave Webb from Chelsea. We won, of course, but there were mutterings among the inmates and we weren't asked back. While we were being given tea and buns after the game, I recognised two of the trusties as people I knew. They were doing time for 'financial irregularities' and felt hard done by for being banged up. One of them explained to me:

'There's a very fine line, Ian, between making a living and fraud.'

A good line, and one that Dick and I would subsequently use in *Porridge*. There was another situation that we didn't get to use. Tom's neighbour was a wine merchant who did something fiscally iffy and went to prison. Inside he met a man who boasted that he had burgled Tom Courtenay's house and still had a souvenir of the theft that he'd be willing to return – for a price. Tom declined, so we imagined that for years the thief's family and friends must have wondered what a statuette for 'Best Actor, *Doctor Zhivago*, Rio Film Festival' was doing on his living room mantelpiece.

Tom and I ate sometimes at a basement restaurant on the Kings Road called The Spot. We were there one night with Rodney and John Thaw and served by a stunning girl called Victoria who had a very, very posh accent. We were smitten. Using all our reserves of northern charm we all asked her out. I vaguely remember that she went out with Tom, but I was the one who was asked, sometime later, to spend the weekend with the stunning posh girl at her mother's country house in Suffolk.

There was just the two us and we went to bed together in one of those typical, charming country house rooms that smelled of potpourri, wild flowers and Jermyn Street soap. This was beyond my wildest fantasies. She told me how happy she was that I was there, kissed me on the cheek then turned over and went to sleep, consigning me from that moment to 'best friend' of Victoria and nothing more intimate. I have been her friend ever since and at least she didn't ask me if Tom was free the following weekend.

Years later Dick, John Wells and I were sitting backstage at the Whitehall Theatre after rehearsals for *Anyone For Dennis.* Somehow the conversation turned to *amour fou*, mad love, and we wondered if any of us had experienced it; met someone so bewitching that we'd leave homes, careers, wives, even small children and take off to Marrakesh or Machu Picchu or Barnsley, or anywhere on the planet she desired. We all agreed we had and then decided to name names. It was the same girl: Victoria.

I was consoled one day after the Suffolk weekend by arriving back at Tom's house to find another young, beautiful girl waiting on the doorstep. Her name was Fiona Lewis and she told me the reason she dropped by was that Tom never returned her calls. I told her – and I'm admitting it almost half a century later – that Tom wasn't a person to get involved with and could I have her number? A few months later I was spending a weekend in another lovely country house, this one belonging to Fiona's parents. She was cast in a film written by Dick and me and starring, yes, Tom. The film was called *Otley* and would be Dick's feature-directing debut.

It was a comedy thriller, a new departure for Tom after the dourness of *Long Distance Runner, King and Country* and *King Rat*, and produced by a brash young American called Bruce Cohn Curtis. Aware that Dick hadn't made a film before and that we were still relatively inexperienced writers, the studio brass asked a famous Hollywood figure, Carl Foreman, to 'godfather' the project and us in particular. A wonderful man, Carl had among his many writing credits *High Noon* and *The Bridge on the River Kwai.* He was also blacklisted for refusing to name names in the infamous McCarthy witch-hunt of the Fifties, a man of honour as well as a gentleman.

Carl admired our script but felt we needed a 'chariot race'. We didn't quite understand; the only cinematic chariot race we were aware of involved Charlton Heston and a thousand extras. He explained:

'You need a sequence that the audience will talk about when they leave the cinema – what about that bit where . . .'

We racked our brains then remembered a line in the existing script, almost thrown away, when Tom's character mentions he has an upcoming driving test. What would happen, we thought with mounting excitement, if the bad guys, the ones who want to kill our hapless hero, show up when he's taking the test? Would that count as a chariot race? It did and was a very funny sequence.

I remember visiting the set after only a week's shooting and asking Dick how he felt. He told me that half the time he didn't know what he was doing but that he was having the time of his life. He made a smashing movie and Tom proved to be a gifted comic talent.

In spite of his screen successes, Tom felt happier on a stage than a movie set. It was his first love and he returned to it frequently, sometimes, when I first knew him, at the 69 Theatre Company in Manchester. I went up to see him in *Peer Gynt* and met for the first time one of his co-stars, the wonderful Fulton Mackay who would later grace *Porridge*. Later I saw Tom in *Charley's Aunt*, in which the youngest cast member was a seventeen-year-old Helen Mirren. Many years later I was back in Manchester to see him and Julie Walters in Tom Stoppard's *Jumpers*. Julie is as down to earth as Tom, which is probably why we had dinner after the show at a brightly lit pizzeria with plastic-topped tables. And that year both of them had been nominated for Oscars, Julie for *Educating Rita* and Tom for *The Dresser*.

It was in Manchester that Tom met the stage manager, Isabel Crossley, who later became his wife and, in 2001, Lady Isabel when Tom was knighted for services to theatre and film.

Tom is a lovely man, and much loved by his fellow thesps,

directors and film crews. He is slightly eccentric and often re-
minds me of a benign headmaster – one, perhaps, who has lost
his spectacles or his chalk. When I see Tom these days, usually for
a meal and drinks, we almost always reminisce about those early
days, about being the odd couple and playing footie and expiring
light bulbs. We talk fondly about past and present friends, cricket,
theatrical anecdotes and, of course, his first love, Hull City.

I visited him in Paris in the sixties when he was filming *Night
of the Generals* with Peter O'Toole and Omar Sharif, his pal
from *Zhivago*. I stayed with them in the elegant town house they
shared on the Avenue Foch and found out that Omar was now an
honorary Hull City supporter as well as one of the world's most
desirable sex gods. He even went with Tom to see a game at the
club's Boothferry Park ground. The more I think of this unlikely
event the more I want to translate at least a moment of it into
script form: the moment when the legions of fans return to their
homes after the game for tea with the loyal, long-suffering wife.

INT. KITCHEN – DAY

*A working-class kitchen, polished and gleaming. Washing on a line
in the small back yard. On the table a loaf of bread, a sugar bowl, a
plate of cold ham, HP Sauce and Branston pickle. The WIFE pours
strong, brown tea as her HUSBAND enters, shrugging off his Hull
City scarf. They speak in Yorkshire accents.*

WIFE
So how was the match, luv?

HUSBAND
Nowt to write 'ome about. Mind you, them two blokes from
Doctor Zhivago seemed to lap it up.

WIFE (*puzzled*)
What you on about? What two blokes?

HUSBAND
Tom Courtenay and the other one. Dark skinned, rode a camel in that desert film.

WIFE
Omar Sharif?!

HUSBAND
Aye, that's him.

WIFE
You're asking me to believe that Tom Courtenay and Omar Sharif were at the match today?

HUSBAND
I swear, duck. Ask anyone.

There is a long PAUSE before:

WIFE
Next match, I'm coming with you.

In 1987 we were going back to London when we met a fellow Brit at the airport, the director, Paul Weiland. He told us David Putnam had just asked him to direct a movie starring Bill Cosby. *'Is he big?'* he asked us.

Yes, we told him, he's enormous. A brilliant comedian and a huge star on TV from *I Spy* and *The Cosby Show,* where he played America's favourite Dad. And his records sold millions. Bill was also a spokesman for Coca-Cola. They owned Columbia Studios and wanted to make the film that Bill would star in. It was called *Leonard Part 6.* The idea was that his work as a secret agent in the previous five parts was too classified to be revealed to the public. It was an in-joke, just as bad as any of the others in the film. Cosby was also the producer, so he was very much in charge.

As it happens, we'd written a pilot for him a few years earlier. Our first meeting was backstage at Lake Tahoe, the second at his cabana when he was vacationing at the Hotel du Cap. We even played tennis with him and thought he was a rather lazy player.

We'd heard whispers about the movie because we were on the same lot at Burbank producing a film called *Vice Versa*. One day we saw a bunch of studio suits coming out of a screening room after viewing an early cut. They looked as if they'd just left a funeral. We got a call from one of those suits. Could we help?

Their idea was to write narration for Leonard's butler in the hope that this could make sense of the plot that made no sense. As our mate Tom Courtenay had been given the role, we agreed. Cosby was not to be told and because it was unofficial and we were 'off the grid' as it were, they couldn't pay us. Instead, how did we feel about a car each? A few days later, enormous Mercury station wagons arrived at our homes, way too big for our garages.

We watched *Leonard Part 6*, dumbstruck. And we couldn't help noticing how often Cosby held up a Coke bottle, or poured from it, or drank from it. We felt very sorry for Paul Weiland, who got all the blame. The star and producer distanced himself from the film the moment the reviews came out. It was a critical and box office disaster – in spite of our narration. We all know what happened to Bill. Oh, and a few months after the film came out, the studio asked for their station wagons back.

Footnote from Dick:

I used to captain an occasional cricket team called the Bushwhackers. I persuaded Tom, at the height of his movie career, to play against High Wych in darkest Hertfordshire. We fielded first and with five wickets down I put him on to bowl. As he set his field the eleven-year-old scorer shouted out:

'Bowler's name, please!'

Tom turned full-face towards him and the handful of spectators in deckchairs and responded with dignity and restraint:

'Courtenay!'

He turned back and prepared to bowl when the urchin yelled out again.

''Ow d'you spell it?'

Thinking Jewish – Dick

Topol

One of my listed credits is as writer on a movie called *Boys Will Never Believe It* under the pseudonym 'Dik Clamant'. If I was going to write under a pseudonym, that would not be my first choice. It sounds like something I might have dictated over a bad telephone line after dental surgery. A more plausible explanation is that a stressed-out Israeli publicist may have dictated it over a bad telephone line in the middle of an air-raid warning *during* dental surgery. The other alias uncomfortably close to my real name is Riccardo Klement, the name chosen by the infamous Adolf Eichmann during his exile in Argentina. Fortunately Mossad kidnapped him and brought him to trial several years before I showed up in Israel.

I never wanted a predictable nine-to-five job. I got a glimpse of that life for a brief period after I left school, taking the same train to London every day and working at Lloyd's getting underwriters to renew insurance policies. Once I became freelance I found I enjoyed the challenge of not knowing where the next job was coming from. It is a great solace when projects are cancelled. A part of me is naturally disappointed but another part is always excited by the prospect that I am now available to do something else.

That's how this job came about, out of the blue. I can't remember what Ian was doing that made him unavailable. What I do recall was suddenly finding myself in First Class on an El Al 747 about to fly to Tel Aviv. Before we took off a very pretty girl sat beside me and said:

'You're either Dick Clement or Ian La Frenais.'

My thought process went as follows:

'I'm married. Ian is single. She's very pretty. I could tell her I'm Ian. I could "be" Ian for three weeks. Who would know? Could I get away with it? She's very pretty. And we're going to Israel. On location. You'll never get away with it. Worth a try though. Live a little, you schmuck!'

Two observations. One: all that took only two point eight seconds. Two: note the way that by calling myself a *schmuck* I was already *thinking Jewish*.

Sometime later we tried to turn this into a script where a writer took on his partner's identity on impulse for the same reasons. We tried to imagine the complications that might have resulted had I succumbed to the horny devil whispering in my ear. Because after two point *nine* seconds, I owned up to my true identity.

A steward persuaded the young lady to give up her own seat and sit next to me, acting like a matchmaking uncle at a wedding along with a raised eyebrow and a knowing smirk. This was not unusual. Every Israeli I met in the next few weeks, male and female, was interested in sex and saw no reason why it shouldn't be encouraged at every opportunity.

I was on my way to Tel Aviv to write a script for Topol. He had just made the movie version of *Fiddler on the Roof* and the theory was that he would be a big star by the time it came out. This film was due to start shooting, in both English and Hebrew, in exactly three weeks. There was an outline of a story but no script. I suppose the thinking was that if you could win a war in six days, why not prep a movie in twenty-one? All the same it took *chutzpah* – another word I'd just learned. At the time it was called *The Rooster* with Topol in the title role playing a man involved with several women simultaneously. Did that make him a *schlemiel*, a *schmendrik*, a *schlimazel* or none of the above? I had no time to find out.

Topol was famous for playing Tevye the dairyman, a much older character. In fact he was only two years older than me. He filled the room with a real presence, brimming with self-confidence. Everybody knew him and he flirted outrageously with every female, flashing his disarming gap-toothed smile. They didn't seem to mind. When I walked through Tel Aviv with him he was given a hero's greeting on every side. I imagine that's what it might have been like if I'd ever had a chance to walk through the streets of Memphis with Elvis. He also seemed to have a hotline to the government. He got a call in the middle of a script conference, listened attentively, put down the phone and told us that a Syrian MiG fighter had just been shot down.

We worked in a room in the Tel Aviv Hilton, high up on the sixteenth floor. One day we broke for lunch on *Shabbat*. Our production assistant was a rabbi's daughter from Milwaukee. She felt unable to summon the lift as it meant using electricity, and started to head for the stairs. Topol teased her for her orthodox beliefs. I hit the button myself to break the deadlock. Apparently a gentile hitting it made it okay and she was spared the long walk.

I decided it might be a good time to grow a beard, something I'd never tried before. After about ten days Topol noticed this and pointed out a hole in the fuzz on my right cheek. For some reason, in a country where beards were commonplace, this seemed like a put-down of my masculinity. That was it for me and beards and good news for Gillette.

I didn't see very much of Israel apart from a side trip to Jerusalem once Jenny and our two children, Andrew and Sian, had flown in for some spring sunshine. Most of the time I was in my room trying to decipher my script notes and get some scenes down. I wrote every day, the pages were snatched from my hand and translated into Hebrew. Incredibly, after three weeks, shooting began.

We visited a location in an orange grove and watched a very long take. I had no idea what the actors were saying or whether it bore any relation to what I'd written. The moment after the director said 'Cut', Jenny threw up. It wasn't the acting that had made her nauseous; it turned out she was pregnant again. It was time to go home.

We called the baby Louis, after Jenny's former boss, the poet Louis MacNeice, and I ended up some months later cutting the English language version of the film in our house, probably breaking all sorts of union rules. It didn't help. The film was a *mishegas*. (That's the last one, I promise.) *Fiddler on the Roof* was released to great acclaim but didn't make Topol a bankable movie star. Maybe you need more than twenty-one days to prep a movie. If you ever chance to see it, don't blame me, it was written by Dik Clamant.

'Nobody Drinks!' – Ian

Ava Gardner

At the end of the sixties Dick and I were working with three American producers resettled in London and operating out of offices in Tilney Street, Mayfair. Elliott Kastner was the senior partner in 'Winkast' together with Jay Kanter, a former agent who'd looked after Marlon Brando, and Alan Ladd Jr., son of the movie star, who would one day become head of Fox Studios and green light *Star Wars*. There was a fourth entity, Gerry Gershwin, who had stayed in California. Gerry, Elliott's partner on projects that included the Paul Newman *Harper* movies, had back problems. He spent much of his time stretched out on the floor of his Malibu pad smoking dope. But when the call from the coast came in, every Mayfair night at 6 p.m., the other three would defer to Gerry's opinion.

We learned a lot hanging around those offices like interns: things about production and deal making which, to us, seemed effortless as they made so many films in such a short period of time. Michael Winner once remarked of this prolific producing period:

'If you were a gorilla walking down Wardour Street with a script in your paw, someone would haul you off the street and give you a deal.'

Winkast gave Dick a deal to direct a movie, *A Severed Head*. I was at a loose end until Laddie asked me to write a screenplay based on a Lionel Davidson novel, *The Rose of Tibet*.

I loved the book and said yes immediately. Laddie and Stanley Mann were producing a movie that year called *Tam Lin* based on a poem by Robbie Burns. It was to be directed by Roddy McDowall and would star the legendary Ava Gardner. They invited me up to the location in Scotland to work on the script there. Hell, yes. Location is always fun even if you're not part of the film and I would meet, surely, one of the great screen actresses of all time.

I met Roddy briefly before the shoot. He was something of a legend in Hollywood, as an actor, child star, photographer, archivist and preserver of Hollywood history. He had been born in Herne Hill in London and acted as a child with comics like George Formby and Will Hay; then he was suddenly transported to California to be in *How Green Was My Valley*, followed by *Flicka* and *Lassie Come Home*. Unlike most child prodigies, however, Roddy didn't disappear into obscurity and worked consistently in films, theatre, television and photography until his death in 1998.

He was also a friend, it seemed, of everyone who was anyone in Hollywood. In his lovely memoir *Dropped Names*, Frank Langella describes Roddy at an A-list party, 'working the room like a cordless vacuum cleaner, sucking up celebrity droppings'. But he was much loved, and a lovely man.

Tam Lin was Roddy's debut as a director. He had vast experience of being 'on the set' but I'm sure what gave him traction was his friendship with Ava. I was told she was very nervous about acting again even though her last film, *Seven Days in May* with Burt Lancaster, was made only two years previously. Perhaps it was because she would be the 'older person' in a cast that was extremely young, except for veterans Richard Wattis and Cyril Cusack. It wasn't only that they were young but they were the products of 'the Sixties', the decade of Swinging London with its sexual liberation and cultural rebellion. They had long hair, short skirts, crushed velvet pants, beads and bongs – a far cry from the Hollywood environment that she'd been brought up in, with autocratic studio heads, contract players and a rigid, if hypocritical, conformity.

Ava, of course, had enjoyed, or tolerated, a lifetime of being in the spotlight. She had been married to the diminutive Mickey Rooney (how did he pull her!), the abusive bandleader Artie Shaw, who had previously been married to Lana Turner (how did he pull those two!) and most famously, Frank Sinatra, Ol' Blue Eyes himself, the Chairman of the Board, whose career was in oblivion when they were first and infamously together, their affair lambasted by the gossip columnists and the Catholic Church.

Through her influence as a major star she persuaded studio honcho Harry Cohn to let Frank audition for *From Here to Eternity* and his career was resurrected. She would break his heart later, of course, especially when she ran off with a Spanish bullfighter, but she always claimed Frank was the love of her life. Roddy told us that the night before the first day of filming, Frank called to wish her luck. This was before mobile phones so I always picture the wee Scottish phone operator in the Peebles Hydro Hotel:

'Miss Gardner, I have Mr Sinatra for you. Putting you through.'

I settled in the hotel and met most of the cast, which included several young talents who would go on to become famous – Ian McShane, Stephanie Beacham, Sinead Cusack, Joanna Lumley and Bruce Robinson, who years later would write and direct the marvellous *Withnail and I*. Jeremy Thomas, who has become Britain's most prolific film producer, was the unit runner. No sign yet of the great star. I worked on the *Tibet* script; wrote in the morning, tennis in the afternoon with Laddie's wife Patty, worked a little more then dinner downstairs with crew and cast. I always like it when everyone on a film, from star to clapper boy, is under one roof.

I became friends with McShane and his wife Ruth. Within a year Ian, Dick and I would work together on the gangster film

Villain with Richard Burton and years later he became Lovejoy and was voted Britain's Sexiest Man. We also were in the same footie team and went to the World Cup in Mexico. In the bitter aftermath of England's 3–2 defeat by Germany, some of us went to a seedy bar. It had a sloping floor so that when someone used the loo their pee would trickle like a stream between our feet. We drank tequila, arm wrestled with farmers who wore machetes in their belts and danced with their women. I don't know how we left that bar alive.

So the great Screen Goddess finally arrived, to little fanfare but great excitement. She had a female companion and her personal hairdresser, Sydney Guilaroff, who was famous in Hollywood and had been MGM's chief hair stylist since 1937. That cut no slack with the British unions and he was not allowed on the set. He did her hair in the morning in the hotel, and she then had a token brush on set while Sydney sulked in his suite. I met him shopping in Peebles one afternoon. He was seriously bored and seriously miffed.

I went to the set on Ava's first day of shooting, keeping a very low profile, which is always advisable when you have nothing to do with the film. And especially when they are shooting a Hollywood legend. God, she was breathtakingly beautiful. I considered her old, of course, even though she was only forty-six. But most of the cast was at least twenty years younger than Ava so she must have felt something like the Grande Dame. Everyone adored her and after initial nerves she began to enjoy herself. So it was that she decided to go out to dinner and Roddy asked me as well as McShane, together with Richard Wattis and Ava's female companion.

We went to a small country hotel somewhere between Peebles and Edinburgh and were given a quiet corner table to avoid the stares of the other astonished customers. I, of course, enjoyed their stares enormously. Hey, I'm a young writer from Whitley Bay and I'm sitting next to Ava Gardner. And tomorrow morning my mother will be the first to know. I couldn't quite believe it. For some reason the sommelier handed me the wine list. Ava wasn't interested in wine and I observed how she very quickly but discreetly connected with a young waiter who would bring her a scotch every so often and slip it beside her glass of untouched wine. Actually, very often. She drank a lot but we all did, and she told stories of other famous people, and Hollywood gossip and dirty jokes and chainsmoked and swore frequently. I was entranced.

When we got back to the hotel she asked McShane and me to her suite where the drinking continued, although now she had switched to vodka. She told us she didn't like liquor very much, she just liked the effect. Ian and I staggered to our rooms at two-thirty in the morning. Next day we compared brutal hangovers. Ava looked like she'd just come out of a health spa after a three-week rejuvenation programme. And a few nights later, when she wasn't working the next day, we did it all again. Same routine; smoke and conversation, ribald stories and the glasses of scotch slipped unobtrusively by her plate. Back to the suite, and staggering, eventually, to bed. And no work on the *Tibet* script the next day.

The film wrapped and everyone went their separate ways, swearing, as on all movies, to be best friends forever. Roddy read my *Rose of Tibet* script and wanted it to be his next project. We met in London for coffees in between his editing schedule and worked on a second draft. Laddie set the project up with Commonwealth United who had financed *The Magic Christian* with Peter Sellers and Ringo Starr, as well as *Tam Lin*. It was decided that the three of us, and art director Don Ashton, would scout locations in Bhutan. None of us knew where it was but we were told by someone who'd been there that there was one great restaurant. We had shots for diseases we'd never heard of, were issued flight tickets and then Commonwealth pulled the plug. I think they had actually gone broke.

Oh well, it had all seemed a bit too good to be true. A script deal, a director attached, a location scout fixed and writing it in a grand Scottish hotel while spending evenings carousing with a Hollywood legend.

I did see the legend again a short time later at a party given by Joanna Lumley.

Then I went to Ava's birthday party at her apartment in Park Place, Mayfair. Quite accidentally I bumped into her at a fat farm in Surrey. She walked around in a white bathrobe with her hair tied up and no make-up, her face flushed from the sauna, and no one recognised her. We shared a grapefruit together. She asked me to a dinner party she was giving for somebody in the near future. It seemed I had transitioned from wide-eyed, stuttering, star-struck fan of Screen Goddess to Friend of Goddess. But I only saw her once again, at an art show in Paris and the meeting was, once more, accidental. A fabulous woman from the golden age.

Tam Lin was not well received or distributed. It seemed to disappear, completely off the grid, into obscurity. Roddy was devastated. Ava bounced back playing the Empress of Austria in *Mayerling*, an acclaimed performance. When I recently checked *Tam Lin* is available on Blu-ray on Amazon for $18.99 and is retitled *The Devil's Woman*.

On that first night with McShane, when we ended up in Ava's suite, I remember the moment when Ian and I decided we had to quit and go to bed. She was quite upset and obviously did not want to be alone. When we walked out of the door her parting shot was:

'*Nobody drinks!*'

Perhaps later she called Frank.

'What Did I Say Yesterday?' – Dick

Peter Cook

I saw *Beyond the Fringe* at London's tiny Fortune Theatre. It remains one of the funniest shows I ever saw. It shocked the older generation, who were especially outraged by the idea that four young men could mock the stiff upper lip tradition that got Britain through the war after only fifteen years of peace. This made my generation laugh even louder and quote lines to one another, like the one when Peter Cook, as an RAF Wing Commander, sends Jonathan Miller off on a mission:

'I want you to lay down your life, Perkins. We need a futile gesture at this stage. It will raise the whole tone of the war.'

Broadway audiences got all the jokes too and they were established as comedic superstars. Peter teamed up with Dudley

Moore and they did a BBC series called *Not Only . . . But Also*.
A second series was being commissioned but the original director
was not available. Frank Muir asked if I would like the job. I was
surprised and flattered and of course said yes.

A lunch was arranged at the White Tower, a wonderful Greek
restaurant on Charlotte Street, sadly long gone, allegedly a haunt
of MI5 during the war. As Frank and I sat opposite the two stars
I felt distinctly at a disadvantage. I wasn't in their league, hadn't
gone to university and they were comic geniuses. This feeling
increased as the lunch went on because Peter was incredibly, consistently funny, which made me feel more inadequate than ever.

I was comforted later when I read that Alan Bennett felt much
the same way. He said it took him a week to come up with a joke,
which he presented to the others like a delicate orchid, whereas
Peter came up with a never-ending bouquet of them.

I got the job and we went to work. In our initial planning session Peter suggested an opening for the first show. He and Dudley
are playing the piano; it is raised into the air, lowered into the
Thames and they continue to play under water.

My PA laughed dutifully and said we couldn't possibly do that,
could we? Peter saw this as a challenge and fixed him with a steely
eye. Why not? A few weeks later, in January weather, a film crew
assembled on the deck of a freighter moored at a London dock
and Peter's idea was recorded on film. He and Dudley played
a few bars before the platform the piano was mounted on was
hoisted by a crane and lowered towards the freezing waters of the
Thames.

A very nasty incident nearly occurred. When the platform hit
the surface, the cables went slack. As they were winched up again,
one of them snaked over Dudley's shoulder and for a horrible
moment I thought it might decapitate him. Once that was over
we filmed the relatively easy underwater part of the sequence in a
Butlin's swimming pool in Bognor.

The work pattern that evolved was as follows: we shot film on location on Monday. We rehearsed the rest of the week, working out the sketches to be taped in front of a live audience, meanwhile editing the show from the previous week and the film for the following week. Saturday afternoon was the only time off. We rehearsed the show in the studio on Sunday, recorded it in the evening, got drunk afterwards and went off with a hangover on Monday morning to repeat the process all over again.

One of these Mondays was memorable. We found ourselves on a train to Felixstowe to film a sketch of 'Pete and Dud'. It was February and it had snowed overnight. This gave us a heaven-sent opportunity. I shot them sitting in deckchairs, gazing out to sea while rhapsodising on the benefits of out-of-season holidays. When they got up the camera followed them trudging across a beach covered in two inches of fresh snow.

The fun fair was opened up for our benefit and we wanted to shoot them as the only customers on the big dipper. The owner had a problem. He was afraid the ice on the rails might slow down the cars and they might not make the rise on the first 'big dip'. My eyes lit up but I knew we could only ever film it once. We quickly set up, well aware that the winter light was fading. The cars were winched up the initial rise. They hurtled down the slope, reached the top, faltered and ran backwards and forwards before finally coming to rest.

Peter hated heights and he and Dudley had to descend a long ladder to get back down to earth but there was no way he was going to let that stand in the way of a golden comic opportunity, the greatest piece of luck I ever had on location and nothing that could ever have been planned.

It's sad to report that this magical moment is lost because the BBC wiped most of the shows to make room on their shelves. For the same reason only a few of the original *Likely Lads* have survived. Two *Morecambe & Wise* shows were recently discovered in a cinema in Sierra Leone so I live in hope that some diligent archivist will discover my own work one day.

All the sketches were improvised. Whatever Peter came up with on Thursday was not always the same as Wednesday. I found out very quickly that my job was essentially to be a brisk and efficient nanny, channelling Mary Poppins:

'That's very funny, Peter, but yesterday was funnier.'

'Why, what did I say yesterday?'

I told him and if he agreed, that was the version we used. None of the 'Pete and Dud' segments, for example, was ever committed to paper. I put five cameras on them and shot them on the fly. Peter delighted in making Dudley 'corpse', while he usually – though not always – remained icily deadpan.

It would be wrong to underestimate Dudley's contribution to the comedy but it's true to say that Peter was the driving creative force. They made a perfect combination because Peter was essentially 'cool', intellectual and cerebral whereas Dudley was, well, cuddly. Women wanted to hug him and take him home. Quite a few of them did.

I can't say Peter and I became close, there was hardly any time for that, though I earned his respect because he credited me with the fact that the second series was a great improvement on the first. I was still in awe of his genius and the speed with which his brain worked. I remember the crew biting their cheeks during a take to prevent them from laughing when we shot a sequence where Dudley played a court jester to his king, who bore more than a passing resemblance to Olivier's Richard the Third.

Conversation with Peter inevitably had a competitive edge. With any new acquaintance he liked to find out whatever made them wince. It might be religion, disability, the royal family, cancer. No matter what it was he would probe until he found the no-go area. It was a characteristic that made me uncomfortable; of course I hid my feelings or he might have used them against me.

At the end of the series there was talk of Peter and Dudley making a movie together. With all the hubris of youth I thought I would be the perfect person to direct it. I lost out – if indeed I was ever considered - to Stanley Donen, a genuine Hollywood heavyweight. The film was *Bedazzled* and Peter played the devil. It was a modest success but when I looked at it again recently Peter's performance seemed very 'one note'. A studio executive at the time thought he might be the new Cary Grant. He had the looks but he wasn't really an actor. His talents lay in wild, unpredictable improvisation, not having to establish and maintain a character over the length of an entire movie. The idea of him as a romantic lead in a 'rom-com', the sort of part that Hugh Grant made his own, seems ludicrous.

Dudley was something else altogether. True, he wasn't tall but he was cute, adorable and funny. Ian used to get mistaken for him. A New York cab driver asked for his autograph. Ian tried to assure him that he was not who he thought he was. The cabbie viewed this as typical behaviour from an overpaid, overpraised actor and subjected him to a string of abuse.

We were looking for locations in the Virgin Islands and at dinner a man kept smiling knowingly in our direction. He finally paid his bill and wandered past our table. He was beyond asking 'Dudley' if he was who he thought he was, he was far too cool for that. He just smiled knowingly at Ian and said:

'I just want to say, the people of Boston really appreciate your artistry. When you hopped across the sand in that movie . . .'

He moved away, chuckling at the memory.

The truth is that the movie he was referencing, *10*, directed by Blake Edwards, made Dudley a movie star. It's also true that Peter betrayed more than a hint of envy. I didn't see a lot of him around that time but he never missed an opportunity to make snide references to his 'vertically challenged' former co-star. Dudley went from strength to strength. He was brilliant in *Arthur*. When the film was remade it only proved how difficult it is to make an incorrigible alcoholic funny and sympathetic. One of the side effects of the role is that people thought Dudley had a drinking problem in real life. Not so. Peter, on the other hand, had different addictions.

Peter retained his conspicuous talent for improvisational comedy and was revered by his peers and the younger generation of comics to the end, but it is sad to reflect that he may have flowered too early. He wrote his brilliant sketch about a man with one leg auditioning for the part of Tarzan when he was only eighteen. I can still see Dudley in my mind's eye, hopping on one leg while Peter, the phlegmatic impresario, gave him the sad news:

'Need I say without overmuch emphasis that it is in the leg division that you are deficient. You are deficient in it to the tune of one. Your right leg I like. I like your right leg. A lovely leg for the role. That's what I said when I saw you come in. I said, "A lovely leg for the role." I've got nothing against your right leg. The trouble is – neither have you.'

Footnote from Ian:

Peter had had a dream of opening a satirical nightclub since university and with the success of *Beyond the Fringe* he had the clout and the money to do so. The Establishment, as he named it, was in Soho, the seediest of the London boroughs, being the only place in England where sex was blatantly commercial with its strip clubs, porn stores, blue cinemas and prostitutes. The premises he took over were formerly the Club Tropicana, an 'all girl revue'.

After Peter's new club opened some local hoods dropped by wanting protection money, or, as they termed it, 'fire insurance'. Peter refused and threatened to put them on the stage during a live performance and repeat their demands to the audience. They left and never bothered 'those upper class twits' again.

The club quickly became the place to see and be seen. It offered dinner at either side of the show – no noisy plates during it – and the Dudley Moore Trio played jazz in the basement. It was always filled with the prettiest girls and was, essentially, a singles bar for satirists. In the year after it opened the club presented three standout acts: Lenny Bruce, Frankie Howerd and Barry Humphries.

It also featured new aspiring comics – the word 'stand-up' had not yet been coined. Two young wannabes were Francis Megahy and Bernie Cooper who, twenty-five years later, wrote us an *Auf Wiedersehen* script.

Dick and I were not used to hanging in 'the hippest spot in town' so when we went to the Establishment we chose an early hour to avoid being refused admittance. We hoped we might connect with someone who would be interested in our comedy sketches – all four of them. We met someone our age at the bar who seemed pleasant and curious. He told us he also wrote sketches and that night he was performing his material himself. We took our drinks into the main room and checked him out.

He didn't exactly set the place alight and afterwards appeared a little dejected and unsure of himself and his talent. He needn't have worried. Within a year he was a household name as the presenter of *That Was The Week That Was*. His name was David Frost.

A few years later he produced *The Frost Report* for the BBC and asked us, I swear, if we had any sketches. I went to his Kings Road service flat and pitched a couple of ideas, one, I remember, about the British abroad and forgetting the sandwiches. He laughed out loud and enthused wildly as David always did.

'Marvellous!'

He didn't use them but then nor did anyone else.

FAQ # 2

'What Are Your Influences?'

Dick & Ian

Dick: I thought we'd already answered this question when we acknowledged our debt to Richmal Crompton and the *William* books, though I suppose she wasn't much help when we started writing movies.

Ian: We were both fans of the new wave black and white British cinema: *Long Distance Runner, Saturday Night and Sunday Morning, A Kind of Loving, This Sporting Life.* Films about working-class resentment and rebellion – a far cry from all those *Doctor* movies with Dirk Bogarde.

Dick: When we were at school all the leading men wore blazers, cravats and suede shoes, unless they were commanding a submarine.

Ian: Television didn't influence me much. What was the point of moving to London and being glued to the box every night? The exceptions were *Hancock* and *Steptoe*. Galton and Simpson were an enormous influence – the first writers we wanted to emulate.

Dick: And *Z Cars*, that was a great show. The cops in it seemed so believable, especially after *Dixon of Dock Green*.

Ian: The rest was pretty awful. Game shows, variety shows, chefs teaching you how to cook *lasagna* and some bloke in wellies telling you how to prune roses.

Dick: If there was anything edgy, Mary Whitehouse would blow the whistle. She called *Doctor Who* 'teatime brutality for tots'. And she thought the Wednesday Plays were 'obsessed with sex, violence and degradation'. Probably why they got twelve million viewers.

Ian: There's another movie that precedes the sixties and had a massive influence and that's Carol Reed's *The Third Man*.

Dick: I couldn't agree more. Every time I see it I'm impressed not just by the visual style but the writing. Graham Greene sets up what it was like to be in Vienna in that post-war era in the opening two minutes.

Ian: It has a brilliant mix of humour and *noir*. Since I saw that film I've always been hooked on thrillers. That and *The Ipcress File* kicked it off. And for espionage it was *The Spy Who Came in from the Cold*.

Dick: We're known for comedy but love writing thrillers. Wish we'd written more. Two of our favourite novelists are Robert Harris and Alan Furst so it was great to adapt their work to the screen with *Archangel* and *The Spies of Warsaw*.

Ian: When we first met we had no credentials to be writers – no college or correspondence courses, no qualifications, not even the burning conviction that this was what we wanted to do. One thing we did have in common was that we had both completed National Service.

Dick: That's true. For two years we witnessed the whole spectrum of the British social class system. Down the line we would mine it, expose it and rejoice in its absurdities and idiosyncrasies.

Ian: So yes, it was a massive influence. I'm convinced it gave us the confidence to accept that first BBC commission. Wish I'd kept a diary like T. E. Lawrence.

Dick: You can put the record straight now.

Ian: Well, for two years I was a Navy Seal conducting black ops behind enemy lines. Think people will find that interesting?

Dick: They might if it wasn't bullshit. Let's try the truth. You go first.

Ian: Why me?

Dick: Because I outrank you.

Queen and Country – Ian

National Service

The common wisdom was to do your military service straight from school, not after university. At eighteen, with A-levels behind you, it would be much easier to adapt than after four years getting a degree during which time you'll have had a taste of freedom, adulthood, living away from home, growing you hair, beer and girls. It was true, I noticed, the grads were miserable, especially the Oxbridge boys, while the rest of us looked on the experience as an adventure or, at least, a bit of a lark.

I imagined instant manhood. I would wear a uniform, I would be armed and surely, over two years, there would be the chance of sex. With a girl, of course, not a squaddie which is what we were dismissively called. People like me, almost all only eighteen, shared the same philosophy – we're lumbered, nothing we can do about it but make the best of it.

The college boys had made their choice in the hope that by the time they finished their studies the government would have abolished National Service. It had been enforced in 1939 but remained after the war and was even increased after Korea from eighteen months to two years. There were still trouble spots in the world and it was possible to be conscripted and killed; in Malaya, Cyprus or Egypt.

That wasn't a possibility that troubled David Hallwood and me as we waved goodbye to our parents at Newcastle Central Station. Around the same time a young Dick Clement was making another train journey with his Penguin paperback and his mother's sandwiches, from Southend in Essex to an Air Force base in Bedfordshire.

David and I had been best friends since infancy and by an amazing coincidence were called up into the same intake of the same regiment and were bound for the same barracks. I say regiment, we were actually assigned to a corps: that was the Royal Army Service Corps, also known as the RASC which, we were told by cynics in a rival corps, stood for 'Run Away Someone's Coming'. We gave that joke to Terry in *The Likely Lads* and have used it several times since.

David and I spent our entire basic training in adjacent beds. The hut was a real melting pot, just as another would be years later in *Auf Wiedersehen, Pet*. There were middle-class boys like us, posh boys from major public schools, working-class apprentices, misfits, petty crims and a gay boy from the London College of Fashion. There was also McNulty from the Glasgow Gorbals, who threatened someone with a bayonet but cried in his bed out of homesickness. We tiptoed around McNulty but one night he smashed all the windows with his bare fists and we never saw him again.

Hudson had set his sights on a career in parliament. He was only nineteen but he smoked a pipe and when he berated a disruptive troublemaker he used the pipe to punctuate all his points about consideration for others, discipline, courtesy, morale and 'playing the game'. The rest of us listened enthralled with the vicarious conviction that this would not end well. It didn't; a moment after he'd made his final point – something about 'knuckling down and pulling one's weight' – Hudson was felled by a single punch to the chin and had to be revived by smelling salts. His pipe was broken in two, but it would have been hard to suck on anyway without his front teeth.

Steele was one of the Oxbridge brigade, all of whom were

deeply distressed by changing dreaming spires for draughty barrack rooms. He had the languid voice of the privileged and his
clothes were hung on Grosvenor House hangers. He had been
medically downgraded because of asthma and was with us instead
of being fast-tracked to a commission in the Royal Fusiliers or
some other snooty regiment. During a class on weapons training
a sergeant asked him if he knew the weight of a Bren gun. Steele
considered the question before answering:

'I've absolutely no idea, Sergeant, but I imagine it's bloody
heavy.'

None of us would have got away with that reply; we would
have all be on the floor doing two dozen press-ups. He seemed
to regard every question or command as an impertinence, but his
casual insouciance just seemed to amuse the instructors, as would
all his responses.

There was Allan, mild mannered and owlish, an Oxford First
who loved the classics and Gilbert and Sullivan. In later years,
every time I read a George Smiley novel, Allan's face would always
come to mind, until it was replaced by Alec Guinness.

And there was Jones. From Shropshire. Abusive, disruptive,
loud mouthed and annoying. He rarely changed his socks. He
farted, belched and scratched his balls.

Surely he must have been in my mind when Dick and I sat
down to create Oz.

We had been brought up as kids on barrack room comedies.
We had laughed at Abbott and Costello in uniform, and Martin
and Lewis, and our homegrown comedians; Peter Sellers and
Terry-Thomas, Tony Newley and the *Carry On* gang. What struck
me after only a few weeks was that all those old clichéd jokes and
situations still persisted. It was as if routine and vocabulary had
never changed since the Charge of the Light Brigade.

So yes, every morning a voice would wake us with the words –
'Hands off cocks, on with socks.'

And NCOs would abuse us, constantly reminding us that we were – ''Orrible little men.' And soldiers who'd served overseas kept ordering us to 'Get your knees brown' or 'Get some in!'

And, heaven forbid we were sick and reported to the MO; whether it was a tooth that needed filling or a leg that required urgent amputation, we would be prescribed two codeine and told to come back on Tuesday.

Drill sergeants shouted at us whether we were on the parade ground or not. Every lunch in the mess a pink-cheeked sprog subaltern would ask how the grub was, chaps, and we'd tell him that it was terrific, sir. On the rifle range the targets were life-sized cut-outs of Hitler and we marched, with the bloody rifles, at the double everywhere. We even had to carry them to lectures and church services.

Ginger Roberts (yes, seriously) had a benign smile and wore bifocals. One day when it rained we were ordered to put on our waterproof capes. Ginger had the brilliant idea of raising his finger under the cape so it looked as if he was carrying his rifle. We all happily followed suit, delighted we were putting one over the system. The sun broke through on a tea break, we took off the waterproofs, our ruse was discovered and we all lost our next thirty-six-hour leave passes.

The most consistent cliché was that criticism, or verbal abuse, was almost always preceded by a question. An example: a sergeant major, a formidable and frightening man, spotted me in the street as I scurried in the shadows trying to avoid detection.

'You!' he commanded.

He meant me; there was no one else in sight. He then gestured with his finger that I crossed the street and stood before him. He appraised me from the tip of my unpolished boots to the badge in my beret. The inevitable question followed:

'What are you?'

'Er, um, not sure, Sarnt Major.'

'Shall I tell you?'

'Yes, Sarnt Major.'

'You are a mobile shithouse.'

And, of course, another question.

'What are you?'

'I am a mobile shithouse, sir.'

Basic training ended and we were all reappraised and re-directed far and wide.

David went off to the dullest part of Germany and I went to OTC – Officer Training School. The first question I was asked was did I play rugby. I said yes and as the current English full back was an old boy from my school I was automatically in the team. Extra rations, tracksuit instead of hairy serge – this would do just fine. Then something happened and I still can't remember exactly what. There was some kind of protest against some kind of injustice. I just went along with what the posher boys decreed and demanded. Next thing our entire class was dismissed from OTC, apparently an unprecedented event.

I wasn't too upset; there were still attractive options. God knows what possessed me but I volunteered for an attachment to the Parachute Regiment, fancying, I imagine, those sexy wings on my sleeve. This was when I learned that my medical had shown I had hay fever, which categorised me as 'Non Tropical'. So no parachute jumps into equatorial jungles and, a comfort, no postings to places with snakes, spiders and bandits.

There were other possibilities. The RASC staffed all British embassies in the world, so when I filled in a form asking for my three preferred choices of posting I wrote: Washington, Oslo, Paris. Which, I'm sure, is why I got Aldershot.

So I ended up in another hut with another bunch of misfits. It was a Resettlement Centre designed to teach trades to soldiers facing demob – real soldiers, not conscripts like my lot. I was made a corporal and my duties were clerical. The departing sergeant showed me the ropes. His name was Stuart Steven and years later he would become editor of the *Daily Express*. Allan, my George Smiley model, was my senior colleague. Our CO was a colonel with a duffel coat and a limp, a war wound no doubt, who was always in a foul mood. He was either in physical pain or his wife was sleeping with the gardener, but every day his mood darkened as the hours passed.

Allan and I were the only educated people in our unit, the others being oddballs from different regiments whose duties were manual and menial. But the ten of us all shared the same hut, hung together, played football, and drank in country pubs. I don't remember all their names but oddly enough I recall all the towns they were from – Bexleyheath, Gravesend, Saxmundham, Worcester, Aberdeen, Leominster, Middlesbrough and Tulla-more, County Offaly. The East Anglian would end up in *Lovejoy* and a couple more in *Porridge*.

For some reason I issued leave passes, most of which I gave to myself. But Newcastle was an awful long journey from Hampshire in those days so I would explore London, mostly the pubs in the West End. I did see a musical, *The Pajama Game*, and saw a very young Shirley Bassey at somewhere in the Strand. The army issued a list of clubs in London that were banned to military personnel. One of them was the Mandrake in Soho so naturally that was the first port of call for me and a couple of mates. I was desperate to know why Her Majesty's Government had blacklisted this club. Perhaps gay men went there, or bohemians or opium users. As we were obviously none of the above the doorman refused us admission. Perhaps it was our haircuts.

There was a pair of humourless sergeants in our unit from the Education Corps; one of them had no chin, the other was from Edinburgh. One day the Scot asked me what I intended to do after the army. Perhaps it was some extraordinary prescience on my behalf or just random bullshit but I told him I was going to write films.

He seemed impressed; it was an answer he'd never heard before.

Up until then I had never talked about 'writing'. I created fantasies and had the gift of making people laugh but nothing more serious than that. During basic training I was assigned for a week to do 'fatigues' on the sports field. I reported to the groundsman and we started painting white lines on the football pitches. He was old and slightly stooped and he asked me about myself. I had not yet read *Billy Liar* but I went into this whole Billy riff, inventing an imaginary lifestyle: a family estate in Northumberland, aristocratic parents, debutante sisters and a badly behaved brother who kept pranging the Jag. The old boy was fascinated, he couldn't wait to pick up the story the next day, which I was obliged to invent. And the day after that. The white lines remained unfinished, so did the weeding and repainting and cleaning out the cricket pavilion.

I sometimes felt guilty about bullshitting the nice old groundsman. But he really liked my stories. He couldn't wait to hear the next instalment of my Downton existence.

And I've been making up stories ever since.

Queen and Country – Dick

National Service

I'm lucky enough to be able to say that I have never fired a bullet at anyone and no one has – so far – fired one at me. Ian's experience is much the same, unless he's keeping something from me. Happily, the nearest I came to combat was when I was on standby to go to Jordan and got issued with tropical kit. Then the crisis passed, whatever it was, and I didn't go.

Perhaps I didn't get shouted at as much as Ian did, though I had my share of it during square-bashing at RAF Bridgnorth in Shropshire. Drill sergeants must all have read the same manual: *Recruits, Humiliation Of: Section 1, Witty Repartee*:

'Did you shave this morning?'

'Yes, Sergeant.'

'Did you use a mirror?'

'Yes, Sergeant.'

'Try using a bloody razor next time!'

Bo-boom. Rim shot.

Then the one standing very close behind the unfortunate Airman (Second Class):

'Am I hurting you?'

'No, Sergeant.'

'I should be because I'm STANDING ON YOUR HAIR!'

Sharing a hut with a bunch of assorted fellow citizens from all parts of the British Isles was, of course, an experience that we tapped into later when we imagined ourselves in the nick or working on a building site in a foreign land. My first hut was at RAF Cardington and included some hard-looking lads from the East End. I was surprised on the first night to hear several weeping into their pillows. I wasn't all that bothered; I'd been to boarding school.

The fact that I'd spent a year in America flagged me in some way. I used it shamelessly in interviews and blagged my way onto an officer-training course on the Isle of Man. As we traipsed down the gangplank Warrant Officer Cooke was waiting to greet us. He looked like a sergeant major in a Whitehall farce, complete with a waxed moustache, its ends bristling intimidatingly skywards. He was nowhere near as terrifying as he looked. In fact he forewarned us that senior recruits would raid us on our first night with a bogus fire drill and we should tell them to bugger off.

I got my commission and the rank of Pilot Officer but no, I was not a pilot (left eye great, right one dodgy), I was in the far from glamorous Equipment Branch. I made one flight across the Atlantic, to Nova Scotia via the Azores. I was utterly superfluous, along for the ride. This was in Coastal Command, from Ballykelly in Northern Ireland, flying low over the sea at a hundred and eighty miles an hour. I spent most of it reading Aldous Huxley and A. E. Housman, studying for an A-level so that I could get into university after my two years were up.

It rained a lot in Ballykelly. I learned how to play poker. I also tried out my charm on the local girls at a dance in Londonderry. While twirling one round the floor I mentioned that I was in the RAF.

'Ah, so you're with the occupational forces of Northern Ireland.'

That was a bit of a non-starter. After a few months I was posted to a base four miles from Stratford-on-Avon. I joined a local Dramatic Society and went to see every production at the RSC down the road. Several members of their company used to drink with us after the show. I was suddenly rubbing shoulders with 'actors',

The family Clement.

Ian's parents.

Ian solo.

'An officer and a
gentleman . . .

. . . and a mobile shithouse.'

CSI Chelsea.

The Lads in their natural habitat. (Topfoto/Arenapal)

'If we stay another month maybe we should buy a car.'

The road to Hong Kong. 'I feel as stupid as you look.'

Moscow with the Elton crew – and Nancy (*front row, right*).

Elton at home? Or is it the Summer Palace?

Doris at the Kremlin.
'Comrade Brezhnev
will see you now.'

Michael Caine.
Cricket in St Lucia.
(PA/PA Archive/PA
Images)

which felt very appealing, as if I was moving among kindred spirits.

Perhaps that was one of the reasons why I never went to university. Instead I joined the BBC as a 'studio manager'. I didn't really know what that meant and the pay wasn't good but I felt that I would somehow be swimming in the right pond. As it turned out, I was right.

I remember my leaving party in the mess with everyone wishing me good luck in 'Civvy Street'. I made a flippant remark, something like:

'From what I hear about the BBC I'll probably have to drop my drawers if I want to get on.'

This did not go down well with a senior officer, one who had only recently arrived at the base. He growled into his gin and tonic:

'I hope you're joking. I happen to find that kind of thing completely disgusting.'

The rest of the leaving party was a bit flat after that.

Many years later Ian and I were flown to Honolulu to do a rewrite on *Pearl Harbor*. Because of the time difference from LA it was still lunchtime when we arrived. We were whisked straight to the film set to meet the director, Michael Bay, various film executives and high-ranking navy brass, determined to make sure that everything portrayed on the screen was historically accurate. Among other things we were told they didn't want any sailors to swear, which hardly seemed historical or accurate.

They looked at us two long-haired limeys with deep suspicion – until I mentioned casually that I had served time in Her Majesty's Royal Air Force. (I omitted to say that this was not dropping bombs but ordering supplies for the Airfield Construction Branch.) Ian followed suit and let them know he had been also spent time in 'the military'.

Their attitude changed instantly. It seemed to reassure them to know that at some time in our lives we had saluted somebody in authority. The fact that it was in another country – and not even in the Navy – didn't faze them at all. And as a matter of record, we rewrote a scene that afternoon that was shot the following morning – our personal record. It featured Kate Beckinsale, daughter of Richard, a link with the past that we all found oddly reassuring.

One aspect of being a writer is that if you hear a good story you instantly ask yourself where you can use it to best advantage. I heard one in the RAF from Flying Officer Mike Caswell. Mike was a proper officer; he had actually flown planes. He was also very funny. He told me about being posted to a remote radar station somewhere in the Hebrides. It had only three other officers, one of them female. When he arrived the first words out of their mouths were:

'Do you play bridge?'

Mike intuited that a lot depended on his answer. There was no nightlife up there and he knew enough about bridge to know that it needed four players. So he reassured them that he understood the basic idea of the game. That very first night they retired to the Nissen hut that served as an apology for an Officers' Mess, sat down and dealt the cards. Mike was partnered with the WAAF officer. He played very badly. He could tell by their dour expressions that he was in no way the officer they had been hoping and praying for.

After an hour or two he was 'dummy', which meant that he laid down his cards to let his partner play them. He was also desperate to relieve himself, so he muttered an excuse and went outside. The trouble was that he had no idea where the loo was so he was forced to improvise.

It was impossible for the two male officers to ignore the echoing sound of rivers of urine cascading against the metal side of the hut. They mumbled excuses for their fellow officer but she would have none of it.

'*Please don't apologise, it's the first time all night I've known what he's got in his hand.*'

It took me eighteen years but I finally found a way to bring that story to a wider audience. We put it in the movie of *The Likely Lads;* Bob and Terry were playing bridge with Thelma in a caravan and Terry had to go outside . . .

I don't think Brigit Forsyth ever got a bigger laugh.

Footnote from Ian:

Just for the record, I fired a Sten gun during basic training in the army and very nearly took the end of my finger off. I still have the scar.

'I Can't Play Comedy!' – Dick

Kirk Douglas

The second film I directed was *A Severed Head*. Not a horror film, as the title suggests, but a project with far loftier ambitions, from the novel by Iris Murdoch and a screenplay by Frederic Raphael. And what a cast my producers assembled: Lee Remick, Claire Bloom, Richard Attenborough and Ian Holm. I felt I was moving up into a different league. I envisioned in-depth articles on my oeuvre in *Sight and Sound*. Perhaps my credit would read: '*Un Film de Dick Clement*'. Just one doubt gnawed at me: who was the audience for this film? I shared this anxiety with Elliott Kastner, one of the producers. He replied blandly that it was nothing I should worry about. Years later it hit me that producers get paid when a movie gets made so of course he would say that.

I went ahead, trying to conceal the fact that I felt out of my intellectual depth. Iris Murdoch visited the set, looking every inch the Oxford bluestocking, no make-up and hair that her husband might have cut with the aid of a pudding bowl. She was warm and enthusiastic and took me aside saying she had no idea that a film-set would be so *completely* like a film-set. During the shoot she sent me hand-written notes that I've kept, perhaps hoping that an obscure American university might make me an offer for them. In one note she was upset after hearing the 'magical object' (her phrase) might be retitled *Affairs and Relations*. She appealed to me to fight for her elegant and famous title, finding the new one vapid, vulgar and very un-Murdoch.

Her title was retained. The film got decent reviews and played at the Curzon. This was a lovely cinema in Mayfair that usually showed foreign movies directed by Bergman or Antonioni. It had very comfortable seats, easy to snooze in, but was a very far cry from your local Odeon.

There was a reason for this. I heard on the grapevine that Nat Cohen, soon to be described as the most powerful man in the British film industry, loathed my movie. Consequently a year went by and no one had offered me another film to direct. How was I going to further my oeuvre? The solution that Ian and I came up with was to write another screenplay called *Orange Wednesday* from the novel by Leslie Thomas. We showed it to various people in the hope that someone would give us a deal.

While this was going on, our agent arranged a meeting with a Belgian producer called Nat Wachsberger. He gave us a book called *Catch Me a Spy*. It wasn't very good so we turned it down and asked him to read our other project instead. After a few weeks we were told that Nat would finance this one as long as we wrote *Catch Me a Spy* first for me to direct. So we took the assignment.

In our experience it's never a good sign if we get bogged down. The best stuff falls onto the page – well almost – but if we stare at each other for two or three days and haven't written anything, it's usually a sign that something is seriously wrong. We did this in a rented house in the South of France. What made it worse was hearing the sound of other people splashing in the pool as we sat in a gloomy room carved out of rock while little black centipedes occasionally fell into our glasses of rosé. We somehow hacked our way through the jungle and completed the screenplay. I rationalised that if the project had any chance at all I would have to give it the light touch, wit and charm of a film like *Charade*.

Then I learned that the main female role was to be played by a French actress called Marlène Jobert. (Her daughter, Eva Green, is a great beauty and an acclaimed actress.) I didn't know her work but she had just had a big hit in France, *Rider in the Rain* with Charles Bronson, and was consequently 'bankable'. The character we had written needed some of Audrey Hepburn's vulnerability with maybe a touch of Judy Holliday's kookiness. Marlène had some of these qualities, but how was her command of English? While I was pondering this, my producer told me that he had found our leading man. All right, I knew I wasn't going to get Cary Grant but maybe George Segal? James Coburn? No, he had cast Kirk Douglas.

I was not happy. Of course I had a lot of admiration for his body of work: *Lust for Life*, *Lonely Are the Brave*, *Spartacus* and all those Westerns – but a light touch? To me it sounded like trying to make a soufflé with meat. But the deal was done, Kirk flew into London and I arranged to meet him at the Grosvenor House Hotel. I knocked at the door of his suite, he opened it himself and

I found myself staring into those blue eyes and that cleft in his chin. And what were his first words, even before 'Hello'?

'I can't play comedy.'

So there he was, voicing exactly what I had been saying to everybody else in a curt, uncompromising growl. I felt like a lawyer hired to defend an alleged murderer whose opening words were: 'I killed the sonovabitch.' Clearly we shared the same misgivings. I don't have the transcript of my response but I must have burbled something about comedy being something I had cut my teeth on and together we could find common ground . . .

But I can't say that we did. Experience has taught me that a problem doesn't go away merely because you identify it. That principle applied, not just to Kirk being the antithesis of comedy, but also to the material itself. Why had Ian and I turned it down in the first place? And why had we decided to do it anyway? So that we could eventually make the film we really wanted to make – which unsurprisingly never happened.

Kirk had every reason to be wary because he didn't trust the material and I had several moments when he took off his jacket, flung it across the room and said something like, 'I've made eighty-seven goddam movies, I think I know what I'm talking about!'

Or:

'Dialogue ends up on the cutting room floor. But in my experience no one ever cut out the bit where I sock a guy in the jaw.'

By now we are in Oban, in the West Highlands of Scotland, a very long way from Hollywood, even though the local hotel had done its best to make him comfortable. Every day he wanted to go over the scenes that were due to be shot, word by word, speech by speech, to the point where Ian, to avoid being spotted, used to duck down – or did he actually crawl, I can't remember – as he passed by Kirk's trailer in search of coffee and a bacon sandwich.

Marlène's command of English was about the same as my command of French, which didn't help. She had a tiny scar on one cheek as the result of a minor accident and it showed up if she was lit from the side. Before every shot she turned to me for reassurance:

'Deek, 'ow is it for my scar?'

She even asked this question before running with Kirk through a herd of highland cattle when the camera was in the next field. She learned her lines and worked hard but the chemistry between her and Kirk lacked sparkle; hardly surprising given that he was thirty years older than she was at the time.

A strange pattern emerged. After lunch Kirk was, if not exactly a pussycat, someone I could relate to. We talked through his concerns, found common ground and shot the scenes. I told myself I had broken through, made contact, got through to the inner man. The next morning it was as if nothing had happened, back to square one. The penny never dropped. It was only in postproduction that my assistant director explained that at every lunch Kirk enjoyed a very large joint.

While shooting a movie you can maintain enthusiasm and blind yourself to its faults. I'd tried to give myself insurance by casting excellent actors like Trevor Howard and our pal Tom Courtenay. I also cast the French actor, Sacha Pitoëff, famous for his leading role in *Last Year in Marienbad.* When he arrived in Argyllshire his opening words were not promising:

'I am not well. I need to go to Paris. Now.'

We were in the middle of a field at the time. I summoned our producer and passed the problem on to him. M. Pitoëff stayed.

I should have known the omens were not good when Ian, directing second unit, managed to drop an Arriflex camera into the depths of Loch Awe, losing several thousand feet of film. All Kirk's scenes were finally in the can, the film wrapped and I started to put it together. It was only when I viewed the first assembly that I had a sinking feeling in my stomach.

I had been careful to choose a profession as far away as possible from what my two elder brothers did. They wore suits and worked in corporate offices. I had no idea what they actually did from nine to five and they had no concept of how I earned a living. That was the way I liked it. Then one day John was offered a job working for Sir John Davis at J. Arthur Rank. Suddenly my brother was in 'Show Business', which up until then had been my turf.

It meant that he was sitting in the screening room beside the other suits when I showed them the movie. As we walked out he muttered that he thought it was a turkey. Tact was never his strongest suit but what made it worse was that I knew he wasn't wrong.

What made the experience even more painful was that I never received the final payment of my fee, a relatively large sum for those days and money I had counted on. I discovered later that Kirk had suffered the same indignity.

In hindsight I have great respect for his professionalism and also his honesty in fessing up instantly to the fact that he felt on shaky ground with his role. We've met a few times since and he is, as he should be at the great age he has attained, entirely philosophical about the experience. Ian ran into him a few years ago at a cocktail party and they reminisced about the movie and the non-payment of fees. Kirk sipped his martini reflectively and said:

'It's only money.'

But maybe he'd just toked a very large joint.

'Has Anyone Seen My Wife?' – Ian

Richard Burton

In the early seventies Richard Burton and Elizabeth Taylor – the Burtons as they were known – were the most famous and fascinating couple on the planet. It's difficult to find today's equivalent as the paps have driven the celebs indoors, behind their gated estates or concierge-guarded New York co-ops; or in the VIP areas of clubs or ushered through the kitchens of fashionable restaurants. It's even hard to snap an airport shot as private jets have become almost commonplace. But the Burtons were always visible as they circled the globe: waving from airplane steps, rubbing shoulders with the punters in London pubs and New York bars, or drinking with the locals in the Welsh valleys. Posing, smiling, waving, Elizabeth flashing her latest diamond. They truly lived up to Max

Bialystock's character in *The Producers*, and his mantra: 'When you've got it, baby, flaunt it!'

After Dick had directed *A Severed Head* we spent more and more time in the Mayfair offices of Winkast, the production company. Famous people would drop by, especially at the day's end when the vodka would flow and the stories fly – Clint Eastwood, Marlon Brando, Donald Sutherland, Elliott Gould, Don Rickles, Roddy McDowell, and rising young stars like Ian McShane and David Hemmings.

We rewrote a script for them, *Special Bookings*, originally written by Graham Chapman and John Cleese that, like most projects, never saw the light of day. Alan Ladd Jr. (Laddie) then asked Dick to direct a movie based on a novel they'd optioned about a London gangster who was also a mother-fixated, sadistic homosexual. The script was terrible and he turned it down. We were then asked to rewrite it. We must have done a good job because the next thing we heard was that another director had been signed and Richard Burton was going to play the lead, Vic Dakin, a character something like the Kray twins rolled into one.

We wondered how on earth we had landed such a star but it has to be said, Burton's great days were mostly behind him then; the wonderful roles in *Becket, Look Back in Anger, The Spy Who Came in From the Cold* and *Who's Afraid of Virginia Woolf?* being replaced by more mediocre movies such as *Candy* and *Boom*. Mind you he must have made a bob or two on *Where Eagles Dare* and as the producer was Elliott Kastner of Winkast he was, presumably, amenable to consider *Villain*, as the film was called.

It was also convenient because Elizabeth would be in London at the same time, making a film with Michael Caine called *X, Y and Zee* based on the novel by Edna O'Brien. Funny aside: one day Richard visited her on the set but arrived during the lunch break, barking:

'Where's my wife, has anyone seen my wife?'

The only response came from the disembodied cockney voice of a spark, high up in the gantry:

'What's she look like, mate?'

The Burtons were surrounded by an entourage, most of them entirely unnecessary, who created such tight security that even their best friends complained they could never get past the guardians at the gate. We managed somehow and went, with excitement and apprehension, to meet the great man at the Dorchester Hotel's Oliver Messel suite. He was polite, offered us coffee and shouted for his wife to join us. Our pulses quickened, we were about to meet the most famous woman in the world, child of Hollywood and *femme fatale*.

'I'm in the bathroom!' replied the Screen Goddess.

She was still in it the next time we went and the time after that. We never did meet the world's most desirable woman. She had, however, made her contribution to *Villain* by choosing Richard's wardrobe for the part, from Savile Row tailors and trendy Chelsea boutiques. Terrible choices. The next day we showed Richard photographs of the Kray Twins taken by David Bailey – the rat pack suits, the slim neck ties, the crisp white cuff-linked shirts, the slither of handkerchief in the breast pocket. He got it and Vic Dakin went to work correctly attired, with a cast that included Ian McShane as the gangster's bisexual sidekick and Joss Ackland, who both gave fine supporting performances.

Richard's entourage constantly assured the producers and director Michael Tuchner that he was 'off the sauce'. Their definition of that obviously ignored the fact that every glass of Richard's orange juice was laced with vodka, but he never appeared inebriated and was a consummate pro. The film went up against the much more stylish *Get Carter* but was received well in Britain and Europe and the critics seemed to like its nastiness. It did not perform well in America, partly because the wife of a studio executive complained that she could not understand the cockney accents and everyone except Richard was hastily revoiced into bland mid-Atlantic mediocrity. Dick and I were so appalled to hear about this that to this day we have managed to avoid seeing this version.

We shot for a day in Brighton with an overnight stay. Sir Laurence Olivier lived there and asked Richard to dinner, which went on into the small hours. Olivier was at the time running the National Theatre with enfant terrible Ken Tynan. That night he tried to persuade Richard, over much wine and a bottle of brandy, to take over from him when he retired. We imagine he said something like: 'Stop being a movie star and come back to your first love, the theatre.' The movie star declined. The National Theatre could never pay for private jets, Riviera villas, diamonds and alimony.

Interesting side note: Richard was given a CBE in the Queen's Birthday Honours list. I was there in the Winkast offices with Jay and Laddie when he stormed in wearing the obligatory morning suit and top hat, straight from the Palace. He was belligerent and angry and wanted a drink. I can only assume he felt short-changed by his honour. A knighthood would have put him on a par with Gielgud, Guinness, Olivier and Richardson. Turning his back on the theatre, and the lifestyle, had cost him the accolade that he obviously coveted.

Just before the film wrapped we were told Richard wanted to make a screen version of a stage play by fellow Welshman Gwyn Thomas called *The Keep*. A screenplay was needed and we wrote it in two weeks. Kip Gowans was assigned as the director. Kip was a very experienced and well-respected AD (Assistant Director) so this was a huge opportunity for him. To discuss the script we were all invited for lunch on the Burtons' yacht. This would have been glamorous if it had been in Monte Carlo or Mustique, but it was actually berthed in the East End of London. It was there so that Elizabeth could bring her two Lhasa Apso dogs to England. As long as they didn't set a paw on English soil and stuck to the poop deck – sorry about that one – she stayed within the strict quarantine laws.

Even without blue skies and palm trees it was still a titillating glimpse of the life of megastars, so we eagerly showed up on a damp, December day and there was *Kalizma*, named after the Burtons' children, bobbing on the oily waters of the Thames, huge, white and gleaming against the cranes and shabby warehouses of Wapping, long before Canary Wharf was built and the area became fashionable.

Once on board Richard greeted us warmly, drinks and handshakes. He was attracted to *The Keep* because it was set in Wales, he knew the writer and he could revisit and replenish his roots. In this sentimental mood he showed us a photograph of a junior school rugby team from South Wales, fifteen youths in baggy shirts with lopsided grins and wartime haircuts. He offered a hundred pounds to any of us who picked him out. I instantly stabbed a finger at a boy in the front row. Richard looked pained.

'No one ever got it before,' he muttered grumpily and promised a cheque next time he saw us.

The salon had rosewood panelling and expensive art hung below muted lights. We recognised a Van Gogh and a Jacob Epstein sculpture. A large floor cushion was flecked with dog hairs. Richard loved to recount the boat's history; she had been on different sides in two world wars and survived them both. In the first one her German captain had an organ installed and liked nothing better than to sail into a gale, lash himself to the keyboard and play Bach as the storm raged around him. The organ still stood there, the pipes polished, the keys the colour of faded nicotine.

Richard drank quite a lot during the meal, his mood shifting subtly from affable to truculent. We were treated to anecdotes and reflections, yarns, confessions and nostalgia. He talked of people and places, of the Hollywood Hills and the Welsh valleys, of producers who were cocksuckers and coal mining cousins who were saints. He spoke of actors he despised and poets he revered. We were star-struck recipients of his wit, wisdom and wine, although his preference was vodka. The subject of our screenplay never came up before he decided he wanted a nap, but insisted that we should stay and watch a documentary:

'In my view it's the most searing indictment of the Vietnam War ever made.'

The projector and screen were on the deck so rain pattered on the top of the makeshift canvas canopy. We shivered in our seats wearing the solemn expressions you assume when you expect to see something harrowing. So we were more than a little surprised to find ourselves watching *Carry On Cleo* in which Kenneth Williams, as Julius Caesar, utters the immortal line:

'*Infamy, infamy, they've all got it in for me!*'

After half an hour we realised we weren't going to see Burton again, or a searing indictment of the Vietnam War, so we took our leave and walked down the gangplank into the Wapping gloom.

Suddenly the Burtons were gone – the pallets of Vuitton luggage, the dogs, the absurd entourage. Gone to sun-kissed villas, snowbound chalets, yachts cruising the Caribbean or the Med, their own or maybe Sam Spiegel's or a Greek tycoon's. *The Keep* was forgotten, surely on the insistence of accountants or agents, none of whom wanted their star stuck in the Rhondda Valley paying guilt-ridden homage to his Welsh upbringing.

We were getting used to projects falling apart but Kip Gowans was devastated and I'm not sure his wife, the actress Lee Remick, ever forgave Richard. He chose another Welsh project instead, *Under Milk Wood*, with Elizabeth playing Rosie Probert. One night in the pub a diminutive local approached her, probably a scrum half. Swaying on his feet, fortified by several pints, he leered at her lecherously:

'*What would you say to a little fuck?*'

According to legend Elizabeth smiled and gazed down at him with those violet eyes:

'Hello, Little Fuck.'

We often wonder what would have happened if Burton had taken up Olivier's offer. What great performances might we have seen? How would he and Tynan or the National's establishment have worked together? Perhaps 'Sir Richard' might have been a possibility. It surely wasn't earned by most of his subsequent films until *Equus* reminded us of his talent.

Oh, the cheque for the bet never arrived. Dick wonders if that's why they call it 'welshing'.

The Man in the Vauxhall Viva – Dick

Edward Heath

I started to direct commercials in the sixties after an approach by James Garrett, who ran one of the first production houses that specialised in the field. He liked the work I had done with Peter Cook and Dudley Moore and made me a tempting offer. Jim ran his empire from a former Jesuit seminary in Farm Street, Mayfair. His producers were an assorted bunch. One of the most entertaining was David Fanthorpe. You could always be assured of a very good lunch with prospective clients if David was producing. At one point Jim asked him to cut back on his expenses to something more reasonable, like six hundred a year. David was indignant.

'*Six hundred a year? I spill six hundred pounds a year!*'

Another was Jeremy Scott. Jeremy was handsome and utterly

charming, the smoothest man I ever met, totally unflappable. American clients saw him as the quintessential suave, sophisticated Englishman, though ironically he was as Scottish as his name suggests. I got an unexpected call from him asking if I could shoot the following day for important clients from the ad agency Doyle Dane Bernbach, who were flying in from New York, in mid-air as we spoke. The original director, Philip Saville, had just fallen out. Happily, the shoot went well. Later Jeremy confided that making a 'switch-sale' so late in the day had been a tricky manoeuvre and he had seriously contemplated calling me 'Philip' for three days and hoping no one would notice.

In 1970 Jim Garrett wanted to land a major new account: the Conservative Party. Labour's sitting Prime Minister, Harold Wilson, had just dissolved parliament and a General Election was pending. Jim arranged a lunch for Ted Heath, leader of the Conservative opposition, and fellow Tory mandarins. His theory was that well-bred Englishmen would not make any important decisions without good food and a plentiful supply of wine. Jeremy was assigned to provide this and chose a stylish but discreet white Burgundy and assorted titbits from Fortnum & Mason. As tempting as they looked, he decided that something was missing that might clinch the deal. He unearthed a bottle of Methedrine tablets that he'd salted away for a rainy day, crushed a few and added them to the quails' eggs and finger sandwiches of foie gras and smoked salmon.

In his memoir, *Fast and Louche*, Jeremy relates how the initial reserve of the Tories gave way to lively and animated conversation verging on exuberance.

Ted had more than his fair share of the canapés and turned an especially alarming colour. Garrett got the gig and I soon got a call from him.

'Can I assume that you're a Conservative?'

No, he couldn't. I had actually voted for Harold Wilson in the previous election. I told him I valued my independence, which gave me the right to sit on a lofty pillar and hurl rocks at either side as and when I thought they deserved it. At the same time I was intrigued by the job he was offering: to make a film of Edward Heath and try to reverse the perception of him as colourless and dull.

My political opinions have evolved over the years. Living as I now do in California, there is no way in the world that I could be persuaded to work for the Republican Party. But I had no particular opinion about Ted so I didn't feel that I was being asked to sup with the devil and I was intrigued by the idea of seeing the political process at close quarters.

There was no question about it: Ted lacked charisma. If you had colour film in your camera he would still look grey. Nor did he fit the mould of the traditional Tory leader. He didn't even talk like them. *Private Eye* mocked his strangulated vowels and dubbed him 'The Grocer', which when you think about it was a typically English kind of reverse snobbery. And he was a bachelor, a word with dubious implications. There would never be a loyal wife at his side for moral support on the podium.

He was MP for Bexley and used to drive himself from Westminster to his Kent constituency in his Vauxhall Viva. I decided to film this to show that he had the common touch. The camera had to be in another car and every time I signalled them to draw alongside and take a shot I had to duck out of sight on his back seat. This was the Leader of Her Majesty's Opposition, driving his own car. In hindsight it's almost quaint to recall the total absence of bodyguards and outriders. The only security I can remember was a silent man in a dark suit. Whenever Jim and I ate with Ted and the mandarins at an Italian restaurant near the studio, he sat on his own, facing the door, but always managed to get through a three-course meal.

In Bexley I filmed Ted doing the daily routine of a sitting

Member of Parliament, chairing committees and talking to con-
stituents. Maybe he still lacked magnetism but he came over as
conscientious and genuinely involved in their concerns and problems. I hastily cut together a fifteen-minute film, shot on 16mm,
and it was transmitted as a Party Political Broadcast. The general
consensus was that it helped to humanise him. Even so, on the
eve of the election the polls gave Labour a healthy lead. But as the
results started to come in they showed a surprising and significant
swing, first in Guildford – well, a Tory stronghold surely – but
then West Salford? By one in the morning champagne corks were
popping.

So am I saying that I played my part in altering British history?
Not really. Mine was only one of several films made, including
a very powerful one by Terry Donovan. My own theory is that
the result had much more to do with West Germany defeating
England in the World Cup in Mexico on 14 June, only four days
before the election. The whole mood of the country soured and
the electorate kicked Harold into touch. Parenthetically, when
Ian and I wrote *Whatever Happened to the Likely Lads?*, we
blamed the same event for the failure of Terry Collier's marriage
to a German girl:

*'Do you have any idea what it was like to be in Germany that
night? Especially after England was leading two-nil. I was standing
on the sideboard singing "Rule Britannia" . . . and then the shame,
the humiliation. To see them all leaping up and down, eyes glazed
with national fervour. I thought they were going to rush out and
invade Poland again.'*

Whether you buy my theory or not I was suddenly on first-name
terms with the Prime Minister. Not only that but Ted seemed to
regard me as some sort of lucky talisman. He wanted me around
when he was about to address the nation and asked my opinion
on the text. I felt flattered but way out of my depth. I was invited
to Number Ten and even to Chequers, the country retreat. I was

there when Lord Carrington, the Foreign Secretary, came in for an urgent conference about an immediate crisis. I never found out what it was but I understood how seductive it is to be on the fringes of power when important decisions are being made in the next room.

Inevitably, we went very separate ways. I still think Ted was essentially a decent man. I think his major flaw was his total mis-understanding of how to negotiate, especially with the unions. He put everything on the table, truly believing he was offering a fair deal: take it or leave it. What he never took into account is that the other side must always be able to show their membership that they've won something.

Since Ted never married there has inevitably been a lot of recent speculation about his sexuality. For the record I always thought that he just wasn't interested in sex, he far preferred classical music, sailing and good claret. Certainly I never felt the slightest blip on my 'gaydar'. His neighbour, the author Leslie Thomas, was very blunt when asked if Ted was gay:

'No, he's bloody miserable.'

But that was years later and I blame Maggie Thatcher.

The Man With His Own Atoll – Ian

Marlon Brando

In the fall of 1972 I was asked to have dinner at the London apartment of Alan and Patty Ladd. I asked Fiona Lewis, a beautiful actress and later accomplished writer. She had been my girlfriend but was now a girl who was a friend. She brought her current beau, the actor Clive Francis, also the illustrator of this book. There was only one other guest: Marlon Brando. There's always a frisson of excitement when you recognise a really famous face but this was a jaw-dropping, heart-skipping moment.

We had drinks, we had dinner, we listened to the Great One talk. He spoke very softly but we clung to every word and rarely ventured one of our own. At that time, he was a truly beautiful man, forty-eight years old, broad-shouldered, thick hair swept back over a broad forehead that would have graced a Roman coin. This was not the Brando of his later years, marooned in middle-age and obesity in his Los Angeles mansion, watching soaps and gorging on butter pecan ice cream. This was the Brando who'd just wrapped *The Godfather* and would soon make *Last Tango in Paris*, willing to be filmed naked while he did unspeakable things with a stick of butter to the sensual and young Maria Schneider.

The dinner conversation was all about Watergate in the aftermath of the break-in of the Democratic National Committee's Washington offices in June that year. It was the sole topic of conversation everywhere; just as the O. J. Simpson trial was the only thing people talked about at Hollywood dinner parties in 1994.

By the dessert Marlon had switched from Watergate to the atoll that he'd just purchased. The word struck a vague chord from geography lessons; it is, actually, a ring-shaped coral reef and Marlon had one. His was near Tahiti where he had made *Mutiny on the Bounty* and taken a gorgeous local girl back to the Los Angeles pad. So the South Seas were a big thing for Marlon and now he had a piece of it. In thrall to his presence, we feigned enormous interest.

The evening was apparently over; Fiona left because she was filming the next day, the Ladds had young daughters to attend to. But Marlon wanted to go on and I was thrilled to be his driver. Along with Clive I took him to Soho because he wanted to see Mongo Santamaria, a Cuban conga player whose band was playing that night at Ronnie Scott's jazz club. I parked – it was possible in those days – and we bought our tickets at the door. No fuss, no VIP treatment, no bruisers with earpieces and shaven heads easing the way. Just three punters getting the best seats they could. And they weren't all that good.

In the smoky darkness of a Soho jazz club no one recognised the movie legend, which kind of disappointed me as I would have enjoyed the speculation of 'Who's that with the guy who wrote

The Likely Lads?' I certainly didn't feel the evening had given me enough attention for My Night with Marlon, so I suggested, after the Cuban's set was over, that he and I went to Tramp. He agreed.

Tramp was *the* club in those days, in fact over the next three decades. We arrived and were ushered to the primo table in the front room, the one to the immediate right of the door where owner Johnny Gold normally sat with his view of all the action. Johnny wasn't there that night so the table was mine. Well, Marlon's. Gradually the looks turned in our direction; curious, disbelieving, shocked. Marlon was used to this, I wasn't. I liked it.

Girls were looking now, girls with whom I had a nodding acquaintance, which meant I nodded, they ignored me. Girls who now made their way to our table and asked, 'Hi, Ian, how are you?' or 'Ian, long time, no see' or 'Hey, what are you up to these days?'

I graciously answered their enquiries, not that they gave a toss, and introduced them to my pal Marlon. We were now the epicentre of the room; people were leaving the disco to register the legend. Marlon asked some girls to join us. By this time I was imagining all sorts of scenarios, all of them sexual. Marlon's suite, flutes of Dom, unbridled whatever.

Never happened, of course. Marlon decided he wanted a night alone and asked me to drive him to his hotel. He did, however, show all the girls pictures of his atoll.

I met him again shortly afterwards when Laddie had given him a script I'd written entitled *The Warm and Golden War*. Marlon was interested. I was thrilled. A tale of mercenaries, the story was set in Eastern Europe against the backdrop of the Cold War. An anti-communist piece, it appealed to Marlon's social conscience, as he was often actively involved in some or other political cause. When he won the Academy Award for Best Actor for *The Godfather* he was into Native American affairs. He boycotted the ceremony and sent instead a young activist, Sacheen Littlefeather, who appeared in full Apache attire and lambasted Hollywood's depictions of her people.

Marlon lost interest in my Cold War script, preferring instead to speak out against apartheid, so he wanted the story to be re-staged in South Africa. No one could see how to do this so the project died and I never saw the Great One again.

When I next went back to Tramp one of the girls who'd been at our table introduced me to her date.

'This is Ian. Ian's a friend of Marlon Brando.'

Some of Us Belong to the Stars – Dick

Michael Crawford

I never went to Film School but I hope they teach pitching. Of course if you're a brilliant writer you don't need to pitch, you just churn out another masterpiece and sell it to the highest bidder. That leaves the rest of us, who occasionally have to turn up at corporate offices with a bright smile on our faces to convince the money moguls that they should give some of it to us and not the people coming in after lunch. I know very good writers who hate pitching and can't do it. The reverse can be true of indifferent writers though I imagine they get found out in the end. I've always found it reassuring to pitch in tandem with Ian because if one of us drops the ball there's an even chance that the other will pick it up.

A few hints: try to mention casually, and with becoming modesty, any previous project that enjoyed a degree of success to reassure them that you have been hired before. Never, ever, reference a movie that didn't make money, even if it's considered a critical masterpiece. If you're pitching in America, don't mention anything you did in England. Their eyes will glaze over. Finally, if you feel you're winning, get out as soon as possible before you bugger it up.

Englishmen of our generation were taught that it was bad form to blow your own trumpet. John Rich, the producer who acquired the rights to the American version of *Porridge,* had none of that reticence. He used to do the warm-up for the studio audience before each recording and shamelessly listed all the previous shows for which he'd won awards, basking in the applause. We were appalled. Wasn't that what agents were for?

There was one notable exception, an occasion when I overcame those inbuilt inhibitions, looked the producer in the eye and said something like:

'We are the best possible writers for this project. Everything we've written up to now has prepared us for this and if you go to anyone else, you're bloody nuts.'

I think I even startled Ian with my vehemence but my conviction was genuine.

We were having lunch at a restaurant called Burke's with an American producer, Peter Witt, the composer John Barry and lyricist Don Black. The project was a proposed musical version of *Billy Liar*. I felt that Billy Fisher's fictional Yorkshire town of Stradhoughton was not a million miles from the milieu that we'd created in *The Likely Lads*. Moreover, we loved Keith Waterhouse's brilliant novel and we knew Tom Courtenay, who had starred in the movie directed by John Schlesinger. We got the job.

We were excited by the fresh challenge of writing the 'book' for a musical to the point where we felt we should do it somewhere completely different. We rented a cottage on a Cornish cliff in The Lizard. We even wrote it on bigger paper. After all, this was for the theatre! It was March. The weather was vile. Seagulls huddled on the windowsill to get out of the rain. There was nothing else to do all day so we wrote and wrote and in five days had the framework of the show that remained intact throughout the coming months.

Billy Liar had already been successfully adapted for the stage by the author with his usual partner, Willis Hall. They didn't want to revisit it, which left the door open for us. We read the play of course, though it struck us early on that the story made far more sense as a musical because the audience could witness Billy's flights of fancy. We borrowed an idea from the film where his parents occasionally became posh and indulgent, mildly amused by his bad behaviour. When in doubt we consulted the original novel, which we still regard as a work of genius. It's very funny with an underlying streak of sadness because Billy ultimately can't find the courage to break away and retreats into fantasy.

The initial job of the book writer is to find where the songs should go and the job they are intended to do. Then the musical team goes to work. Once the songs are written the text is adjusted to make them fit. Perhaps the most assertive voice in the early stages belonged to John Barry. He had been down this road before when he wrote the music for a stage version of *Lolita* in partnership with Alan Jay Lerner. It had failed memorably and John was determined not to make similar mistakes this time. So right from the get-go he told us that Michael Crawford was going to play Billy Fisher.

We had worked with Michael before on the first film we ever wrote, *The Jokers*, though we could hardly say we bonded much as Mr Winner had no use for writers hanging around the set. Michael had been in the movie of *Hello, Dolly!* with Barbra Streisand but his main claim to fame in the UK was through his TV role as Frank Spencer, the accident-prone hero of *Some Mothers Do 'Ave 'Em*. The series was notable for some hair-raising physical stunts in the tradition of Harold Lloyd and Buster Keaton that Michael performed with great verve and considerable courage.

He brought this energy and commitment along with him, which was just as well as Billy was hardly ever off the stage. Subsequent attempts to revive the show have failed because it is so difficult to find an actor who can sing, dance, be funny, look young and, most importantly, put bums on seats.

The show was tried out in Manchester. We moved into the Midland Hotel and in between rehearsals wrote an episode of *Porridge,* the one where Fletch helps Godber make it through the night. About a week before it opened, Michael had a fall and

fractured his wrist. He killed any talk of postponement and declared that he would soldier on.

We attended the dress rehearsal. It was running very late.
Tempers were frayed. The final scene of the first act was a tribute to Fred Astaire and Ginger Rogers. The girls in the chorus
were supposed to have gorgeous dresses trimmed with feathers.
They made their entrance without them. Onna White, the chore-
ographer, stopped the show and went ballistic. Where were the
goddam feathers? Ian listened to her screaming abuse at everyone
within earshot and muttered to me in the stalls:

'I think Onna's at the end of her feather.'

So on opening night we had never had a complete run-through
and Michael had his arm in a cast. The curtain didn't go up on
time. The audience was growing restless. Then someone stepped
through the curtains and announced that the reason for the delay
was a bomb scare. No one stampeded for the exits. The news was
strangely reassuring. *It wasn't our fault!* The curtain finally went
up forty minutes late and very soon Michael was singing 'Some of
Us Belong to the Stars'. The response of the audience confirmed
that they agreed.

The first night in London was marred for me because my dear
mother, sitting in the royal box of the Theatre Royal, Drury Lane
with Frank Muir and Edward Heath, suffered a mild heart attack
and had to leave at the end of the first act. Frank, incidentally, was
a tower of strength. Once I made sure that she was out of danger
I waited up for the reviews. They were outstanding and Michael
received the accolades he deserved.

What is it that makes a star? A crucial element is an innate sense
that centre stage is where you belong. In film terms, yours should
be the first name on the call sheet. You need dedication and drive.
Michael had all of that. Eight times a week, for two solid years, he
went out there and gave it his all. After a few months he went for
some easy laughs when a little bit of Frank Spencer crept into his

performance and he had to be reined in. He occasionally showed the downside of stardom, making demands and occasionally picking a feud with someone in the company. He never challenged Brian Pringle or Avis Bunnage, who were brilliant as his parents, or Elaine Paige who was outstanding as Rita, the most confrontational of his three fiancées.

'You rotten, lying, cross-eyed dog! Get back in the cheese with the other maggots!'

Her role was a far cry from Evita, whom she played four years later, but she was destined to be a star just as Michael was. When we watched him a few years later in *The Phantom of the Opera* it was as if he had totally reinvented himself. His voice was more operatic. He was even a different shape with the broad chest of a tenor but the star quality was the same.

For us, having *Billy* running in the West End was the time of our lives, probably the most euphoric period of our career. We had offered our services to the theatre and on our first time out we had a hit. I did some really silly things, like calling the box office just to listen to the engaged tone. I would turn up at the theatre before dinner and stand at the back for ten minutes to make sure the audience was still laughing at some of our lines. That's the kind of instant feedback the theatre gives you that you can never get from film or television.

Naturally we wanted it all over again. We wrote a musical about Laurel and Hardy with Jonathan Pryce and Richard Griffiths set to play the leads. It fell apart. We wrote *Jailhouse Rock* in collaboration with Leiber and Stoller, until the producer one morning told us she was going in another direction with another score and another book. Leiber and Stoller withdrew their support and the show was produced without the title song.

We wrote *The Face of a Woman* about Helen of Troy, with a score by Brian Johnson and Brendan Healey. It never happened. We wanted to do *The Commitments* on stage but Roddy Doyle, the writer of the original novel, always blocked it – until he announced that he was doing it himself without using any of our screenplay.

Don't think for a moment that the desire has died. The flame still burns, which incidentally is one of the songs in our new musical *Jukebox Hero*, which happily has not stayed on the shelf and recently had its world premiere in Toronto. And we have Michael to thank for lighting the flame.

The Beautiful Boy and the Beautiful Game – Ian

George Best

One night, sometime in 1972, George Best was bundled into the back of my car at Tramp, the Jermyn Street club, and stayed in my flat instead of his hotel, where he was hounded by press and paps. Heady stuff to be a friend of a famous person, even more so to be caught up in their own personal psychodrama.

Let's back up.

The most impersonal and cryptic description of George on current online bios reads: 'Irish soccer player, starred for Manchester United and was named European Footballer of the Year in 1968, before a hard-partying lifestyle took its toll on his career and health.'

The period of his 'hard-partying lifestyle' resulted in one of the most famous George anecdotes and I have to repeat it for those readers, if any, who have not heard it. The newspapers scented, as they love to do, a celebrity in decline, and were filled with stories of George's drinking, love affairs and problems with the club – Manchester United not Tramp.

It was at this time that George checked into a London hotel suite after a night at a casino. Well after midnight a waiter brought up expensive champagne nestling in a silver bucket of crushed ice. George was lying on the bed surrounded by bank notes that he'd won earlier and a former Miss World stood in the bathroom doorway in her underwear. The waiter shook his head sadly and asked:

'So George, where did it all go wrong?'

George was born in Belfast, Northern Ireland, in 1946. Twenty years later England won the World Cup and the country became crazy about football, having become crazy about pop music three years earlier when we heard the first 'Yeah, Yeah, Yeahs' from the Beatles. George epitomised both, an athlete who looked and behaved like a rock star. Slender, sexy, long-haired, he was indeed christened by the European press in 1966 as 'El Beatle'.

On the sporting side the Irish Football Association would describe him later as 'the greatest player ever to pull on the green shirt of Northern Ireland' and the scout who first spotted him at the age of fifteen sent Manchester United's manager, Matt Busby, a telegram which read, 'I think I've found you a genius.' Ten years later the genius had scored 179 goals for his club, their top scorer in the league for five consecutive seasons.

I suppose I knew George at the outset of the hard-partying lifestyle that would take its toll. I saw a lot of him when Dick and I were in Manchester when our musical *Billy* was playing before transferring to London. Most nights after the show we would head for George's nightclub, Slack Alice. As we usually took several girl dancers from the chorus we were guaranteed a warm welcome, a primo table and George's company.

He always seemed surrounded, as many celebrities are, by a coterie of agents, advisors, friends and hangers-on. So many people wanted a piece of him – friendship, money, an interview or a partnership in a business, usually a bar or a boutique or a sporting goods store. The girls, a constant presence, just wanted the piece that was in his Carnaby Street pants. George, fuelled by a night's vodka and chat, was happy to oblige.

I did have my own serious chats with him, although it was usually at a late hour and after alcohol. He was sly, funny and intelligent. He was aware of the phony friends. He was conscious of the conflict between what he did on the field and the life he enjoyed off it, and savvy enough to know that conflict would not end well. He was very aware of his own imperfections, one of his most famous quotes being:

'I spent a lot of money on booze, birds and fast cars – the rest I just squandered.'

He also knew he was an alcoholic but believed he could easily handle it. Sadly, alcoholism plagued him his entire life.

And so, halfway through the 1972–73 season, he flattens himself on the floor of my car and we drive off through the West End streets. A few days earlier he had not shown up for training, was suspended by the club, transfer listed and, according to the tabloid headlines had 'disappeared', which meant he was in London, at his favourite table in his favourite bar. He joined me, probably because I was with a stunning girl and she was part of the deception to get him away from the waiting press.

It didn't work because the next morning two *Daily Express* reporters walked into my bathroom while I was shaving and asked where George was. I told them I had no idea and asked them, nicely enough, if they could fuck off. Later I left the flat in George's coat, a flat cap and dark glasses. I was tailed to Sloane Street then leapt on a number 22 bus. George, meanwhile, left the flat unobserved and was picked up by a mate and resumed training in April.

When he signed a book deal to write his autobiography I remember Michael Parkinson urging him not to pen the average, predictable 'And then I joined United' sports bio. He thought George's book should be much more of a satirical, tongue in cheek, piss-taking piece on the nature of football and fame. He referenced the great American gridiron quarterback, Joe Namath, who made no secret of his love of women and booze as much as football. His nickname was Broadway Joe and he titled his memoir 'I can't wait for tomorrow because I get prettier every day.'

What would have happened if Joe and George had hooked up and hung out together? I imagine they would have bedded even more women than Barry Sheene and James Hunt did in the year they were both were world champions of their respective sports.

George, or Besty as he was affectionately and enviously known, failed to show up for training again in 1974, was dropped by then manager Tommy Docherty and United were relegated at the end of that sad season. In a decade of declining talent and fortune, George would play for several clubs in South Africa, the Republic of Ireland, the United States, Scotland and Australia. I actually met him at Los Angeles airport when he was on his way to join the San Jose Earthquakes. He had no idea what they were like or even where San Jose was, but it was another payday, another field to display his gifts, another, hopefully, fresh start. Trouble is there would also be another bar filled with boozy expats just dying to buy their hero a drink. And then another . . .

A year or so before he died, I heard that he sometimes used a small pub in a quiet side street in Chelsea so one lunchtime I dropped by and there he was, alone and unrecognised, nursing a white wine spritzer at a corner table. I had to remind him who I was but he was pleased enough to see and talk with a face from a happier time. I found it very sad.

Late in his life George was voted eighth in *World Soccer*'s one hundred greatest footballers poll. Brazilian football legend Pelé considered him the greatest player of all time. At his public funeral in Belfast he was referred to as 'the beautiful boy with the beautiful game'.

His self-deprecating humour as well as his brilliance was a source of his popularity but his enduring appeal was best summed up in a piece by Mark Garnet and Richard Weight who observed:

'The British like their heroes to be tragic ones; possessed of enough glamour and talent for stardom to be lived vicariously through them: yet flawed and vulnerable enough for the public not to be threatened by their success.'

Exactly.

One Ronnie – Dick

Ronnie Barker

When we were researching a movie about Harpo Marx we drove into the California desert to meet his widow, Susan. She greeted us graciously and as we sat down to lunch almost the first thing she said was:

'Don't expect me to tell you anything bad about Harpo because there isn't anything to tell.'

The same remark applies to Ronnie Barker. Ronnie is the only actor who ever gave me a car. I've dropped hints to many others since but none of them even offered as much as a wheelbarrow. Technically, it was only half a car. He gave it to Ian as well so we had to timeshare. It was a massive Jaguar saloon with fuel tanks on either side. Ideally a petrol tanker should have been running alongside at all times.

He gave it to us when he was about to go to Australia. Ronnie often spent a year abroad, probably for tax reasons. When we first knew him he had his life planned out often two or three years ahead because he loved to work. And then he suddenly stopped. We wanted to know why. He told us that Peter Hall had asked him to play Falstaff in a season of plays at the National Theatre. He was initially flattered then began to worry about the commute from Pinner, where he lived, to the South Bank every day. And then he thought:

'If I'm more concerned about the journey than the art, I should give it up.'

In many ways it was a tragedy because Ronnie was a brilliant actor. Notice that I didn't use the word 'comic' in that phrase. When I was set to direct my first movie, *Otley*, I wanted to cast him in the part of a professional assassin, the part eventually played by Leonard Rossiter. My theory was that if you can play comedy, you can play anything. He thought of Norman Stanley Fletcher as his favourite role, something that gives us great pride.

Porridge came about because the BBC commissioned a series called *Seven of One*, designed to showcase Ronnie's talents. We were asked to write two of them. One was called 'I'll Fly You For a Quid', in which he played two roles: the father and grandfather of a gambling-mad Welsh family. For the other he told us that he had always wanted to do something set in prison. This gave us something of a problem because we had just written a series called *Thick as Thieves*, in which Bob Hoskins came out of prison to find his wife living with John Thaw. So we compromised and wrote *Prisoner and Escort* about a man *going* to prison as opposed to coming out. The prisoner was, of course, Norman Stanley Fletcher and his escorts were Officer Mackay and Officer Barrowclough, brilliantly portrayed by Fulton Mackay and Brian Wilde.

The BBC brass asked us which one of these shows we'd like to turn into a series. We discussed this with Ronnie over lunch at the rehearsal room canteen in Acton. We tried not to be distracted by the all-girl dancing group, Pan's People, sitting in their leotards at the next table.

It wasn't an easy choice, like deciding which one of your children you think shows more potential. In the end we thought a series set in prison was the greater challenge. Accordingly we went to Wandsworth, Brixton and Wormwood Scrubs to see what real prisons looked like. The experience thoroughly depressed us. The main impression I took away was that most of the prisoners carried with them a sense of defeat. How could we possibly make anything funny out of something so grim?

Then, in my mind's eye, I saw Ronnie making his entrance as Fletcher. Among his many great qualities is that he brought with him a sense of comedy before he said a word. What we had to agree on was his attitude. Ronnie's original conception was a character something like Sergeant Bilko in *The Phil Silvers Show*. If this was before your time, check it out on YouTube: it was a brilliantly funny American show where the main character is a crafty wheeler-dealer forever working the angles, in his case in the army.

We loved the show, but it wasn't what we wanted to write. It seemed important to convey that prison is not a great place to be. Our Fletcher had the attitude of an old lag who'd been there before:

'Bide your time and keep your nose clean. Little victories, that's what keeps you going in here.'

I compared him to *The Good Soldier Schweik*, another expert in survival, in his case during the First World War. I got some strange looks when I mentioned this. I will now confess that I never finished the Czech original but I remembered the blurb on the back of the Penguin. We never met anyone in an English prison anything like our Fletch but oddly enough we did when we did the American version of the show.

When we did location filming at Chino Prison in California

we were assigned a prisoner to be our guide and official photographer. He was about the same age and build as Ronnie. The
guards told us he was in for murder but as it was a one-off crime
of passion they viewed him as a safe bet not to repeat. He was
a hopeless photographer but clearly viewed the assignment as
a welcome change from routine. He was helpful and happy to
answer our questions. He also had Fletcher's instinctive sense of
looking for an angle. He eyed our camera car and asked whether
it had insurance. We didn't see why anyone would want to steal
such a specialist vehicle. He raised an eyebrow.

*'Are you kidding? Give me half an hour and a spray gun and I'd
have that thing looking like a hippie wagon.'*

When Ronnie read the scripts he went with our approach right
away. The only thing we lacked was a title. They can be tricky, they
either come or they don't. He came in one day and announced
that he had the perfect one. We had one too. A heated argument,
for about six seconds, ended in a coin toss, won by Ronnie.

'Porridge!' he announced triumphantly.

Uncannily, that was our title too.

We needed a younger character, someone to receive the benefit
of Fletch's wisdom and experience. The casting of Richard Beckinsale to play naive Lenny Godber was a stroke of genius – not
ours but our director's, Syd Lotterby, the same Syd who saved my
bacon whenever I stumbled directing *The Likely Lads*. When we
were writing the first series we felt that we needed one episode set
entirely in a cell. It was a challenge but, after all, prison is about
being locked up. So it was virtually a two-hander, called 'A Night
In', in which Fletch helps Godber to cope with prison, reminding
him that there are no locked doors to the imagination. The two
actors were brilliant together and the episode was both funny and
touching.

The sequel to *Porridge* was *Going Straight*, where wily recidivist
Fletch tries to deal with life on the outside and stay on the straight

and narrow. Perhaps understandably audiences preferred him in a captive situation, but the series was good enough to win its own BAFTA award and the final episode, where Godber marries Fletch's daughter Ingrid, is one of our favourites.

Richard really deserves a chapter of his own. The term 'laid-back' didn't exist at the time but if it had there should have been a picture of Richard next to the dictionary definition. I don't know how he got his first job because he was terrible at sight-reading. When we sat round the table to read a new script the cast groaned collectively if Godber had a long speech. Richard took it in his stride. When we went back to rehearsal two days later, he was word-perfect. I really like actors but some (no names here) can be self-absorbed, neurotic, obnoxious, vulnerable, egotistic and insecure – perhaps not surprising when they so often suffer rejection. Whatever drove Richard was different because he showed no sign of being driven by ambition or ego. He was a wonderful actor with enormous charm who tragically died before reaching the heights he was destined for.

The studio audience can have a strange effect on some actors. The first laughs on the day of the recording can throw their timing off completely. It's a strange, hybrid medium, an awkward cross between theatre and film, but nobody worked an audience better than Ronnie. Strangely enough, he didn't like to 'warm them up' beforehand, needing to concentrate on the job in hand. But if anyone fluffed a line or there was a technical hitch, he instantly stepped into the breach and made them laugh – and relax.

He was a very talented writer. For *The Two Ronnies* he initially wrote under a pseudonym, Gerald Wiley, so that his offerings would be judged for their merits, not on his name. I'm still in awe of his technical ability. Go to YouTube again and check out some of those sketches that rely on verbal dexterity, like the one where he plays a spokesperson of the Society for the Prevention of Mispronunciation. It's like watching a tightrope walker, or a show-jumper heading for a perfect round. One mistake and the entire performance is ruined.

Did he offer up lines of his own on *Porridge*? Of course, but always with the greatest respect, flashing us a look to see if we approved. I can't remember ever saying no after we stopped laughing. I directed the movie version of the show and discovered that in addition to his other talents he was technically savvy. When blocking a scene he was often ahead of me, usually sensing where the camera had to be for the master shot.

Some comedians are always 'on', needing the constant re-assurance of laughter. Ronnie was not a comedian, though he was extremely funny when he chose to be. I rented a house in Gloucestershire one year and invited him and Richard Briers and their wives to dinner. I wish that evening was on YouTube because it was one of the funniest of my life and I can't remember a word of it.

Some years later we took our friends Maurice Gran and Laurence Marks to have lunch with Ronnie at his house in the Cotswolds. On the car ride we told them categorically:

'Whatever you do, don't ask Ronnie why he retired.'

Before we'd even raised a glass to our lips that was the very first question that Laurence put to him. It's something we're constantly asked, even today. He was essentially a very private man. I've been racking my brains to find something negative about him. I finally remembered. That Jaguar he gave us needed a new silencer.

Footnote from Ian:

So much of the critical attention given to *Porridge* is focused on Ronnie and Richard that I feel it's only fair to say something about the other two stars.

Fulton Mackay was a lovely man, brim-full of life, love and enthusiasm; a well-rounded, spiritual man. Syd Lotterby told me that Fulton would rehearse for ever if he let him, never too tired to have another try to see if he could make his performance even better. It came from a deep desire for perfection and at the same time a zestful energy for doing something he loved. I first saw him when I saw Tom Courtenay play *Peer Gynt* in Manchester. Fulton played the Button Maker and I remember Tom telling me that he was a wonderful actor and one of the nicest people he'd ever worked with.

He did some things in *Porridge* that were inimitable, like Mr MacKay's reaction when he realises Fletch has put one over on him: first a cold fury that he's been had, followed by a mute warning of dire retribution to come. Dick and I make each other laugh by remembering his reading of a line from the movie where he is showing the ropes to a new screw:

'The Prison Officers have a club. It is known . . . [a long drawn-out emphasis on the word while his left hand paints the name on an imaginary door] . . . as "The Prison Officers' Club".'

When an actor makes a part his own to that degree you can't imagine how you wrote it in the first place without seeing him in your mind's eye. But I remember him too as a painter and philosopher, enormously kind and always optimistic.

Brian Wilde belonged to that stock of character actors whose work, understated and subtle, is always excellent and consistently unheralded. I think of Brian as the civil servant overlooked for his expected promotion; the man in the raincoat at the bus stop, jostled aside and left standing in the rain; or the clerk who lives with his invalid mother and pines, secretly and hopelessly, for the girl in the accounts department.

Brian's characters don't stand out in the crowd; they blend in with the background. Brian was a little bit like that himself. We never got to know him well but grew to respect his dry humour and superb acting instincts. He brought more to the character of Prison Officer Barrowclough than we put on the page. He ennobled him with compassion and a sweet-natured perseverance that never lapsed into being pitiful or ridiculous. With his furrowed brow and lugubrious features he made us laugh unexpectedly – and frequently.

Inevitably, the success of the series thrust Brian more and more into the spotlight, much as he tried to shield himself from its glare. But at least a large and enthusiastic public got to recognise his craft and his talent.

When we revived *Porridge* in 2017 there was some inevitable resistance on the lines of 'Why would you want to revisit a classic?' We felt it was a challenge too good to resist. An early decision was to transplant it from the seventies to 'Now'. Nor did we want to ask any actor to impersonate Ronnie so Kevin Bishop played Fletch's grandson, incarcerated for computer hacking. It was a marvellous performance and so were those of Mark Bonnar and Dominic Coleman as the Prison Officers and Jim Hill as the old lag, Joe Lotterby, named in honour of our old friend Syd. Ronnie would have applauded all of them.

FAQ # 3

'Why Did You Move to America?'

Ian & Dick

Ian: 1974 was a tremendous year. We had two series on the air, *Whatever Happened to the Likely Lads?* and *Porridge.* We had a hit musical in the West End and Newcastle got to the Cup final. So remind me, what possessed us to move to California?

Dick: When people asked at the time our standard response was, 'We're going to do an American version of *Porridge.*' In hindsight we were incredibly naive to assume that this meant it would actually make it on-air.

Ian: I know. We rented houses, leased cars, sent out change-of-address cards without realising that the American TV business is a graveyard of unmade pilots. Plenty are commissioned. Some actually get made. A tiny proportion is picked up to become a series.

Dick: Yes, the odds are a bit like the chances of newly hatched baby turtles scurrying across the sand to make it to the ocean before seagulls gobble them up.

Ian: It was even riskier for you. You had to find a house big enough to accommodate a wife and all those children.

Dick: Yes, we had four now after adopting Sam. He and Louis took the move in their stride, being so young, but Sian and Andrew weren't at all sure about it.

Ian: Your rented house was rather grand. Maybe that's why we made friends so quickly. You used to throw barbecues on Sunday and then we'd play badminton on the lawn.

Dick: It sounds rather refined and English but it really wasn't. Everyone was well pissed by the time they started hitting shuttlecocks.

Ian: Being there was exciting, though – working in 'Hollywood' and driving there every day to the studio in a convertible down Sunset Boulevard.

Dick: I think we're the only Brits who adapted our own work into 'American'. But our producing partner John Rich had done this before with great success when he adapted *Till Death Us Do Part* into *All in the Family*. Johnny Speight had nothing to do with that, he stayed home, banked the money and bought another Roller.

Ian: We needed a new title for *Porridge*. We kind of liked *Greybar Hotel*, which is old prison slang but the studio thought that was too 'edgy'. They were having doubts about the whole concept. One exec suggested setting the series in Hawaii, as if a glimpse of a palm tree through a barred window would make prison more palatable. Finally we settled for *On the Rocks*. I'm still not sure why.

Dick: Slade, our old Victorian nick, became Alamesa State Penitentiary and Norman Stanley Fletcher became Hector Fuentes. I guess they thought Puerto Rican was the American equivalent of cockney.

Ian: Just to make sure everything was politically correct, even in

1975, we had to have an African-American character, an Okie and a hippie white Jewish kid to share the cell with Señor Fuentes. Totally believable. In fact the most realistic thing about the series was the pre-filming in a real hard-core prison called Chino. This was the same prison where Roman Polanski was sent for pre-trial evaluation. Having seen it with my own eyes I can understand him skipping off to Paris.

Dick: Do you remember that inmate being admitted while we were there? He was Hispanic, very tall in a white suit with a cigar clenched between his teeth. We assumed he was a drug dealer. When he looked in our direction we all peed our pants even though his hands and feet were manacled. Amazingly, the prison authorities let us and our actors mingle with the mainstream. We wore prison blues with our fictitious prison – Alamesa – stitched on the pocket.

Ian: One lunchtime a real prisoner joined our table. He registered the name and asked if that was where we'd just shipped in from. We nodded yes. He shook his head knowingly and said: 'That's a tough joint.'

Dick: There was nothing gritty and realistic about the show but we completed the casting, rehearsed and shot the pilot. One of the ABC executives was a young Michael Eisner, later to become CEO of Disney and currently trying to resurrect the fortunes of Portsmouth Football Club. He gave us a broad smile, a thumbs-up and said: 'Lightning in a bottle!'

Ian: I still don't know what that means.

Dick: Nor me. But they commissioned a series. Our baby turtle had survived! But could it swim?

Ian: We broke another precedent and wrote all two-dozen episodes ourselves. In all American shows there is a 'writers room', which is a room with a lot of writers in it. *On the Rocks* had only you and me in a tiny office fortified by a cheap red wine called 'Hearty Burgundy'. And there was no 'commissary'. Twice a day a Mexican truck came round selling tacos, burritos, burgers and tuna salad. Everyone called it the 'roach coach'.

Dick: It was bloody hard work too. John Rich sweated over every line making sure that we had written everything 'American'. It's easy enough changing 'boot' into 'trunk' and 'bonnet' into 'hood', but we were still new to American speech patterns so inevitably we made mistakes. I remember you lost it when he challenged a line for the fortieth time saying it was a British construction. You came back with, 'So is London Bridge and that's in the middle of fucking Arizona!'

Ian: To compensate for the roach coach we explored famous restaurants, relics of a fading Hollywood era. In all of them an ancient waiter, realising we were out-of-towners, would tell us: 'That was Frank's table.' Or 'Mr Sinatra always sat there.'

Dick: Frank obviously ate out a lot.

Ian: Socially we were meeting just as many exiles as locals.

Dick: You especially in that football team you joined.

Ian: It was great. We had a kickaround Wednesdays and Saturdays and played in a league on Sundays. Half the team were British rock stars who'd come to LA to avoid taxes or paternity suits. I always played right back as it's one of those positions where you're not required to display brilliant gifts of ball control.

Dick: I remember the team you played for in London had an annual dinner where you were given the 'Jekyll and Hyde' Award, a trophy for the player who displayed the greatest difference in character on and off the field.

Ian: We were mixing with the music and movie community. We met people we'd been in awe of for years and others who would become stars in the years to come. I even went on a vacation to Mexico with Bernie Taupin and Alice Cooper.

Dick: Did that involve live snakes and dead chickens?

Ian: No, but there was a lizard on a tennis court bigger than a Westeros.

Dick: We also met our fair share of bullshitters, especially those people who feel compelled to claim they know everybody. Remember the Guy Fawkes party on the beach at Malibu? It was given by the staff of Elton's Rocket Records so they were mostly Brits. Everyone was standing round the bonfire with drinks when this American publicist ankles over and asks who the party is for. We told him Guy Fawkes. He thought about it only for a moment and said: 'I've met him. Didn't he have a deal at Paramount?'

Ian: In spite of the social situation, the work was becoming more and more frustrating. We missed the way we'd worked back at the Beeb, where we recorded the show and were having our first drink in the bar by 9.15. With *On the Rocks* we were doing retakes until after midnight long after the audience had gone home. Our leading man didn't have the comic charisma of Ronnie Barker, but how many people do? It got to the point where we were sharing out the lines among the cast to make it more of a gang show. Somehow, our ratings were still just good enough to keep us on the air but alarm bells were clanging.

Dick: That's why they sent us to Milwaukee to meet Rita Moreno.

Ian: Milwaukee! Breweries, churches and cheese. Never been there before, never been back since. And we saw Rita Moreno playing the lead in *Bells are Ringing* with Tab Hunter in a tent.

Dick: Rita was a big star. We were very excited. She'd been in the movie version of *West Side Story* – how cool was that? And she'd just had a big Broadway hit in a show called *The Ritz*. The networks were looking for a show for her. She's Puerto Rican, and so was our leading man. So one of the suits suggested she played Hector Fuentes's cousin and visited him in prison. The rest of the episode would feature her. This is what they termed a 'back-door pilot'.

Ian: It wasn't half-bad. Rita was great. And shortly after that the network hauled us in for a meeting. How did we feel about a second season of *On the Rocks*?

Dick: We didn't sugar-coat the problem we had with our leading man. I remember saying something like: 'If only he had the energy and spark that Rita Moreno showed us.' And about ten days later John Rich got a call. How did we feel about a second season? *With Rita in the lead!*

Ian: Unbelievable! It was a bit like suggesting another series of *Porridge* with Barbara Windsor taking over from Ronnie Barker. No one had given a thought about what Rita was supposed to be doing in a men's prison. We never even considered it. There was a lot of money at stake but we turned it down.

Dick: It's one of the silliest suggestions I've ever heard from a network, though there are others. There was a script conference about an American version of *Fawlty Towers* where an executive asked: 'Could you maybe put in a line to suggest that deep, deep, *deep* down, Basil really loves his wife?'

Ian: Remember that note we got from a studio exec on another project? 'We asked you for a grey suit. You have delivered a grey suit. But what we now realise is that we really need a brown suit.'

Dick: It was a relief to go back to the UK to do a third season of

Porridge. Back in the bosom of the BBC and working again with that wonderful cast.

Ian: Shamelessly, we took plots we'd written for *On the Rocks* and translated them back into English. Then we did it in reverse again when we tried to do an American version of *Whatever Happened to the Likely Lads?* But what was the equivalent of North Shields?

Dick: I came up with the idea of Steubenville, Ohio as I'd been there during my year at school in the States. It's a bit like the town where they made *The Deer Hunter*. So we went there to film the titles for the show with the two leading actors and Tony Richmond, an old mate from the UK, to do the actual filming.

Ian: It was just what you'd promised us – full of churches of every known denomination and even more bars. Every single sign had at least one of its letters missing.

Dick: On a misty February morning we looked down from a bridge to the murky waters of the Ohio River. Large white letters had been painted on a concrete slab reading 'STEUBENVILLE MARINA'.

Ian: We all lost it. There was nothing remotely nautical in sight, not even a rubber dinghy. The two words just didn't belong together.

Dick: The show didn't gel either. All the grainy, blue-collar grittiness was in that title sequence. There was no sign of it in the rest of the pilot episode.

Ian: We weren't at all sure that the move to California was working but we found ourselves talking to an immigration lawyer called Ron Bonaparte. I'm amazed we never worked that name into a script.

Dick: And then you met someone.

Ian: I met Doris, a beautiful girl from Paris who, within months, had moved in with me bringing a five-year-old son, her mother, a housekeeper and a Yorkshire terrier. And a few weeks later her brother Sam was sleeping on the sofa. Forty-five years later, she's shown no sign of leaving.

Dick: It's ironic that you, the perennial bachelor, were settling down at the same time that my first marriage was in serious trouble. Jenny had never been happy in America and we decided to split up. No one in my family had ever got divorced so there was no road map. The next few years were the most turbulent and painful of my life, especially as my four children were six thousand miles away. I was a mess, desperately missing them and unable to move forward or back. I even saw a shrink for a while. How Hollywood is that?

Ian: I don't remember that. Did he advise you to see less of me?

Dick: Not exactly. He helped for a bit. Then one day I showed up and he was out of sorts because he'd had a bust-up with his father. I did my best to show him where he'd gone wrong and then I thought, 'He should be paying me for this session!' Part of my brain couldn't help thinking that this was a sitcom moment.

Ian: I always found the best therapy was work.

Dick: Yes, but you also had tennis. You were suddenly being invited to large houses to play with people like Larry Gelbart and Mel Brooks. I was very jealous and decided to take up the game myself. It's taken its toll over the years and cost me two half-knee replacements but I'm still playing three days a week.

Ian: It's good that you chose tennis over drugs. There were drugs everywhere. It was routine to be offered them at business meetings, lunches, dinners, parties, screenings, concerts.

Dick: I'm glad you didn't start dropping acid. What if you'd had a really bad trip like Syd Barrett? I'd have had to write the third series of *Porridge* all on my own.

Ian: I remember going to an apartment in New York and our host had already cut two lines of coke and laid them on a glass-topped table. You shook your head, no thanks. The host persisted: 'Hash? Speed? Mescaline?' Your reply was priceless: 'Do you have a Heineken?'

Dick: Did you have to tell them that, it makes me sound so English.

Ian: Well you are.

Dick: We both are. When the World Cup or the Olympics come around there's never any question about who we're cheering for. And we've never stopped working for the home country. The truth is it's still very comfortable writing *British* English, with all those different dialects. We wrote *Auf Wiedersehen, Pet* here; quite a lot of *Lovejoy* and *The Rotters Club*. We talked to Jeff Lynne a lot to make sure we got the right Brummie cadences.

Ian: So yes, we're still here in LA, in spite of wild fires and the constant prediction that the next quake will be 'The Big One'. We live in the same canyon, up in the hills, so it's a very planet-friendly commute from my house to yours every morning.

Dick: But it might also explain why the following chapters take place in Moscow, Vienna, London, Dublin and Gateshead.

After Midnight in Moscow – Dick

Yevgeny Yevtushenko

I can't pretend that Yevgeny Yevtushenko and I were close. Of all my chance acquaintances, he is the only poet, the only Russian. He died quite recently and I doubt that he ever remembered our encounter but it echoes vividly in my mind.

It happened in Moscow because Ian and I were filming a documentary record of Elton John's concert tour in May 1979, *To Russia With Elton*. The Soviets were wary of rock 'n' roll. The only precedent was Boney M, who had been there the previous year. The authorities probably gave their blessing because the first half of the concert was Elton performing solo piano; far less threatening than, say, the Who or the Rolling Stones.

Three years earlier I shot a series of commercials in Paris with Petula Clark. The producer for the American agency was Nancy Campbell and I fell head over heels in love – well, I like to think that she did too, though it took her a little longer. It was not an easy courtship as she lived in New York and I lived in LA making frequent trips to London, but I eventually persuaded her to up sticks and move in with me. When her mother flew in from Ohio to check me out she was not impressed – well, she seemed to like me, but not where we lived.

'You told me he had a house. This is a hut!'

It's a little bigger now but we still live there, more than forty years later.

Nancy was as curious as all of us about the way the Russians would receive us.

None of us had any first-hand experience of living under Communism.

Remember, this was a decade before the Berlin Wall came down and the Soviet Empire crumbled. The Cold War was still chilly. Our first introduction to a difference in basic philosophy came on the Aeroflot flight to Leningrad. After quite a while, no food had been served, no attendants were in sight. Eventually someone went looking for them – and found them eating behind a curtain. It was made clear that once they had finished they might get around to attending to the passengers.

In Leningrad we stayed at the Europa Hotel, an elegant relic of another era, still thriving today under another name and a lot more expensive. In accordance with my status as co-director of the film, I was given a suite with a grand piano and a chandelier, but the authorities had a puritan attitude towards unmarried couples sharing. Nancy was assigned a dingy room at the far end of the corridor, which was guarded by a formidable 'Key-Lady' who sat at her desk to ensure that there was no *'henky-penky'*. Sometime after midnight Nancy went to her bathroom and saw an enormous cockroach. That did it. She marched defiantly past the Key-Lady and joined me in my spacious suite. We were woken some time later by a flash from the chandelier. I mentioned this to someone at the British Embassy when we got to Moscow and he shook his head.

'Silly buggers, they should've used the infra-red.'

The fans behaved like fans everywhere. Elton's albums had never been released in the Soviet Union but they applauded each of his hits from the opening bars. When we talked to young kids after the shows we learned how. Someone did his military service in, say, Poland. He bought Western records there – Elton, Led Zeppelin, Genesis – and he'd make copies for his friends,

sometimes down the phone. At the conclusion of the first performance some of these fans rushed down to the front of the
stage, just as they had in Birmingham a few weeks earlier. This
was frowned upon. At the second concert the front three rows
were occupied by bull-headed men in ill-fitting suits, like security
officials at football matches who sit with their back to the game
scrutinising the crowd. Elton was told not to kick over the piano
stool again and not to play 'Back in the USSR'. He ignored this
and got an ovation every time he sang it.

In the second half percussionist Ray Cooper joined him on-
stage. However many times we saw the show we never wanted to
miss Ray's entrance, halfway through 'Funeral for a Friend'. An
enormous screen like a giant garage door slowly began to rise and
the silhouette of Ray was revealed. He was utterly still as Elton's
chords built and built until suddenly, dramatically, lights illumi-
nated him beating the shit out of kettle drums!

Dressed in a dark suit with cropped hair, stubble and rimless
glasses he looked like a Russian dissident newly released from the
gulag. When he'd finished with the timps he tossed the mallets
aside as if he had no further use for them and moved to the tubu-
lar bells, looking at the audience with a manic glint in his eye. The
moment was worth the price of admission.

We were dazzled by Leningrad's architecture, especially when
we filmed at the Summer Palace, which had been totally restored
since the war, something that could only have happened under
Communism. The authorities insisted that we took a night train to
Moscow and emphasised that no filming should take place during
the journey. Harvey Harrison, our cameraman, saw this as a challenge and took lyrical shots of the countryside in the dawn light
that ended up in the completed film.

The hotel in Moscow, the enormous Rossiya, was a complete
contrast to the Europa, with all the charm of a federal penitentiary. It was hot. We were thirsty. We eventually found a bar on

an upper floor and ordered beers. A sour-faced lady told us that if we wanted beers we would have to sit on the terrace. We duly obeyed. A few days later we took some new arrivals up to the bar, sat on the terrace and put our order in. This time the same woman told us sternly that if we wanted beers we had to drink them *inside*. I suppose this was the only part of her life over which she had any control and by God she planned to use it.

Elton was offered a VIP tour of the Kremlin and our wives managed to tag along. They were shown all the royal, historical and artistic treasures left over from the Tsars. As they stumbled into Red Square Elton confided to Nancy that he was shocked to discover that he had a bigger Fabergé collection than the Kremlin.

We were very aware of being constantly under surveillance. Elton was assigned a personal assistant who was clearly gay, doubtless in the hope that it would lure him into some indiscretion. Someone opened the wrong door in the concert hall and saw more than a dozen outsize tape recorders, their reels revolving steadily, recording who knew what. Very soon if any of us said something even remotely subversive we would look up at the ceiling and say:

'Did you get that, Boris?'

We quickly found out this wasn't even original; everyone did the same. Two tour managers were attached to us, Helena and Natasha, who had been to the West with the Bolshoi Ballet. We all fancied Natasha – well, maybe not Elton – and she took us into her confidence one day.

'Be very careful what you say in front of Helena because she's KGB.'

We thanked her, grateful for the inside tip. A few days later we were feted at the British Embassy and mentioned this to a young man in a suit. He gave a condescending smile.

'Yes, well of course so is Natasha. Oldest trick in the book, you see. Page One in the Spy Manual.'

After two weeks we were all ready to go home, tired of being under constant supervision and especially tired of the food. Only caviar seemed plentiful, at least for us VIPs. The buffet table often consisted of a few sad potatoes and a lone tomato. At Aragvi, Moscow's poshest restaurant, we nicknamed one dish 'smashed chicken' because every mouthful managed to contain at least one splinter of bone.

Our last night was the most memorable. After the performance Ray approached Nancy and me and asked if we wanted to go with him to meet Yevtushenko. It seemed too good an opportunity to turn down so we skipped the wrap party and drove off in a Russian limo.

I'd never read his poetry but I knew there were two schools of thought about him. His detractors thought that he had sold out to the Politburo and was being used by them to make the regime look more liberal. Others thought that he was playing them very cleverly at their own game, the only possible way to survive.

He lived in the Artists' Colony, the theory supposedly being that the regime could keep a close eye on all longhairs and subversives at the same time. It was some way outside Moscow and it was after midnight when we arrived at the poet's dacha, quite a modest rustic structure by Western standards but luxurious here. Yevtushenko was tall and lean. He was forty-six and spoke excellent English. His wife, Jan, was Irish, which surprised us. They proudly showed us their new baby. Another surprise was that his other guests were American, young Jewish students from Yale.

He produced a black and white photograph of the place where he was born. At best it was a hamlet, a small pond with a pair of ducks and a few wooden dwellings, somewhere in Siberia. It was hard to imagine anyone having a sentimental attachment for a place so bleak and remote but he looked at it with nostalgic yearning.

We sat at a long table and he poured some Georgian wine, which he said was very rare:

'Even Mr Brezhnev has only one case of this.'

He made a toast, a very long toast. We raised our glasses. At one point I started to lower mine and was told that this was not the custom – they should all be held high until he was finished.

He told us about a dream. He was in a graveyard. The tombstones, instead of dates, showed a length of time: a year, a month, a week, sometimes only a few minutes or seconds. There were many, many blank stones. An old man tending the yard explained that this was the length of time that these people had given to others during their entire lives.

He addressed each of us in turn, starting with Ray, whom he revered as a genuine and brilliant artist. He moved on to the students from Yale and dished out similar praise, hesitating only when he got to me, probably because he wasn't sure who the hell I was. He concluded by saying that none of our tombstones would be blank because of the generous amount of time we had given to others.

His delivery was dramatic and hypnotic – the Russian accent didn't hurt – which is why the story made such a profound impact on me. The rest of the evening was equally memorable. The young men from Yale were quiet and serious. At about three in the morning he invited them to sing. They intoned a chant *a capella*, a forgotten part of Russian culture they had travelled all that way to reintroduce. Their resonant *basso profundo* voices were unforgettable, haunting and strangely moving.

Yevtushenko suggested that the perfect way to end the occasion was to visit Boris Pasternak's grave. I think we must have walked there – I don't remember getting into cars. We made our pilgrimage in the dawn light and stood solemnly around the railing where the great man was buried. I found out later that the railing features in a poem he wrote about it. Pasternak's son was buried next to him, his wife outside the railing some distance away under the trees, a very Russian kind of male chauvinism that was not lost on Nancy. It was very quiet in the dawn light and I remember thinking that I had never, ever, felt so far from home.

Over the next year or so I told a lot of people about that extraordinary evening, never forgetting to mention the dream about the unmarked graves. Then one night I was half-asleep in a rented flat in London when some dialogue on TV woke me up with a start. The words seemed eerily familiar:

'I had a dream. I found myself in a graveyard where all the tombstones were marked in a curious way: 1822, 1826 . . . 1930, '34, always like that, always a very short time between birth and death.'

By now I'm sitting bolt upright, fully awake, staring at the black and white movie.

'In the graveyard, a very old man. I asked him how it was he'd lived so long when everyone else in the village had died so young. But no, he told me this – it's not that we die early, it's just here on our tombstones we do not count the years in a man's life but rather the length of time he kept a friend. Let's drink to friendship.'

This was delivered in sonorous tones by none other than Orson Welles in his ill fated movie *Mr. Arkadin*, also known as *Confidential Report*. It was released in 1955, twenty-four years before we were in Russia. I was stunned. After all the times I'd told my friends how moved I'd been by the toast, I now realised that Yevtushenko had ripped off Orson Welles!

I was able to quote the entire speech verbatim because years later Nancy tracked down the Criterion Collection version of the movie that is, to put it kindly, less than a masterpiece. I checked out the moment in the film that had woken me up and shaken my belief in Yev's artistic integrity. And yet, as with most things Russian, there are always two schools of thought.

Mr Arkadin precedes the speech by saying it's a Georgian toast.

Maybe history's most infamous Georgian, Josef Stalin, used it to honour guests at dinner parties, eyeing each of them in turn, their elbows aching as they held their glasses high, while he decided which ones to purge.

The wine we drank that night long ago was Georgian but the poet was born in Siberia, several time-zones away, Zima Junction, to be precise, so it isn't likely that he heard the toast as a boy at an uncle's funeral. On the other hand, would he really have been able to get hold of a bootleg copy of *Mr. Arkadin*?

I'm still in two minds about him.

Goodnight, Vienna – Ian

Peter Sellers

Our relationship with Peter Sellers was based almost entirely on two dinners. In between we had a couple of script meetings, a few phone calls and did production revisions and rewrites in his hotel suite. The dinners were extremely pleasant, productive, affable and at times hilarious. Why wouldn't they be, you may well ask, but Peter had a reputation for being unpredictable and impossible so we approached the first meeting with some apprehension. At that time, the late seventies, he was one of world's biggest stars and the career and financial clout afforded him by the phenomenal *Pink Panther* franchise gave him every right, I assume, to be as demanding and difficult as he wished.

The first dinner, in April 1977, was in St Tropez; the second, the following year, in Vienna. For the first one Universal Studios and the Mirisch Company flew us to France to discuss with the great star a remake of *The Prisoner of Zenda*. There had been many previous retellings of the classic Victorian novel: several films, some of them silent, stage plays, a stage musical and television adaptations. The most respected was made in 1937 with Ronald Colman and Douglas Fairbanks Jr. and described by film buff Leslie Halliwell as 'a splendid schoolboy adventure tale'. Stewart Granger and Deborah Kerr starred in the fifties version. There was an even a Bollywood version made in 2015, starring, you've guessed it, Salman Khan and Sonam Kapoor.

With Sellers aboard, ours was to be, of course, a comedy. That was the general idea. Peter would play three roles, the old decrepit King of the fictional Ruritania, his foppish son, and the unwitting lookalike, Sid Frewin, a London hansom cab driver with Peter giving his best, authentic cockney accent. Voices are not just Peter's forte; they are the portal to his characterisations. He told us, on another project:

'I haven't got the voice yet. I need to get it or I won't know the character.'

He has admitted in many interviews or conversations that he had no real identity outside of the roles that he played, which is probably why his behaviour could at times be neurotic or compulsive.

And so we met in Saint-Tropez, at a restaurant called L'Escale on the old port, which in the summer would have been packed with French showbiz royalty, models and yacht-owning sheikhs. We would have been refused a table, unless of course we were with Peter Sellers. I asked Bill Wyman to join us. He was living in the South of France at the time and knew Peter socially. So the four of us sat down to dinner with the understanding we would leave 'work' until the next day.

Dick and I quickly learned that the key to making Peter

comfortable and amiable was to tap into his reserve of sentiment and nostalgia, most of which revolved around his early days before stardom; his days after demob from the RAF in Music Hall, before the remotest possibility that he might end up the superstar he became. Days of weekly revues in the provinces, 'treading the boards' with fellow comedians, singers, impersonators, novelty acts, jugglers and acrobats. Long Sunday train journeys, theatres that were faded relics of Edwardian times, cheap theatrical digs, fried food and draft beer, lightened, perhaps, by the occasional skirmish with a chorus girl in some draughty room with a gas meter.

Peter didn't in fact spend much time on the road as he landed a regular spot at London's Windmill Theatre, doing his routines between tableaux of posing nude models. They were allowed to be nude as long as they didn't move. If one of the girls had sneezed the Lord Chamberlain would have closed down the show the next day. Peter loved to talk about that distant time. He had an especially fond spot for ventriloquists (vents) and their weird relationships with their dummies, sorry, partners. When I was a schoolboy there were vents who had their own radio shows, like Peter Brough and Archie Andrews in *Educating Archie*. None of the millions of listeners could see, or care, if Peter's lips were moving or not. It was as absurd as BBC announcers being made to wear formal evening suits when they read the news.

Sellers' favourite story revolved around a vent called Jimmy Tattersall, who used several different dummies in his act, one of which was a life-sized old lady operated by remote control, which caused constant stress and anxiety. She was supposed to appear from the wings at the climax of his act while he was singing 'My Old Dutch' and walk into his arms.

One night Jimmy told him: 'Trouble is, Peter, in all the time I've been doing this I've never felt in complete control.'

His worries were well founded. On several occasions the old lady malfunctioned, took a savage left turn and ended up in the orchestra pit.

I ventured a story that I'd heard from Mike King, a member of a singing group who had played the same circuit as Peter, albeit a few years later just before the halls surrendered variety acts to rock 'n' roll tours. They shared the bill with several other acts including 'The World's Strongest Man'. Except by now the world's strongest man was way past it and clinging on to his reputation by his very worn fingernails. So Mike would always hover in the wings at the climax of the Strongman's act when he would throw a cannonball into the air and catch it on the nape of his neck. Every time it landed he would give an agonized gasp:

'Jesus Chriiiiiiiiiiiiiist!'

Peter loved that; we had one in the win column. So far so good. We'd finished the escargots and were now onto steak frites and the second bottle of vastly overpriced Provençal plonk. But Peter's stories had loosened him up enormously. And we still had our ace to play: the Goons. The seminal radio show that made British household names of Peter, Harry Secombe, Spike Milligan and Michael Bentine. Now we were on safe ground, reinforced by the fact that Bill could recite whole sketches verbatim.

There is no one of our generation, and a few subsequent ones, who wasn't massively influenced by *The Goon Show*. At school we would imitate all the voices as part of our daily vocabulary. What made it even better was that our parents were puzzled by the Goons, even indignant. It was absurdist, surreal humour and there had been nothing like it. But mostly, which at our young age we didn't recognise, it was outrageously subversive, targeting the most respected British institutions, values and beliefs.

Let's remember the war, in which all four Goons served, was only recently over and victory still being savoured with pride and swelled chests. But the Goons, channelling Spike Milligan's scripts, mocked the war and especially the portrayals of it in British films with their portentous narration:

'The English Channel 1941. Across the silent strip of grey-green water, coastal towns were deserted. Except for people.'

This was against a background of fifties Britain, with its rigid social hierarchy, sexual repression, conformity and absolute respect for the Establishment, that coalition of Parliament, Church, the Military and the Law, all targets of Goon ridicule. Ten years later they would be the same targets of *Beyond the Fringe*.

Jonathan Miller happily admits Goon influence:

'They did an enormous amount to subvert the social order. After all, half their shows are a send-up of British Imperialism.'

I told a story as dinner wound down. When I was in the army, listening to *The Goon Show* was a weekly ritual. Almost everyone, except sentries and cooks, gathered in their quarters at the appointed hour to tune in. The show, along with music and announcements, was piped through to the camp from the guard room and the choice of programme was in the hands of a duty corporal. One such evening, waiting expectantly for *The Goon Show* at 8.30, we were horrified to hear classical music instead. Obviously this evening's corporal was a bit of a highbrow. Two of the burliest soldiers in my quarters pulled on their boots and headed for the door. I'm not sure if one of them grabbed a bayonet but I was probably embroidering the anecdote for Sellers' benefit.

I looked out of the window and from every building pissed-off 'delegates' were heading for the guard room. They were out of sight for a moment, the classical music still filling our ears. Then silence, leaving us time to imagine the dire retribution raining down on the hapless Mozart-loving NCO. Finally the familiar sounds of Goon lunacy filled our ears and the entire barracks.

Peter loved that story.

'You must tell Spike, please tell it to Spike.'

L'Escale wasn't very full when we arrived but it was empty

when we left except for yawning French waiters looking at their watches. A splendid night, one to remember and savour; we felt we had established a rapport with Peter that would serve us well for our mutual venture into Zendaland . . .

Vienna, a year and a bit later: *Zenda* was about to shoot and permits had been issued, granting the crew access to all the magnificent museums and palaces.

We were staying at the Bristol Hotel, a relic of the Vienna of *The Third Man*. There we had dinner with the director, Richard Quine. We had never met him before, never exchanged notes, thoughts, ideas, all the issues essential to a working relationship between writers and director. Perhaps he was too tied up with locations and casting although I suspect it was because Dick and I were perceived as 'friends of the star' and so Richard figured he could recuse himself with script issues. Big mistake. We needed input; we needed a voice that wasn't Peter's because his view of things could change on a dime, depending on weather, the state of the world or his current emotional state and that of his new young wife and co-star Lynne Frederick.

Don't get me wrong, we liked Lynne, she seemed a stabilising and calming influence on our erratic star and she was well suited to play Princess Flavia. She came with Peter to dinner number two in a very old-school Viennese restaurant named The Three Hussars. It was, we learned, Hitler's favourite. Peter also brought his regular dresser. Jeffrey was gay and funny and a match for Peter's anecdotes. He had been a performer in a previous life and gone through the same vaudevillian routine of a life on the road in the same dull, grey provincial Britain of the fifties.

Peter urged him to recount a story of a certain week in the city of Leeds, a town in those days of several woollen mills and few smiles. His landlady was a woman of a certain age with a refined Yorkshire accent and massive hips. She forbade female company

in rooms, and alcohol and noise or anything that might suggest
fun was being had. She especially reserved her frown of disapproval for 'theatricals', always assuming their behaviour would be
inappropriate. And – crucial plot point – her house was being
repainted while Jeffrey was there.

This particular evening he left for the theatre. The landlady told
him, as she did every night, that if he was late there would be a key
in a plant pot in the back yard. He set off and then remembered
he'd forgotten something. Instead of bothering her with the front
doorbell he headed straight for the yard and the pot. He walked
into the kitchen and found the landlady spreadeagled across the
kitchen table with skirts hitched up while the youngest of the
painters and decorators took her from behind.

Jeffrey stopped, frozen in disbelief and embarrassment. The
landlady, flushed and flustered, quickly regained her composure
but didn't alter her position.

'Oh Mr Jeffrey,' she sighed, 'you must think I'm an awful flirt.'

The four of us analysed why it was so hysterical and agreed it
was the use of the word 'flirt', which normally suggests fluttering
eyelashes or pouting lips or sideways glances, coquettish gestures
all far removed from being bonked from behind on a kitchen
table in Leeds.

And so the night ended on another high note and work and
the script were never mentioned. Which is all very well except
Prisoner of Zenda was about to commence principal photography
and a harder look at the problems night have served us all better.

We made fixes, cuts and changes with Peter and Lynne and
maintained good terms. We tried to capture in our script the
speech patterns and language of the Victorian original; thus the
King's counsel, General Sapt, on returning to Ruritania, quotes
Sir Walter Scott:

*'Breathes there the man with soul so dead, who never to himself
has said, "This is my own, my native land."'*

This draft elicited a very fast and cryptic response from one of the Mirisch brothers back in Tinsel Town:

'What's all this "Yea, yea, verily verily" shit?'

We left Vienna on good terms with Peter and began work on another project to which he agreed to attach himself. This was *Chandu the Magician*. After we'd written it he suddenly, without warning, jumped ship and made the awful *The Fiendish Plot of Doctor Fu Manchu*.

We saw a *Zenda* rough cut and were both deeply unhappy, so much so that I have never since seen the film from beginning to end, except on fast-forward looking for appropriate clips for a lecture. It opened to mixed reviews although Philip French in the *Observer* found it 'A mess of porridge' and you have to wonder if he was alluding to the writers, by now so associated with that word. When it opened in cinemas in New York I had a phone call that woke me up deep in the night. It was the actress Kelly Le Brock who told me she and some friends had just seen the movie and thought it was hysterical. Was she serious? I asked her if they were all stoned.

'Oh, God yes, we'd smoked a ton of weed.'

If, dear reader, you are tempted to stream *Zenda* or watch it on late-night television I suggest you follow her lead.

Peter bounced back with a startling performance in Hal Ashby's *Being There*. The film won him many Best Actor awards including the New York Film Critics Circle and a Golden Globe. He was also nominated for an Oscar but that prize eluded him and went to Dustin Hoffman for *Kramer vs. Kramer*. If we don't count *Fu Manchu*, and let's not, it is a massive consolation for Peter and his fans that he saved the best for last. He died at the absurdly young age of fifty-four, ironically having a fatal heart attack on the day in London when he was scheduled to have a reunion dinner with fellow Goons Spike Milligan and Harry Secombe.

But thank you Peter, for giving us so much laughter over the years. And two great evenings.

Footnote from Dick:

Almost everyone who worked with Peter – even Blake Edwards – found him notoriously difficult. I remember a conversation with writer/director Paul Mazursky, who directed some wonderful films including *Harry and Tonto*, *An Unmarried Woman* and *Down and Out in Beverly Hills*. Earlier in his career he and his co-writer Larry Tucker wrote a script called *I Love You, Alice B. Toklas*. When Peter signed on to star in it, he insisted that the director should be either Fellini or Bergman – this for a hippy-trippy comedy set in Malibu. Agents went through the motions, assuring Peter that they had been in touch with Federico and Ingmar's people, but sadly they were unavailable.

Paul briefly got the job himself but then got a call from his agent, who told him that he was off the picture because Peter was convinced that he was having an affair with his wife Britt Ekland. Paul vigorously denied this. All he had done was visit Peter's house for a script conference. Britt had been there of course, but she hadn't lingered after hello. His agent listened to his protestations then asked:

'Okay Paul – but was she worth it?'

A Pillar of Salt – Dick

John Wells

I heard laughter from the bathroom, early one morning. Since laughter is, as it were, my business, this demanded investigation. It turned out that Nancy was reading *Private Eye*, one of the 'Dear Bill' letters. Let me explain what these were.

Denis Thatcher, after a lifetime as a pillar of industry, had been looking forward to a retirement filled with playing golf and drinking gin and tonic with his pals. This was totally buggered up when his wife became Prime Minister. This put him in a spotlight he had never sought. His views were even further to the right than Maggie's and he was prone to indiscretion. He therefore needed to be kept on a tight leash and bridled against it. Thank God Twitter was still a thing of the future or who knows what havoc he might have wrought.

John Wells and Richard Ingrams gleefully seized upon this core situation and conceived the idea of a weekly series of letters in *Private Eye* from Denis to his friend 'Bill', usually thought to be William Deedes, former editor of the *Daily Telegraph*. The letters allowed them to comment on current events with a satirical slant. They were irreverent and very funny.

Ian and I read them to each other and thought they deserved a wider audience, perhaps in the form of a play. We got in touch with the writers. Richard Ingrams declared firmly that he did not want to be involved. John Wells later ascribed this to his 'life-long love of the theatre', something he did not want to besmirch.

John clearly felt differently and agreed to meet us in a Soho pub.

He looked like a professor already late for a tutorial at one of our lesser universities. He was slightly untidy, his hair flopping over his forehead, with a vaguely distracted air until he found something funny, at which point his laugh was unrestrained and loud enough to stop clocks. We got on well and agreed on a name for our venture: *Anyone For Denis?* Robert Fox agreed to be our producer, his first, but by no means his last theatrical production, and I found myself directing it.

John came up with a plot. Maggie was away for a Euro conference, giving Denis the opportunity to invite his chums, Maurice and the Major, for a weekend of unbridled drinking at Chequers. As in all good farces, his plans were sabotaged by his wife's unexpected arrival.

Ian and I sat down to collaborate with him – not on the words, which were very much his province. Logistics was where he could use our help. There could be only one set and no more than eight actors, three of whom would have to play two parts. We discovered that John had no idea how to get people on or off the stage, how to tell the audience who they were or how to give the actors enough time offstage so they could change from one character to the other.

On the other hand we soon realised that he was intellectually way above us. He translated plays from French and German. He had taught at Eton. He told us that he usually improvised the 'Dear Bill' letters while someone else wrote them down. The play began to emerge in the same way. Take, for example, Denis informing Bill on the phone at the start of Act Two that it would not be a good idea to drop by:

'Lacking the brush of a Leonardo I find it hard to paint an adequate picture, but suffice it to say that if you were to turn up at this precise moment you would be about as welcome as a pedlar flogging rubber johnnies at the front door of a monastery. Margaret has

just toddled off upstairs to practise her killer looks in the bedroom mirror. I'm afraid one of these days, Bill, she may turn herself to stone.'

But who should play him? It was typical of John that he waited a while before saying quietly, with unassuming modesty, that he would be willing to throw his hat into the ring. It was so obviously the right idea that I wondered why I hadn't thought of it before. John was an actor. He was a terrific mimic with an unparalleled genius for improvisation. Not only that but, as the playwright, he wouldn't have to ask anyone's permission to change the text if occasion demanded it.

It was Ian who had the brilliant idea of opening the play with Denis on the phone to Bill, the aural equivalent of a 'Dear Bill' letter. That was one of the main reasons for the play's success. Curtain Up, Denis enters, picks up the phone and talks to Bill about the latest scandal or whatever was in the headlines of the *Evening Standard*, so what he said changed nightly. John played the audience like a stand-up comedian for as long as it would take and finally put down the phone. The rest of the play was the same every night, but an illusion of topicality had been created.

Another major reason for success was that Angela Thorne captured every nuance of Britain's Prime Minister: her walk, her posture, her every cadence. Not only that but our venue was the Whitehall Theatre, just off Trafalgar Square and a stone's throw from Number 10 Downing Street and Clubland. We had a hit on our hands and it felt good.

John still looked more like a mathematician who had just proved an especially tricky theorem than the star of a West End show but he knew how to enjoy success. He generously gave me a case of rather good claret. I came home one afternoon to a rented flat in Pont Street to find it cordoned off and a policeman on duty outside the front door. When I asked why he said there was a suspicious suitcase underneath the Mercedes parked opposite.

He nodded towards my car, a vintage BMW that I used on visits to London. I owned up that it was mine and he had the wrong make. He muttered into his lapel mike:

'I have the owner of the suspect vehicle with me now.'

I was more concerned about John's case of claret, which was still in the boot and almost certainly worth more than the car. In time a robot arrived, retrieved the suspect suitcase, took it into an alley and presumably blew it up. I think it contained dirty laundry.

The play ran long enough to merit our Prime Minister's attention. I imagine that her aides persuaded her that she should see it for herself to show the country that she had a good sense of humour, something nobody had ever glimpsed. She never understood why most people found it funny when she famously said, referring to her Home Secretary, Willie Whitelaw, a staunch supporter of hers:

'Everybody needs a Willie.'

Whatever persuasion was used by her PR gurus the result was that we received word that she would like to see the play and be pleased to entertain the producers, John and myself at Downing Street after the performance.

I sat in the stalls a few rows behind her on the night she came. I never once saw her shoulders shake with mirth or raise a hand to stifle a laugh. I did notice that her hair never moved, as unbendable as her will. After a decent interval John and I walked down Whitehall to Number 10. I decided not to mention that she would be the second Prime Minister I had met. I had heard she was not especially fond of Edward Heath.

She greeted me with a gracious smile, the very one that Angela captured so perfectly in her performance when she greeted the Euro-Delegates, Monsieur Vouvray de Chambertin and Herr Heinrich Schubert. Her voice was soft and soothing as she said:

'I gather your play is a great hit with members of the Establishment.'

My response came from some dark corner of my brain:

'It's always been the habit of the Establishment to hug its critics to its bosom.'

I wasn't trying to be clever but the result was instantaneous. I was turned into a pillar of salt. Her smile faded and she turned her attention to whoever was next in line. I ceased to exist.

The rest of the evening was more cordial. I especially enjoyed talking to Willie Whitelaw himself, the very same Willie that everybody needed. He was an old-fashioned patrician Tory in a grey double-breasted suit that looked as it had been made for him in 1948. He was affable and charming and seemed to be enjoying the occasion. Nor was he especially discreet. He confided:

'Denis is a very, very nice man. It's also true to say that he's not a million miles away from how he's portrayed on stage.'

Satirists are usually thought of as being motivated by anger, using their wit to denounce hypocrisy, deflate pomposity and expose vanity in all its forms. I never felt that John was that kind of satirist. He was essentially too kind, too willing to see the funny side. His colleagues at *Private Eye* mocked him for his social skills. He seemed to know everyone, including Princess Margaret, though he never introduced us.

In some ways John was curiously old-fashioned. He never drove a car, for instance. I thought he had some of the nostalgia for times gone by that he put into Denis's mouth:

'To be able to toddle down to the boozer on a Saturday morning, buy a round of drinks and still have change left out of an old brown ten-bob note. Stroll into the grocers and be called "Sir" by a fellow Englishman with polished boots and properly parted hair, stub of pencil behind one ear, long white apron, the kind of cove who used a wire to cut the cheese with.'

The main quality I remember is a sense of mischief. I was never bored in John's presence. He died far too young and I still miss him.

When Allan met Tracey – Ian

Tracey Ullman/Allan McKeown

I first got to know Allan McKeown on the set of *Catch Me a Spy*. It was cold and wet and he was the unit hairdresser. He was in low spirits, having to deal with two problems. One was our leading lady, Marlène Jobert, who was never quite happy about the way Allan styled her hair; the other was suffering from the effects of surgery for piles he'd had only two weeks previously. So you could say, correctly, that he was trying to cope with two pains in the arse at the same time.

He started his career at the age of fifteen as an apprentice in Vidal Sassoon's salon in Mayfair. He was really called John McKeown but Vidal already had a John and gave him his new name. In the seventies Allan began styling hair for the movies. He gave Vanessa Redgrave a very elaborate 'do'. She liked it. The following morning he wanted to try something new. She explained that as she was completing the scene that was shot the day before it would have to be exactly the same.

'I can't possibly re-create that. I'm an artist!'

In spite of this shaky start he became Elizabeth Taylor's stylist of choice and for a while he moved in the Burtons' seductive, luxurious, absurdly glamorous orbit.

At that time Tracey Ullman was an eleven-year-old girl living in south-west London having been born in Slough. When she was six her father died in front of her with a heart attack, which affected her take on life from that day onwards.

'When that happens to you as a child, you can face anything, because you're always waiting for the other shoe to drop.'

As a way of easing her mother's depression she and her sister Patti would perform a nightly review in the bedroom, mimicking friends, family, neigbours and celebrities. Even at that early age she realised she could impersonate almost anyone.

Meanwhile Allan's ambitions went far beyond a pair of scissors or even his own salon. To my amazement he was suddenly in advertising, producing commercials for James Garrett. He produced the shoot in Paris where Dick met Nancy. In our office there's a picture of the three of them and Allan's girlfriend at the time, walking along the Boulevard Saint-Germain looking very young and very slim and wearing flared trousers.

I always felt whatever Allan was doing was a stepping-stone to the next: producer to studio head, perhaps; or CEO of a corporation, tycoon, even Chairman of the Federal Reserve. He was extremely ambitious and self-confident but he always loved the creative community and having creative people around him. Our first venture was the film of *Porridge*, which Allan and I produced and Dick directed. Chelmsford prison in January; Dick, wearing what looked like an Afghan warlord's coat in freezing weather.

This was when Allan explained to me the crucial difference between producing and directing:

*'In conditions like this, producers go to lunch. Somewhere warm
with a wine list.'*

Three months later we were all in the Cold War Soviet Union
making *To Russia With Elton* where Allan spent considerable time
trying to seduce our very attractive KGB handler, Natasha.

A few years after this the three of us were partners in Witzend
Productions with an office in Hollywood and another in Soho.
LA was party central in the seventies and we did our share. Allan
had a Rolls-Royce for a while but he didn't have a licence to drive
it after being arrested for not pulling over for three ambulances
and a fire engine. He was probably on the phone working on
a deal.

He could be a little naughty and unpredictable after a couple
of drinks too many. Flying on a business trip to Sydney we drank
those silly drinks with umbrellas on the stopover in Honolulu.
Back on board Allan berated the crew for not upgrading us into
first class until he was told, quite forcibly, that if he did not behave
the plane would make an unscheduled stop in Fiji where he would
be placed in custody.

America never really panned out for us in the eighties but in the
UK Allan was on a tear and during the next two decades Witzend
or Select TV was a fantastic place with which to be associated.
Under Allan and Tony Charles an amazing roster of shows was
produced, and a stable of writers created, the most prolific of
which were Maurice Gran and Laurence Marks, always affectionately, known as Lo and Mo. The series kept on coming – *Shine
on Harvey Moon, Roll Over Beethoven, Astronauts, Girls On Top,
Pie in the Sky, The Other 'Arf, Auf Wiedersehen, Pet, Birds of a
Feather, Lovejoy, Westbeach, Freddy and Max* and *Full Stretch*.

Allan's energy and enthusiasm infected us all and the office
in Derby Street was always buzzing. Script meetings, casting,

pitches, seminars and weekend retreats in country hotels. Allan wheeled and dealed and made believers of everyone. He was the Ringmaster, our Mr Kite. And Hazel was our Girl Friday, her desk an oasis of calm among all the raucous rivalries and competing egos.

Tracey and Allan met on a Witzend pilot at Elstree Studios. It was called *A Cut Above* and was set in a hairdressing salon. 'I have to say,' he told me one day, 'I rather fancy that Tracey Ullman.' The show didn't survive but Allan's feelings persisted. Sometime later we produced *Girls On Top*. Tracey was the first person cast but by then she was a rising talent having done *Three of a Kind* with Lenny Henry and David Copperfield and had made hit records. Ruby Wax was alongside her and one night we went to a pub in Battersea to check out two aspiring female comics, Dawn French and Jennifer Saunders. I think John Sessions was one of the other acts.

The girls joined the show, which centred around their adventures sharing a London flat. Their landlady was played by Joan Greenwood, whom Dick and I, along with legions of teenage boys, had fantasised about in the fifties in the era of Ealing comedies. Joan liked lunch every day at an Italian *trattoria* near the studios where she drank white wine, smoked and told us stories.

I became, along with Ben Elton, a script editor on *Girls*, which meant trying to curb their anarchic and freeform instincts and stick to some kind of basic plot. The girls often derided my efforts, in the nicest way of course. When I arrived at Dawn's flat in Shepherd's Bush for a script session they would greet me chanting:

'Here's Ian – structure, structure, structure!'

Script-editing is a thankless task because you usually annoy the original writer. In the prolific Witzend nineties Dick and I were often overcommitted. I remember a night at Tony Charles's house, where I always stayed in London, when together with Tony and

his wife Audie we worked till two in the morning rewriting an episode of *The Other 'Arf,* which starred John Standing and Lorraine
Chase. Next morning Tony handed in the script, handwritten on a
legal pad and covered in wine stains.

The *Girls On Top* cast were all brilliant but Tracey had the edge;
she could dance and sing and was an outstanding mimic. In 1987
Jim Brooks brought her to Hollywood and she became star of
The Tracey Ullman Show. This made her the first British woman
to be offered her own sketch show in the States and the UK, an
astonishing achievement. That was also the show that introduced
The Simpsons. When Dick and I saw the pilot episode we jointly
offered Tracey the same piece of advice:

'You have to get rid of that silly cartoon segment.'

(This wasn't the only time that we were spectacularly wrong
with a prediction. We assured all our English friends that there
wasn't a snowball's chance in hell that Donald Trump could ever
become President.)

I was Allan and Tracey's best man when they were married in
Los Angeles in 1983. Allan, with a wife and very soon children,
became a different man. Family life gave him stability and balance
and he became a devoted husband and father.

Working on *Tracey Takes On* in the nineties was a great experience. Dick and I had never written a sketch show and rarely
worked with a writing team except as editors. It was as if we'd
been home schooled for years and were suddenly released into
the noise and mayhem of Junior High. The routine was the same
every season. We spent a long weekend in a Santa Barbara Hotel,
spit-balling ideas about theme and content. Then every Monday
we would meet in Tracey's office, discuss that week's show, pitch
ideas, delegate who wrote what and meet at the end of the week.
Dick, Tracey and I would choose the final content, her decision
being decisive, and edit the material.

What made it exceptional was that she would do all the voices in sketch read-throughs and have us helpless with laughter. Along with Ronnie Barker, Tracey has to be the most brilliant, versatile comic talent we ever worked with. The show, made by HBO, garnered a stack of Emmy awards and nominations.

Allan and Tracey had two children by then, Mabel and Johnny. A very young Mabel accompanied Tracey to Florida where she was appearing in a play. Mabel sat in the stalls, observing rehears-als and soaking up the luvvy culture of the theatre. She witnessed another performance of sorts on the flight home to Los Angeles – a Flight Attendant going though the safety procedure of seat belts, life jackets and exit doors. When she finished and was walk-ing down the aisle Mabel grabbed her arm and told her:

'You were marvellous.'

No, Mabel did not become an actress, she went into politics instead after some years at Leeds University where, Tracey told me, she graduated in 'Advanced Arguing'.

Allan and I fell out when we revived *Auf Wiedersehen, Pet.* The rights had reverted to the original creator, Franc Roddam, who set new machinery in place. Allan felt he should have been involved. He was right, but he blamed me for it not happening; for him, the damage was irreparable and we didn't speak for some years, although I would often see Tracey socially, and she was as friendly with Dick and me as always.

We made our peace eventually, thank God. We were like one of those married couples who divorce then reunite years later. Our friendship had deepened and, I think, made us both more appre-ciative of what made us friends in the first place. Although I still do have a few questions about the petty cash . . .

Mortality had something to with our reconciliation as Allan's illness was beginning to take its toll. He had lived with cancer for twenty years, never with anger or self-pity, always with resilience and his trademark humour. In 2013 he decided to stop chemo and heavy duty meds and come to terms with the inevitable. He arranged it so that the family would all be together, Johnny from college, Mabel from London, during the most sentimental holidays of the year. With exquisite timing he died on Christmas Eve.

If Allan ever gets the chance to read this I'm sure there will be only one question on his lips: Is there a series?

Diversion for a Spider – Dick

Robert Morley

Directing commercials gave me a welcome break. I was often faced with the challenge of reassuring nervous advertising executives, often over a good lunch. Casting made a welcome change. I was given a chance to work with the very best film crews. It was also a useful discipline to have to tell a story in only thirty seconds. Every time I got the call to see if I was available I had to negotiate with Ian for 'time off'. He was very good about it. On one occasion, for a shoot in Milan, he came with me so that we could finish a script. He did most of it but still allowed me to keep my half of the fee.

Partly to pay him back I pulled him in to collaborate on a series of commercials for Double Diamond featuring the slogan 'I'm

Only Here For the Beer'. One night I dreamed one of them. I often have ideas in my sleep but usually, as I float back to consciousness, they disappear like a mirage. This one was about two thirsty Brits turning up for a holiday in an unfinished hotel on the Costa Brava and realising that the picture they'd seen in the brochure was 'an artist's impression'.

The agency bought the idea and I went to Almeria, a favourite location for spaghetti westerns. When I settled into my hotel I found there was no soap in the bathroom. I called down to reception and asked them to send some up. After quite a while they sent me some soup.

I needed to talk to my assistant director about the shoot the following day. He'd sent a note saying he was in room 403. I went down there. A sign on the door said 'DO NOT DISTURB'. Who the hell did he think he was? I was the director and he was my AD. I needed to go over the call sheet. I ignored the sign and rapped on the door.

Silence. I rapped again, more insistently, then a third time. Something suddenly didn't seem right. I checked the note he had left me. He was in Room 304.

The door of Room 403 was unlocked and I found myself staring at the cadaverous face of Jack Palance. He was four inches taller than I was. He squinted down at me through those deep-set eyes. He looked rumpled, curious how anyone could possibly contemplate disturbing him by knocking on a door with such a clear warning about not disturbing him. He wasn't happy about being disturbed. This was the man who shot Elisha Cook Jr. in *Shane* in cold blood and looked happy about it. Who had played roles like Revak the Barbarian Celt, El Tigre, Attila the Hun and, yes, Dracula.

Jack never said a word. He didn't have to. I backed away, waving my hands in the air like a footballer trying to convince the referee that he never meant to make a studs-up tackle.

'Oh, is this the fourth floor? Sorry, I thought . . . I was looking for three-oh-four . . . Really sorry. I'll kill Nick for getting the room numbers mixed up . . .'

I reached the sanctuary of the stairs and scurried out of sight.

I made a number of commercials with people I had already worked with, like Ronnie Barker, Peter Cook and Dudley Moore, Frank Muir. But I had never met Robert Morley, the character actor famous for his roles in movies like *Beat the Devil* and as Katharine Hepburn's preacher brother in *The African Queen*.

One of the biggest shoots I ever did was with Robert, a series of commercials in Paris for an American company, Burlington Industries. He was an outsize teddy bear of a man, much loved by Americans for his air of quirky British eccentricity. I came to love him for different reasons. The first of these was his generosity. The New York clients had no idea who I was or what I had done before, but Robert always gave me a plug saying things like:

'You must realise that this is a very clever fellow.'

He then listed my credits. Sharing the limelight in that way is, in my experience, a rarity in actors. He occasionally lost his temper, but instantly apologised and found a way to blame himself. His plummy upper-class vowels might lead you to think he was a patrician Tory. Not a bit of it, he was firmly of the left. Perhaps some of the grittier members of the Labour Party dismissed him as a 'champagne socialist', but he never wavered from his convictions in my hearing.

He told me how he bought his house in Wargrave just after the war. He walked into it and found a man laying tiles in the kitchen. He asked if he knew who the owner was.

'Me,' said the man, without looking up.

'I don't suppose you'd like to sell it.'

'I might if you gave me a thousand quid.'

'How about nine hundred?'

'Done,' said the man. Still on his knees he offered his hand. Robert shook it and lived there the rest of his life.

After the shoot for Burlington, hawking carpets and curtains among other things, I was asked to direct him for British Airways. One of these was a hair-raising shoot in a helicopter. Robert made his affable pitch with the green fields of England behind him – then the chopper took off to reveal that he was standing on the edge of the white cliffs at Beachy Head.

When *Billy* was about to move into the Drury Lane Theatre we were worried about whether the show would play in such a vast space. Robert was very reassuring:

'Marvellous theatre, dear boy – I did a death scene in *Fanny* for two years and you could hear every word at the back of the upper balcony.'

He had an Oscar nomination when he was thirty for his role in *Marie Antoinette*, though he had a philosophical no-nonsense attitude about the business of acting. In his view:

'Acting is not a sacred call. Good actors act to live, they don't live to act.'

He probably got into fierce arguments with fellow thespians about that one, but Robert loved nothing better than saying something irreverent and provoking an argument. He got bored when he was in a long run and on occasions could be very naughty. He was upstage on one occasion, looking out of a window while his fellow actor, Bill Franklin, had a lengthy speech. Halfway through it, Robert stopped him suddenly with something like:

'Sorry to interrupt, old chum, but come and look at this spider. It's quite unusual. Have you ever seen one like it before?'

Bill, familiar with these unexpected diversions, dutifully walked over to take a look and ad-libbed a few lines until Robert said:

'Sorry, where were we?'

But he wasn't finished. After the interval the audience settled in their seats and checked their programmes, which told them that the second act was taking place *three months later*. Once again, the same two actors were in the middle of a scene with Robert at the same window when he made a second interruption:

'Good Lord, this is extraordinary. D'you remember that spider I mentioned three months ago? *Well he's still here!'*

Among his other talents he had written and directed for the theatre. He asked me to direct him in a play he had co-written with Rosemary Anne Sisson called *A Ghost on Tiptoe*. In the end the dates clashed with other commitments and I had to decline. Three years later he was in another play at the Savoy Theatre called *Banana Ridge*. I asked him how it was going. He thought children were the most appreciative audience. When I mentioned that I had some he organised tickets.

Andrew was thirteen and Sian twelve at the time. Our seats were in the stalls, about six rows back. A moment came when Robert had to excuse himself because he had dinner guests. I don't know what the line was supposed to be but on this occasion he looked straight down at us, waggled his bushy eyebrows and said:

'I must get on because the Clements are coming to dinner.'

True to his word he took us all out afterwards to Joe Allen's. Instead of asking my son and daughter a few token questions he spent the whole meal talking to them about their hopes, aspirations and views on everything under the sun. It saddens me to think that it was probably the last time I saw him but I treasure the memory of his warmth, wit and generosity of spirit.

Sex Is in Its Infancy in Gateshead – Ian

Auf Wiedersehen, Pet

Dick nudged me and lowered his voice.

'Please, God, let him be able to act just a little.'

We were in a rehearsal room in Paddington and the young man he was referring to had arrived to audition after a preliminary casting call in Newcastle had shortlisted a handful of hopefuls. His name was Jimmy Nail and he was up for the part of Oz in our new series about migrant construction workers.

The producer Martin McKeand and director Roger Bamford warned us it was a long shot. Jimmy had not acted before, he'd wandered into the Newcastle casting while he was killing time in his lunch break from his job as a glazier. Oh, he'd also done time in prison but he already had an Equity card because he sang with a band called the Crabs.

There were two other actors from the North East at the Paddington session, reading for other roles, but Tim Healy and Kevin Whately had experience in television and theatre and there was no risk attached at all. They were quickly offered their parts but Jimmy Nail? Oz was arguably the most difficult of all the roles to pull off; it was too much of a risk to go with a first timer, and yet . . .

A year earlier, living in sun-soaked Southern California, we'd never heard of migrant construction workers until Franc Roddam took us to lunch in a West Hollywood bistro. Franc had directed the greatly acclaimed *Quadrophenia* and was about to make *Lords of Discipline.* He had already acquired a home in the Hollywood Hills and from his bedroom window he could look down on his gorgeous neighbour, Daryl Hannah, swimming naked laps in her pool. Life was good.

But Franc, like myself, was from the North East of England with strong ties to the region. He had recently been there and had a few drinks with an old mate, Mick, now forced to work on building sites overseas. Franc thought it might be the basis for a series. And by the end of lunch and two bottles of cabernet, *Auf Wiedersehen, Pet* was born.

A deal was closed some time later with Central Television by our producing partner Allan McKeown with the endorsement of Margaret Matheson, Central's Head of Drama. Although there was not a woman in sight, certainly not one with a strong identifiable role, I think the political aspect appealed to Margaret. Prime Minister Thatcher pontificated about opportunity and prosperity but there was precious little of either for working-class blokes like Mick, which is why they were forced to graft overseas.

What appealed to Dick and me was the fact that the workers were housed in hostels or, better still, huts on the site. It reminded us of POW camps from Second World War films, the irony being that the reason the Brits were there now was to rebuild some of the cities their dads had flattened in the first place! And it was the perfect captive situation, which so much of our work has celebrated. Likely Lads Bob and Terry, trapped by their environment and class barriers; Fletch and his fellow lags in *Porridge*, prison being the ultimate captive situation. And now: a hut in Germany, with disparate characters trying to forge liveable relationships with total strangers in suffocating circs. Yes, we told Franc at the end of that lunch, this is for us.

Given that you are stuck in a claustrophobic hut, the last person you need is a loud-mouthed, uncouth, misogynist yob with holes in his vest and sweaty feet. Jimmy Nail looked all of these things, complete with holes in his vest, which was why the moment he walked into that room we prayed we'd found Oz.

Jimmy was cast, as were Tim, Kevin, Pat Roach, Gary Holton, Christopher Fairbank and Timothy Spall. We had trouble finding Wayne, the rock 'n' roll cocky cockney. Then I went to a party and met Gary. He was cheeky, funny and had a Ronnie Wood haircut. After about fifteen minutes I gave him the number of the casting agent and made him swear to me he would call. For Moxey, Dick and I considered taking another flyer by using Ray Cooper, the brilliant drummer and percussionist whom we had met when we made our film of Elton John's Russian tour. Knowing Ray might be nervous we made his character a man of few words. Several scripts had been finished when Ray changed his mind and from then on we scrambled to increase Mox's vocabulary.

With three episodes written Dick was offered a film to direct and I was left with the daunting task of finishing the series alone. I managed most of them but we enlisted the splendid Stan Hey to take care of the others including the final episode when the hut, with all their savings and possessions, was burnt to the ground.

Martin McKeand and I went to Dusseldorf to research and scout locations and we took Mick along as our technical advisor. He was arrested by German Immigration at the airport for unpaid legal fines from his last trip there as a brickie. It was a perfect Oz moment, so we didn't mind bailing him out with our per diem and personal credit cards.

Writing the series in Los Angeles – how absurd that seems – Dick and I needed to call Mick from time to time and ask him crucial questions like 'What is a damp course?' and 'How much does a hod carrier get paid?' But Mick didn't have a phone so he used a public one at an appointed hour once a week. Which is why he was standing outside a red telephone box at eleven at night when a police car pulled up. The local officers knew Mick and assumed that at that hour he had to be 'loitering with intent'. Mick responded to them indignantly:

'I'm waiting for a call from Hollywood!'

I don't know how unlikely that sounded to case-hardened Teesside cops, but at that very moment the phone rang, and it was us.

The series was officially set in Dusseldorf but location filming began on a construction site in Hamburg, a smaller version of which was duplicated on the back lot of Elstree studios. So was the infamous hut, small, cramped, hot, a perfect setting for the actors to assimilate the claustrophobia of the real thing. For a while Jimmy, still reeling from the fact that he'd been hired and was now officially an actor in a (hopefully) major drama series, became Oz, on and off the screen. Twice Martin and I persuaded the hotel manager not to throw him out and once not to have the German police arrest him.

It was agreed that I should have a word. I told Jimmy that as much as we loved our character, the series would survive without him. We could easily contrive a situation where Oz is killed in a work-related accident; a crane perhaps, or an excavator: perfectly plausible on a building site and a potent, dramatic twist to that week's episode. Jimmy was genuinely shocked and his behaviour rapidly improved.

I was also asked to have word with Gary Holton whose behaviour, while not aggressive like Jim's, was becoming slightly 'erratic'. Meaning he was high but we didn't know what on. We went to a bar early in the evening so that we wouldn't be disturbed. It was in the Reeperbahn, Hamburg's notorious red-light district, which we planned to explore later with the rest of the lads. Halfway through our conversation a naked man and woman entered and started making love on the floor a few feet from our table. I carried on our talk because I wanted to make a point and Gary and I managed to ignore the copulating couple. Their act,

I suppose, was the reason our warm bottle of Blue Nun cost me eighty quid.

Meanwhile, Jimmy began to appreciate that the fates had handed him a rare and possibly life-changing opportunity. He confided this one evening to Tim Spall who had become a bit of a mentor to him. He told Tim he loved the camaraderie between the actors but he still couldn't quite believe that he was being paid to, well, be himself. Tim smiled and said:

'You're home, Jim.'

Jimmy never forgot that.

Two years later Jimmy Nail, acting creds established, music career off the ground with his great voice, would grace the cover of *GQ* magazine. What would Oz have made of that?

We had no idea how the press and public would receive the series, and no expectations of it being a hit, given the nature of the material and the rawness of its look. Reflecting on a visit to a German brothel Oz confided to the others:

'I'll tell you one thing, sex is in its infancy in Gateshead.'

How on earth could we get away with a line like that? And if that was typical of the series' tone, who on earth would watch it? Happily, millions did and the reviews were excellent.

It changed lives overnight. Only half the series had aired when I went up to Newcastle to see a match. Local sports journalist and passionate United fan John Gibson arranged the tickets for Jimmy, Tim Healy and me and we met for lunch in the Swallow Hotel. Tim arrived, ashen faced, and told us:

'I was buying underpants in Marks and Sparks and I was mobbed by hysterical women.'

Gary Holton went on the road with a band and Jimmy got a record deal. And Series Two was commissioned, where we took the misfits to Spain.

The reason for Spain is that during the eighties many British villains settled there, as no extradition treaty existed at that time between the British and Spanish governments. Most of them were in the hills and small towns around Marbella in an area known in the tabloids as the Costa del Crime. We had the idea that the lads were refurbishing a gangster's villa.

On a fact-finding trip Dick and I, together with Stan Hey and director Roger, checked out a pub in Fuengirola called The Office, which was rumoured to be a villains' watering hole. An unattractive tavern, it had as its centrepiece an imitation gold bar above the bar itself, a tribute of sorts to the Brink's-Mat robbery in late 1983 when thieves took off with £26 million worth of gold bullion, diamonds and cash from a warehouse near Heathrow. That's over £87 million at today's rate. And it's more than possible that some of those thieves were in The Office that night.

We received curious, suspicious stares. Questions were asked. Roger explained politely why we were there and also said that we were the writers of *Porridge*. That reference was like a computer password. We were surrounded by fans and the drinks were on the house. Most of the customers seemed to defer to a small man in a pink angora sweater. This was Ronnie Knight, former club owner, friend of the Krays and ex-husband of actress Barbara Windsor.

Ronnie, I read once, denied being a gangster, preferring the phrase 'lovable rascal'. He would, in later years, return to England and do a bit of porridge himself. But at the time he and his mates all thought they were living in clover, soaking up the sun and sipping sangria. We went back to The Office on Sunday lunchtime for a karaoke party where along with half the expat London underworld we sang Neil Diamond songs.

When the episode 'Marjorie Doesn't Live Here Anymore' aired, 16 million viewers tuned in, a record for Series Two, and especially gratifying as this episode was my and Dick's favourite. But this series lacked the grit and greyness of the original. It wasn't as real, perhaps because swanning around in Speedos in the sun had none of the rough texture and setting of a building site in Germany.

The cast knew it, and so did we. Jimmy grabbed me in the loo at Central's Nottingham studios and voiced his own opinion. He was hostile, truculent, slightly pissed but absolutely right. I've respected his opinions ever since.

But the ratings and popularity remained high throughout and a mantelpiece of awards testified to the show's strengths. The cast was bonded for life especially in the light of two tragedies: Gary Holton's death from drugs before he'd finished shooting Series Two and Pat Roach's death at the beginning of series five. He had battled cancer for a long time but I believe, as do the other cast members, that the resumption of *AWP* in 2001 added years to his life. It was those bonds that encouraged Franc and Jimmy to consider an *Auf Wiedersehen, Pet* revival. Dick and I had strong reservations. Reservations of another sort were made in a Mayfair restaurant. What occurred to us afterwards was how much the actors loved each other, and loved working together. They had all become successful, they didn't need to do another *AufPet*; they wanted it.

There was another factor. Since the late nineties we had become involved with a charity show called *Sunday for Sammy*, a biennial event supporting young creative talent in the North East. Sammy Johnson had been an actor who died tragically young. He was Spender's sidekick in the eponymous series, which Jimmy Nail and I wrote and created, so I had got to know him before his illness. Dick and I wrote a sketch for the show, bringing some of the characters back together after a chance meeting at an airport. Oz, Dennis and Neville, the Geordie Boys, walked on stage to a resounding ovation. Every member of the audience was on their feet. The actors were floored; we were floored. It was astonishing and emotional. That response was the root cause of the decision to do it all again.

If you bring a famous series back after a number of years it has to have some special hyper-element to distinguish it from the previous work. In American television parlance it has to 'Jump the Shark', meaning taking things to a more provocative level. Franc and Jimmy's idea did that. It was based on the outrageous proposition that a Native American tribe in Arizona needed to build a bridge across a gorge to enable punters to get to their gambling casino more easily. So they decided to buy the famous Transporter Bridge that spans the River Tees in Middlesbrough and hired our lads to do the job. As far as Dick and I were concerned that was A Bridge Too Irresistible and we were in. When the series went out a lot of people were upset by the thought that a North Eastern landmark was gone for ever.

It was a joy to revisit those characters and to be reunited and on location in the American West. We had also created another character, played by the brilliant Bill Nighy, and a new friendship was forged. We had the wrap party in a motel in Page, Arizona, still part of a Navajo reservation. Alan Yentob flew out, representing the BBC, and asked me, late in the evening, where the next series would be set. Slightly drunk but without hesitation I told him – Cuba!

And so, a few months later, Dick, Franc, Jimmy and I flew to Havana after an eight-hour rain-delayed flight from Gatwick. We arrived at three in the morning. We could smell coffee, the ocean, tobacco and the tropics. My drunken remark to Alan had led to this. Now, where the hell was the plot?

We loved being in Havana, dusty, dilapidated and sexy, like an ageing whore who used to be beautiful back in her day. There had been no spare parts for the American cars since the fifties and most of the scaffolding we saw was not there to renovate buildings but to keep them from falling down. The streets were crowded, the people seemed to be always smiling, every bar claimed to be Hemingway's favourite and there was always music playing somewhere. Our best walks were in the narrow streets of the old town and the Plaza Vieja. The diet seemed to consist of rice and beans. Salad was unheard of and at night we ate in people's homes where the enterprising owners had made their living rooms into mini restaurants. They're called *paladares* and they were fun and unpredictable.

Our guides, a lovely married couple from the Cuban Film Board, showed us everything we needed to see and also took us to a rehearsal of the National Ballet Company and another of the Buena Vista Social Club. But as the days went by we could not think of a logical and credible reason for our lads to be working here. We became increasingly stressed.

On our last night we went to a charming *paladar* in a decaying neo-baroque building with broken masonry on the stairs and a tethered goat in the hall. We ate well, drank well and became increasingly tetchy. Cuba had been a bad idea. The following afternoon, before our overnight flight, we had been invited to tea and a reception at the British Embassy. None of us wanted to go but didn't know how to get out of it.

We showed up, sipped tea, ate finger food and made polite conversation. Then we discovered in a chance conversation that there was a government agency in London who contracted building firms to renovate British consuls and embassies. All over the world! A last-minute reprieve and inspiration, we were elated. *Auf Wiedersehen, Pet* Series Four would be in Cuba!

In 1990 *AWP* won an Achievement of the Decade award. On its return in 2002 it was nominated for The People's Choice Best Drama and in 2015 it was voted the Favourite Television Programme of all time in a *Radio Times* readers' poll.

'Howway the lads', as they say 'up there'.

Over the years the *Sunday for Sammy* sketches have become more surreal and absurd as we began to imagine our heroes in historical situations. They worked on the Trojan Horse, dug a tunnel in the Colditz POW camp; built an extension to Nottingham Castle where they ran into Robin Hood, and helped build the Roman wall dividing England from the marauding Scots. That piece contains my personal favourite *Auf Wiedersehen* line.

Explaining the gig to the others Dennis tells them that the Romans have hired them to build a wall from Corstopitum to Wallsend (a Newcastle borough and birthplace of Sting). Neville is puzzled, as in those days there was no such place as Wallsend.

'*I know*', says Oz. '*But there will be when the wall ends there.*'

All the Money in the World – Dick

Bill Mark

Bill Mark was a Texas oilman but he didn't wear a ten-gallon hat or a bootlace tie with a turquoise clip. He was tall, though not Texas-tall, quietly spoken and stylishly dressed. In fact he bought his suits from Doug Hayward in Mayfair, which is how he happened to come into our lives. Doug's clients included Michael Caine, John Gielgud and John Le Carré. He was a shrewd business-man and nobody's mug but Bill talked him into investing in an apartment block in Florida. And no, he didn't lose his sea-island cotton shirt. Audie Charles, wife to our production colleague Tony, worked for Doug and mentioned to him that this agreeable chap kept coming into the store and seemed rather lonely. So they invited him to Sunday lunch.

Sunday lunches with Audie and Tony Charles are legendary, oc-casions I look forward to on every visit to London. They still live in the same house in Barnes, a constant factor in an ever-changing world, and are among our dearest and most trusted friends. Tony started off in the rag trade before becoming an agent, a profession far better suited to his talents, then came into partnership with us producing television shows. Bill seemed intrigued to learn all this over the roast lamb. Our names cropped up in conversation and he said he was a big fan of *Water*, the film we wrote for HandMade Films that I had recently directed.

Bill sent a case of wine as a thank-you for lunch along with an enormous TV, which they returned. He offered Tony a business proposition to make a promotional video for land he and a partner had bought in Tennessee. The day before Tony was due to fly out there Bill said he had sold it to a Japanese group but he paid the sum they had agreed – in cash – for the time Tony had spent on it.

In 1988 we all met for the first time. Bill explained that he was in business with wealthy Arabs who had money they had to invest by a certain date or they would run into tax problems. They were interested in setting up a company to make TV shows and movies. Would we like to think about going into partnership with him?

Not long before Christmas we all met again round the same dinner table in the Charles house. Bill told us how well his meeting with the Arabs had gone the day before. The amount of money they wanted to invest was $30 million. He talked about how we could 'float' that sum and make it grow. I tried to look as if this was the kind of conversation I had every day. In truth I was financially strapped, dealing with tax demands and debating whether I could afford to keep my London flat.

Then he dropped another bombshell. In return for setting up the deal there would be a 'bonus' fee of a further $2 million, which he felt we should split four ways. As I wrote in my diary: 'This made it difficult to think straight.' He said we would have to go to Geneva in a few weeks, perhaps leave the money in Switzerland.

Around this time a producer gave us a slim novella called *The Commitments* about a bunch of kids in Dublin who wanted to start a soul band. We were hooked instantly, told him we wanted to write the screenplay and flew back to Los Angeles on Pan Am. After Christmas Ian and I had lunch with Alan Parker in Hollywood. We told him about Bill and our sudden and unexpected ability to finance movies. When we mentioned *The Commitments* his eyes lit up.

'Why don't I do that one?'

There it was, that simple. We had no ulterior motive when we sat down to eat, none at all. But as we walked out of Tutto Bene on Fairfax Avenue we had a genuine interest from one of the hottest directors in the business. He read the book right away – it didn't take long – and called us to say that he loved it. Naturally we reported everything to Bill, who was delighted. This would be our first project together. He talked of flying to LA with Tony on a private jet. I stopped thinking about putting my flat on the market. Ian spent a lot of time looking through the windows of the Bentley showroom in Berkeley Square.

Then we got word that Bill was in hospital in Houston. His key meeting had been postponed but he reported that he had invested the money in a Canadian bond that would bring in $300,000 interest per month. He had to go to New York and then London to deal with emergencies. There was no e-mail in those days, no mobile phones. We communicated by fax, which was far from perfect. Not only that but he didn't have a permanent office or a regular secretary called Janice with whom to leave messages. Ian began to call him 'The Shadow'.

We went back to London and met him again for yet another lunch chez Charles. No, nothing was signed yet but there was the prospect of even more capital. His Arab colleagues had checked out our past work. They had watched *Water* and *Vice Versa*. We pictured them in our minds, screening our movies in the desert in their burnouses, tossing pistachio shells over their shoulders and laughing at our jokes.

He came to LA again with a Lebanese banker. We introduced him to our lawyer and our accountant, Marvin Freedman. Marvin was a canny old fox and said he found him an odd mix of sophistication and naivety. We asked ourselves if it was we who were being naive. You're probably asking the same question. It began to feel as if this was an enormous con game; that we were being set up for something – but what? It wasn't as if we were being asked to sign documents and hand over the deeds to our houses.

Alan Parker's agent confirmed his very real interest in *The Commitments*. But where was the money? And where was Bill? He had disappeared again. He was in Miami, or was it Riyadh? He called one day from Maracaibo and we had to open our atlas to find out it was in Venezuela.

Here are some entries from my diary:

April 18: *We spoke to Bill whom, it seems, had sent us a fax we never got. He's saying 'end of next week' again but a draft contract Monday. Earlier Tony had chewed him out saying 'Forget it'. Audie left the room covering her ears.*

April 24: *Message from Bill to say one of the backers has died. No contract arrived as planned. Yet another snag and dealing with a recording made it tougher. Why won't he call us at home? Not as if we'd care about being woken up.*

April 25: *Another message from Bill – off to Saudi to deal with it directly. 'There is a problem; not terminal but under Arab law all his assets are attached.'*

May 24: *Bill called from Switzerland. Formed the company in Liberia. Spent over $100,000 setting us up. I said we have to meet. Went off with promises for tomorrow . . .*

May 26: *Breakfast at Richoux [London]. Tony and I are polite. Have to have the money next week, we say. Also better communications. A new telephone is promised. But it's the first meeting where 'au fond' I don't trust him. If I see a check I'll faint.*

May 30: *Bill gave me the name of a different lawyer today. Just as well as the last one didn't seem to exist.*

We had a meeting with him in London at his office in Berkeley Square. This was reassuring, an actual office, with a boardroom.

He told us about oil tankers on the high seas. The moment they docked we would get our commission. But when we went back to Berkeley Square the following day, there was no trace of him. Nor did any nightingales sing. Presumably he had rented the office for the day.

Around this time I played tennis with a fellow writer, Marc Abraham. He had just joined a new company called Beacon Pictures and they were looking for material. I mentioned *The Commitments* and Alan Parker's interest. We couldn't wait for Bill any more and they ended up financing the movie.

Bill wasn't finished. There were more meetings, more schemes, more dazzling sums of money. Some vestige of me still wanted to believe in him in spite of all evidence to the contrary. By now we had run up legal fees. Ian and I paid half and thought it only fair that Bill chipped in for the rest. He agreed. We gave him the outstanding account. We never saw him again.

I don't feel anger when I think of him. Of course, it would have been nice if the money had come through and I hadn't had to sell the London flat. Better not to think about what it's worth today, though of course I do. But he gave me – and Ian – a gift. For a brief period we thought we had access to finance. Without that belief we would not have been able to induce Alan Parker to make *The Commitments*, a film we are immensely proud of and one that changed the course of our careers.

To this day Bill remains an enigma. Why did he do it? Was he dangling our names to his Saudi friends to convince them to part with their funds? Did they exist at all? Or was Audie's original diagnosis the correct one? He was lonely. And for a few months he had a bunch of really close friends.

The Bollix – Ian

The Commitments

The Commitments, I've been told, has been voted Ireland's most popular film of all time. It said as much in a programme note at a twentieth-anniversary screening given by the Barnsley Film Festival in 2011, with Dick and myself along as guest speakers. We didn't realise there was such a festival and I don't think the good people of Barnsley did either. There was such a small turnout we asked all the audience to the nearest pub, bought them drinks and did the Q&A there. Even so it brought back many vivid memories.

I often wish we could turn back time and be in that Dublin rehearsal room for the first reading of the script by the young, raw cast. I'd love to be back in the pub later that night when the Guinness flowed, the jokes came thick and fast and the *craic* was brilliant. And I'd love to be back in the moment when Alan Parker first shot them singing as the Commitments. Was it 'Mustang Sally'? Probably not but who cares, any number will do.

Roger Randall Cutler had optioned the novel, written by an Irish schoolteacher called Roddy Doyle. It wasn't even a novel, it was a novella, which means a very thin book. I read it that night, called Roger the next day, told him I loved it and had given it to Dick. He said it would have to be shot on a shoestring so there would be hardly any money for a script. I said that's okay, I still love it.

So did Dick, as I knew he would. There wasn't much of a plot but it was filled with great dialogue and definable, sometimes hilarious characters. As Dick has recounted in his piece about Bill Mark we were bolstered by the knowledge that we had untold wealth and could make financial offers. It was very small potatoes for Alan Parker but we tried to make a virtue of that, persuading him it would be a perfect antidote to all the big-budget productions he'd been involved with and all the inherent headaches and problems.

We wrote the first draft and gave it to Alan in Portland, Oregon where he was shooting *Come See the Paradise*. He loved the script and said he would make it. And then the untold millions disappeared and so did Bill Mark, leaving us no forwarding address and an unpaid legal bill. But we had Alan 'interested' and on that basis we quickly found financing, gave ourselves a pat on the back and a co-producing credit. And off to Dublin's fair city.

Early on Alan challenged our very first scene. 'You've put it in Howth, which is picturesque and on the sea. Movies establish their credentials in the first five minutes. We need to begin with something gritty and working class.'

And he was right; the scene changed to a market place and a grainy, blue-collar texture informed the film from that moment. The leading character in the piece is a young, council estate visionary called Jimmy Rabbitte who decides to manage a band. Not a pop band or a show band but a soul outfit. The reason, he tells his first puzzled recruits, is simple:

'The Irish are the blacks of Europe, and the Dubliners are the blacks of Ireland. And the Northsiders are the blacks of Dublin. So say it now, and say it loud. We're black and we're proud!'

There is a scene in the film where Jimmy (played by Robert Arkins) is holding auditions at his parents' house. Dozens of hopefuls show up, claiming to play every kind of instrument with musical influences as wide apart as Jethro Tull and Jarvis Cocker. Alan's auditions weren't much different, a riotous succession of actors, musicians, misfits and the unemployed parading their talents and pedigrees.

A sixtyish male showed up for the part of horn-playing veteran Joey the Lips. He held a stained, battered trumpet in his hand. Alan asked him how long he'd been playing. The old timer replied: 'Oi bought it on the way here.'

Alan's choices of his cast, and his rehearsal work with their inexperienced, unrefined talents, was remarkable. Only the three 'Commitmentettes' and Johnny Murphy, who would play the trumpet player, had acted before. The boys hadn't. Almost all of them, including manager Jimmy, were in bands or in between bands, and the money most of them were paid on the film went back into their bands. It seemed to Dick and me that Alan was giving himself an enormous amount of extra work and worry, as well as the obvious risks. The result was brilliant and we cannot praise or admire him enough. I think most other directors were impressed when they saw the film, asking themselves, as I'm sure most of them did, 'How did Alan manage that?'

During the first week's readings, mostly awkward and self conscious, Alan asked the cast to keep switching scripts and reading other parts, even if it meant a man was reading a female role. It made it more fun as well as challenging and gradually confidence increased, performances improved and Dick and I could tailor rewrites to enhance both. I think at least two of the actors were dyslexic, which made the early process painfully difficult for them. Alan saw beyond this and visualised how they, and everyone, would come across on the screen. Thanks to his instincts and patience all of them scored and the whole process from early beginnings to first screenings was exhilarating.

There was pressure at one point, as there always is with films of limited budget and no box-office names, to cast at least one well-known actor, even in a cameo. Perhaps Michael Caine could be the older horn player? Or what about Bob Hoskins? Alan refused to consider these kinds of suggestions, although he did give some thought to the notion that a real life Rock Star might help, not playing himself, but acting a role.

Van 'the Man' Morrison was the obvious choice, being a God to the musical Irish. He was sent a script and agreed to a meeting with Alan at which his manager demanded breakfast before even a 'Hello' or 'Good morning'. Van thought it would make much more sense if the kids played *his* music, not soul. Perhaps he had a valid point, but as he also found our script 'shite' there didn't seem much point pursuing the issue. Van was decidedly not our man. And the issue of a 'star' was dropped.

The cast would all play and sing the songs live; nothing would be pre-recorded. There was a shadow band on hand to perform the songs as they should be played and tutor and advise the actors. One day one of these musicians brought along his son, who sang one of the numbers. Alan called Dick and me a day or two later. He felt strongly that for an audience to believe our kids could actually make it, then that belief had to spring from the singer. Not the lead guitarist, or the drummer, or the bass player – it had to be the frontman. And he'd been blown away by the young man who sang on the session.

'He's nothing like you wrote and he's only seventeen, but just listen to the voice.'

We did. Andrew Strong was cast and we happily rewrote his character to accommodate his natural personality. Every time we hear him, in the film or on record, we know it was one of those inspired, transformative calls. And the cast album was an enormous commercial success. Memo to ourselves: next time we negotiate a musical deal, try and get a piece of the record.

There was a wrap party at The Point on Dublin's waterfront. As drunk as they were the Commitments played a blistering set. And they did the same at the after party of the New York premiere, and Los Angeles when Wilson Pickett himself did a couple of numbers. Alan threw an afternoon party for all of them and guests, at his house above the Sunset Strip. A memorable moment came after heartthrob Liam Neeson joined the girls in the Jacuzzi and the drink flowed. Bronagh Gallagher raised her glass to the sun-bleached California sky:

'I can't fuckin' believe this. I'm drinking tequila in a hot tub in Hollywood and Liam Neeson has his hand on me thigh.'

To which Angeline Ball piped up:

'And mine too!'

The finished film was everything we hoped, and it never dates. It won us great reviews, awards and opened doors, and to this day Dick and I are frequently referred to as 'those guys who wrote *The Commitments*'. We are immensely proud of that. Roddy provided wonderful material, which we happily plundered along with our own words, and we gave the story shape and structure. But this is Alan Parker's movie. No question. Perhaps one of his best. Thank you, Alan, for that great trip. It was, for all concerned – 'The Bollix'.

And they all went their separate ways. Bronagh and Angeline worked with us again in a short-lived television series while Maria Doyle combined singing with her Black Velvet band with a wide variety of acting roles. The lads went back to their own music. A few years later some of them reformed the Commitments and toured, for legal reasons, as the Committed. I caught them at The House of Blues in Los Angeles and we drank and reminisced happily backstage later.

Glen Hansard, a former busker, played the role of Outspan Foster in the movie. Later he teamed up with Czech singer and instrumentalist Markéta Irglová, and they appeared together and wrote the songs for the Irish film *Once*. Their song 'Falling Slowly' won Grammy and Oscar nominations. Glen came to LA with his mother, Markéta and her parents, and my wife and I gave a dinner for them at our home, after which they played us songs. We had asked some other musicians to meet them and pretty soon a jam ensued, with piano, guitars, a violin and Ringo playing saucepans. A magical evening.

Three nights later we watched the Oscars on television and Glen and Markéta won for Best Song.

Dick and I wanted to do a stage musical of *The Commitments* from the moment the film was released. There was enormous interest from theatre producers but Roddy would not release the rights until he wrote his own version many years later, basing it on his original material and not our screenplay. We were very disappointed not to be included but, as the Irish say in their infinite wisdom:

'Fair fucks to you, Rod.'

Two or three years after our 'fillum' was made Johnny Murphy showed up in Los Angeles with a touring version of *Waiting for Godot*. We took him to lunch and he told us a lovely story, a testimony to the enduring affection the Irish have for our movie. He was in a small town in Ireland when there were suddenly shouts and cries of alarm as three masked gunmen ran out of a bank. Johnny froze as the robbers ran past him. One of them stopped, pulled off his ski mask and exclaimed:

'Jaysis, it's Joey the Lips!'

A Scheme of Merriment – Dick

Kingsley Amis

I haven't had many bosses in my life, one of the advantages of being freelance.

For a brief period, however, I was a 'staff' director at the BBC, having directed *The Likely Lads* and a script by Marty Feldman and Barry Took called *Barnaby Spoot and the Exploding Whoopee Cushion*. I don't think that one's on YouTube, possibly just as well.

Frank Muir was appointed Head of Comedy, a title he found suspect. He was fond of quoting Dr Johnson: 'Nothing is more hopeless than a scheme of merriment', well aware that creating one was precisely his job description.

The first time I went to meet my new boss he put me instantly at ease. We had something in common after all: he'd been writing much of the comedy I'd listened to for years in partnership with Denis Norden.

'I feel a bit like a poacher turned gamekeeper. I'm much more used to standing where you are now, trying to read BBC memos upside down.'

He and Denis were famous for the outrageous puns they invented on the radio panel show *My Word!*

My all-time favourite is the origin of the phrase 'East is East and West is West'. Frank invented an elaborate story about a family obsessed with playing cards. The eldest son got into trouble and had to flee the country. After many years he returned to find his parents, brother and sister in the middle of a game. His father was so overcome with emotion that he collapsed and died. The son sat in the chair he'd just vacated and picked up his hand. The others stared at him, aghast. How could he be so insensitive? He explained:

'He's deceased and whist is whist.'

I asked Frank if they were they given the phrases in advance. He told me they used to make them up off the cuff but the trouble was they always ended up being dirty.

It was Frank who suggested that Ian and I wrote a new series called *The Further Adventures of Lucky Jim*. I was, and still am, an enormous fan of Kingsley Amis's first novel. How could we say no? We wrote seven scripts and Kingsley came to all the recordings. He seemed very happy with them, especially when it came to going to dinner with the cast afterwards where he always managed to sit next to the prettiest actresses.

Fifteen years went by and the BBC asked us if we would like to do the series all over again, transplanting the hero, Jim Dixon, from the sixties to the eighties. We revisited our old scripts, threw out one or two, polished them up and wrote one entirely new one that we were particularly pleased with. A director and recording dates were set.

It seemed no more than common courtesy to ask Kingsley to lunch and see if he had any notes. Ian, for some reason I can't recall, cried off and I took Nancy instead. We met in Covent Garden at a fairly trendy restaurant called Inigo Jones.

Kingsley was now sixty, heavier than I remembered him, more florid of complexion. His political views had also put on weight. I knew that he was a vocal supporter of the current Prime Minister, Margaret Thatcher. I made a mental note to steer clear of her policies.

After the introductions we sat down to what I felt sure would be a lengthy, probably bibulous but affable lunch. He took some time over choosing scotch, finally settling on Macallan. We summoned a waiter and put in our orders. Kingsley took a deep breath:

'Now we come to the unpleasant part of the day's proceedings. I loathe the scripts.'

Imagine in your mind the strongest emphasis on the word 'loathe'. I was stunned. This was not what I was expecting. Where was the affable Kingsley from fifteen years ago, laughing dutifully at all our funny lines? There was more, much more. I don't recall exactly what he said but he left nothing out: the limp plots, the feeble characterisations, the predictable situations, the lamentable, cliché-ridden dialogue. It poured out of him in a torrent while I was thinking: 'Where the hell is Ian and why isn't he here to take at least his fair fifty per cent of this abuse?'

Finally, after what seemed an age, he ran out of things to say. I sat in stunned silence for several seconds, wondering how to respond, which aspect of his tirade to dispute first. Then Nancy did a wonderful thing. She put a consoling hand on his arm and said quietly:

'That can't have been easy to say.'

This wasn't true at all. He'd found it incredibly easy to say, as if he'd been rehearsing for weeks in front of the bathroom mirror. But those seven words had a miraculous effect. It was like watching the air go out of a balloon. He was, literally, disarmed. Nancy has a wonderful quality of being able to get people to open up. I remember a bartender in Saint-Tropez agonising about whether to get married or stay single. It took her ten minutes to sort that one out.

Kingsley told her everything. Essentially, he was lonely. His second wife, the fellow novelist Elizabeth Jane Howard, had 'bolted' and he was living with Hilly, his first wife and her third husband, Lord Kilmarnock. This had all the makings of an upper-class sitcom, one that, happily, no one ever asked us to write.

He was jealous of his son's success.

'Martin gets invited to country-house weekends. I don't. Not any more. I used to love country-house weekends.'

What also emerged was that he found it depressing that *Lucky Jim*, his first 'hit', was being rehashed yet again rather than his more recent work. I'm guessing here but perhaps it made him feel like yesterday's man, someone whose best work was behind him and with none of Martin's relevance. All this was revealed over a long lunch in which we drank more than our fair share of good wine. I let him choose as he had written things like this about Chablis or Pouilly-Fuissé:

'Closely resembling a blend of cold chalk soup and alum cordial with an additive or two to bring it to the colour of children's pee.'

When *Lucky Jim* was first published Kingsley was thrown in with the group that the press conveniently labelled 'Angry Young Men'. He was often bracketed with Evelyn Waugh, even though he wrote, about *Brideshead Revisited*:

'I may have missed the irony but I cannot believe that a man can write as badly as that for fun.'

When Waugh was interviewed on *Face to Face*, the classic TV show where John Freeman put celebrities under a psychological spotlight, he admitted that the characteristic he least liked about himself was irritability. Kingsley certainly had that in common

This little-known French *hameau* is twinned with Whitley Bay.

Dick and Nancy 'then' . . .

. . . and 'now'

On the river: a boatload of Clements.

Ian and Doris 'then' . . .

. . . and 'now'.

Highland fling: Billy Connolly's birthday.

with Waugh. Jim Dixon's fury is simmering just below the surface, but it's always funny. When I first read it I was struck by its refreshing irreverence. One phrase always stuck in my head when Jim, hearing someone singing a song, described it as 'some skein of untiring facetiousness by filthy Mozart'.

We were the last people in the restaurant when I finally settled the bill. I hope the BBC reimbursed me. It was at least four o'clock but Kingsley was by now enjoying himself and wanted more. He suggested we walked across the road to the Garrick Club for port. On arrival he addressed the hall porter:

'*Lady in trousers. Would you recommend the tradesman's entrance?*'

The hall porter thought this might be desirable. Nancy had to make a detour before she could join us for one, possibly two glasses of port. Whatever we talked about it wasn't the scripts and I don't recall making a single change to any of them as a result of Kingsley's notes, by now lost in a fog of alcohol. Nor do I remember if I had a hangover the following day but if I did I could never have described it as well as he did in *Lucky Jim*:

'*He lay sprawled, too wicked to move, spewed up like a broken spider-crab on the tarry shingle of morning. The light did him harm, but not so much as looking at things did; he resolved, having done it once, never to move his eyeballs again. A dusty thudding in his head made the scene before him beat like a pulse. His mouth had been used as a latrine by some small creature of the night, and then as its mausoleum. During the night, too, he'd somehow been on a cross-country run and then been expertly beaten up by secret police. He felt bad.*'

Not Fade Away – Ian

The Rolling Stones

When I lived in my first London flat – the one in Earls Court next to the Indian restaurant – we had two neighbours. A thirty-something man called Paul lived in the basement. He had a mid-Atlantic accent and said he was a deejay. In those days a disc jockey was someone who put vinyl records on a turntable in dimly lit clubs, not a millionaire spinner pumping out EDM to fifty thousand ecstasy-fuelled ravers in a soccer stadium.

In the flat down the hall lived the first pop star I ever met. His name was Mike O'Neill and his band was called Nero and the Gladiators. He was Nero, even though he couldn't have looked more different being very skinny and always sniffing, as if he had a permanent cold. The band had two hits in the early sixties, which is probably why he moved out pretty quickly and I never saw him again. Google tells me he played for lots of other groups including the Blue Flames and the Ivy League. I hope his cold got better. He was a very nice guy.

The Rolling Stones were just beginning to register on the pop radar and someone told me they hung out in a coffee bar on the Earls Court Road. I went there almost every day but never had a sighting. The first one I did see was Charlie Watts, who was travelling on the up escalator at Holborn tube while I was descending. He looked rather surly. Years later I read an interview with Lord Lichfield's butler. When asked who was the nicest guest he ever encountered at his master's estate during his frequent house parties, he replied: 'Mr Charlie Watts, sir.'

So perhaps I caught Charlie on a bad day, or maybe he was just sick of strangers staring at him on escalators.

I bought the first Rolling Stones album when I moved to a basement flat in Chelsea. I remember the sleeve notes were written by manager Andrew Oldham and said something pretentious about the Stones being 'a way of life'. Well, it was a life I fancied but the nearest I got to it was trying to shimmy in front of a mirror like Mick Jagger singing 'Not Fade Away'. I loved that track, even though I was confused to know what it meant. I hadn't heard the earlier Buddy Holly original, so the Stones' version came right out of the blue and I played it, and the whole album, endlessly. I was fascinated by them, as much as the Beatles, and have shamelessly been fascinated by them for the following fifty years.

By the time the Stones had become Britain's second favourite pop group, the 'Swinging Sixties' were in full flow, although it did have its detractors who found the whole scene frivolous and full of empty spectacle. Bernard Levin described London as:

'Full of pimps and ten per centers, whores and pedlars, decorators and actors, the froth and scum of a decadent, doomed society.'

Obviously Bernard wasn't getting laid, which must have been especially galling as almost everyone else was. Well, everyone at the party.

Robert Freeman was Cambridge educated, tall, good looking, with the kind of long hair that never gets frizzy. (That was important in the sixties.) Bob was a renowned photographer and director of commercials. He shot the first Beatles album covers so was tight with the Fab Four. His studio was in a dodgy part of Notting Hill at a time when most of it was dodgy, long before the Richard Curtis era. It was always filled with models, film crews and hipster hangers-on. Bob used me as an actor in one of his commercials that was art directed by Alan Aldridge and featured top model Paulene Stone. They blow-dried my hair and gave me a crushed velvet black jacket to wear. When I saw it in the cinema it didn't make a lot of sense. I didn't even understand what it was selling.

Bob asked me to write a screenplay based on an idea that didn't make a lot of sense either. He had this notion of four beautiful young women kidnapping a film star and keeping him in a geodesic dome. Well, why not, if it meant moving into Bob's orbit. One day he arranged to pick me up on the Kings Road and did so in his Studebaker Avanti, the coolest car imaginable and perhaps the only one of its kind in Britain. He was now casting the film that makes no sense so I assumed the girl in the front seat was a possible. She squirms up and I wriggle under her unbelievably long legs. She was Anita Pallenberg – model, sixties poster girl, and main squeeze of Brian Jones of the Rolling Stones!

Later that night we went to Sybilla's, the hot club of the moment. I wore the crushed velvet jacket and dared to think I might have crashed the party that was the sixties.

Through Anita I met Brian, shy but affable, curious, and rather endearing; obviously some time before he was messed up on drugs. They were house hunting like a young married couple looking for their dream home, a place to settle and raise kids. Brian drove a Rolls-Royce Silver Cloud. They were – nice.

My wife Doris, through her first husband Eddie, was living in Paris in the early seventies and related to French rock royalty through in-laws Johnny Hallyday and Sylvie Vartan. So of course she met all the Stones long before I did and even hung out at their Paris recording sessions. When we were a couple some time later, Sabrina Guinness introduced us to Bill Wyman and his partner Astrid. I think it was in 1976. Bill, the archivist of everything Stones-related, will no doubt pin down the exact month, day, hour and what colour shirt I was wearing. I know we had dinner in a small restaurant in Vence, high up in the hills above Nice with Astrid and drummer Dallas Taylor. Bill had bought a house there when the Stones moved to France for tax reasons and made the brilliant *Exile on Main Street* album. We became, and have remained, great friends.

'Je suis un rock star. J'avais une résidence – j'habite là – à la South of France.'

So sang Bill on his solo single in 1981. We had great summers there, cricket on the box in the afternoons, dinners on the terrace, wine and blues later. And few people have a greater knowledge, or love, of that music. He faithfully archived every Stones gig, album review, article, triumph or scandal. Whether in Vence, his house in London or his historic, moated, medieval – and seriously haunted – mansion in Suffolk, Bill was almost always found hunched over a computer in a small cloud of menthol cigarette smoke assiduously researching and recording the past. Nowadays there's no longer any ciggie smoke.

Bill also, literally, dug up the past, mostly on his Suffolk land, turning up an archaeological treasure trove of Roman and Saxon artefacts, many of which are secured in museums.

In the early days of my fan addiction, when my only access to the group was through television, photographs and articles, I was always curious about Bill's persona; the long, inanimate, aquiline features framed by curls that looked like a cavalier's wig. He offered less than the others in interviews but the publicity machine might have framed that strategy given that Bill was twenty-six, married with a son and his real name was Perks. In the Beatles camp other PR gurus were concealing Cynthia Lennon.

He was also the stillest pop star I'd ever seen in performance. No doubt those lidded eyes were scoping the totty in the front rows but otherwise no other muscle seemed to twitch, except for his fingers on that vertical bass.

Bill got me tickets to the band's gigs and authored my transition from punter to 'Friend of Stone', hanging out backstage, with its own structured hierarchy of privilege. There is access to an outer bar and Astro Turfed lounge area with wine, beer and a buffet of chicken wings, crisps and coleslaw. But, with a different pass, there is also an inner bar: better wine, sushi, sofas and celebrities, small talk and the smug satisfaction that you must be someone or how else could you possibly be backstage at a Stones concert. Not too smug, of course, because there's also the knowledge that behind another tightly guarded door is an inner, inner sanctum where the dressing rooms are, and perhaps a putting green or a massage room with aromatherapy oils and waterfall music. To have access to this means you really are close to Mick or Keith or Ron or Bill. I might have breached this firewall of unimaginable exclusivity but Bill left the band!

He quit the Stones in 1993, which astounded me as it did any rock fan. How on earth can anyone leave the greatest band on the planet? Bill said he couldn't tour any more because he hated flying but I think he wanted to reinvent himself somehow and he chose a completely independent path. With his wife Suzanne's support he did so with remarkable success, becoming an author of seven books, a producer, photographer and archaeologist and father of three beautiful daughters. And he tours every year with his great band, the Rhythm Kings. Rock on, Bill.

The Stones continued seamlessly, of course, and simply hired another bass player who has been with them ever since. But Daryl James is *with* the Stones. Bill *was* one. And Mick is the guvnor. Or so it's always seemed.

I don't remember how or when I first met Ron Wood. Sometime before Scorsese's film *The Last Waltz*, because I remember him talking about it and making preparations to be there. Doris and I spent a lot of time at the Woods' rented house in Malibu, which is where I met Keith Moon who was going through a mellow period at the time (Malibu does that to you) and didn't cause any mayhem. I have a photograph of six-year-old Michael flanked by Woodie and Moonie who look like benevolent but slightly demonic babysitters.

The trouble with being 'Friend of Rock Star' is that when the jams start you are completely irrelevant, unless there's a spare tambourine, but some chilled-out, hippie beach babe usually got that. All you can do is listen, open bottles of wine, roll spliffs and take pizza orders. I left the spliff-rolling to my future brother-in-law Sam, a genuine hippie who, as a Vietnam vet, knew far more about marijuana than I did. They were magical evenings being in the company of many gifted talents. I remember one summer morning when my houseguest, Sabrina Guinness, berated us all like the headmistress of a posh English girls' school.

'Come on, everybody! Have you forgotten we're having brunch at Neil Young's?'

All these years later I keep wondering – did Neil Young really 'do' brunch?

When Woody's wife Chrissy's pregnancy got nearer the time, the Woods moved into town and stayed with us in our house off Benedict Canyon, only four miles from Cedars-Sinai hospital where Jesse James would be born. The jamming didn't stop, nor the parties, all of them impromptu and, for me, exhausting as I had to be round at Clement's at 9.30 every morning and rose early. Usually around the time Harry Nilsson arrived.

We exiles, plus some Italian waiters and odd misfits of the LA scene had a soccer, sorry, football team. We played in a league on Sundays, and had a kickaround Wednesdays and Saturday afternoons in a small park in Beverly Hills next to a fire station at the foot of Coldwater Canyon. One Saturday, seeing me kitted out, Chrissy asked if I could take Woody. He needs to get fit, she told me, so I scrambled around trying to find spare boots and shorts while she woke him from his vodka-fuelled hangover to tell him the news.

The kickaround, like the professional game itself, connected us to home. As did the thought of English beer, the great British breakfast, Marmite, Branston pickle, *Morecambe & Wise* on the telly and the *News of the World*; they were the portable memories we'd brought with us to our exile in sun-scorched California. After the game we'd drink in a pub on Sunset Boulevard called the Coach and Horses and we all proudly displayed 'GB' plates on our American cars.

Rod Stewart was the most famous and affluent player on the pitch but also one of the most gifted. No one was more astonished than Rod to see his former Faces pal Woody take the pitch, his skinny legs in borrowed socks and boots, his shirt several sizes too large. As his oldest pal he could not recall him ever taking exercise. I felt good that I'd brought about this, perhaps, life-changing moment.

Woody did okay in the first half, and through a brilliant sense of positional play managed to avoid contact with the ball most of the time. But he ran and tackled like an eager, skinny schoolboy. At half time we split into our two separate, sweaty groups. From his shorts he produced a slim, small vial in which was a colourless liquid.

'Should we do a drop of this, then?'

It's amazing that in the drug culture of the time how many people would try something then ask what it was afterwards. And so our team elected for the strange liquid in the vial and eschewed the slices of orange that someone's halter-topped girlfriend offered us. Was it liquid cocaine? Is there such a thing? Or was it something someone had bought off a hairy-assed biker who'd tooled up to the Hollywood Hills from his meth lab in the desert? We'll never know but we played the second half at the frenzied pace of a Mack Sennett two-reeler. We were the Keystone Kops with a soccer ball and left the opposition bewildered and confused, if not by our skill, certainly our speed.

It had worn off after pints in the pub and when we arrived home Chrissie hugged me gratefully and thanked me for ensuring her old man had had a healthy runaround in fresh air. To this day I have no idea what it was, and nor has Woody. These days he's blissfully married to Sally with scene-stealing twin daughters. His cigarettes are electric and his strongest tipple is Red Bull.

His buddy on tour was Keith. There was always something conspiratorial about the pair of them; scruffy street urchins trying to get up to something wicked behind the grown-ups' backs. In a Toronto rehearsal room I watched them shooting pool for an hour while they chatted, smoked, joked and tippled. I never saw one ball potted. But maybe that wasn't the point.

Mick once inhabited the same guest room in my house that the Woods had when waiting for their baby. Mick was there because he was holed up in the throes of a romantic assignation with a lovely, leggy friend of ours. He emerged only occasionally to eat and check the cricket scores. I could never quite equate cricket's gentility with renowned rock star flamboyance. But then Alice Cooper plays golf. Mick loves cricket and is very knowledgeable about it. And we've known each other ever since that brief stay in the yellow bedroom.

Along with Prince, Mick is the most mesmerising performer I've ever seen on a stage: the definitive frontman. Watching him recently he seemed as antic and agile as he was on those mega stadium tours of the seventies. Reviewers always talk about his showmanship but less often about his voice. It's changed in texture over the years but it's exceptional: sexy, teasing, raw and nuanced, never more brilliantly demonstrated than on the Stones' recent stripped-down album *Blue & Lonesome*, a tribute to their enduring love of the music that was their roots and inspiration.

For all that I would say 'close acquaintance' describes my relationship with him. Mick is charming, wise and witty but keeps his distance, and his guard up. And that unknowability is an essential part of the mystery, the aura, the power that's made him a mega star for fifty years. No one has been as exposed, no one more interviewed, chronicled and photographed. And he still remains a secret. A different set of rules seem to apply to him, as they always have.

Sometime in the early sixties some journalist penned the question: would you let your daughter marry a Rolling Stone? Well, why not? Five sexy, cute boys, about to become as rich and famous as the Beatles. How could a doting mum disapprove of quiet, unassuming Charlie, who would one day be Lord Lichfield's butler's favourite guest? Or Brian, who could have won the sixth-form poetry prize. And Mick, a grammar school boy with one year at the LSE and an adorable smile. Yes, Bill was older but surely that meant more mature and he'd never touched drugs.

Keith Richards, of course, was the exception No, you would not let your precious Katy or innocent Melanie hook up with that boy with bad teeth and hair that's a stranger to a comb and who scowled more than he smiled. Keith looked, as he always has, a badass. That's why we love him. The Stones were always seen as an unruly and untamed alternative to the Fab Four but in truth they were just as carefully groomed, managed and marketed as their Merseyside rivals. It was the Who and the Kinks who were the real subversives and misfits. And Keith.

Keef has been the rebel consistently through half a century of rock 'n' roll, booze, drugs and attitude. His audiences never want him to change, remaining for them some sort of talisman of what they envy but could never have been themselves; cheering him on as he crabs across the stages of the world playing his raunchy riffs with a fag in the neck of his guitar and a bottle of liquor on the nearest amp. He knows, above all things, that he's a survivor. Whatever shit he's been through, and he's been through more than any of the rest of us, he's come through it. Not unscathed, but still standing. There will never be a Sir Keith.

I saw him once upon a time in a Kings Road restaurant called the Casserole. Excited to be in the presence of, then, an aspiring rock god, I was also surprised because it was lunchtime and I never imagined Keith Richards 'did lunch'. He sat in sullen silence with a knot of friends and he wore silk scarves wrapped around his neck. Bracelets jangled from his wrist and he smoked rather than ate. No, his expression told me, I don't do lunch and I've no idea why I'm fucking here. Keith is a charming, clever, witty rascal. Backstage at last year's Coachella he offered me a very large spliff and a very large vodka. What's not to love?

I've bought every Stones album since 1964 and seen almost every touring show since the mid-seventies. I didn't catch the 1978 tour. The one that was never out of the media with its rumours of excess and debauchery; the one with the entourage of syco-phantic Manhattan socialites like Halston, Andy Warhol, Jackie O's sister Lee Radziwill and Truman Capote. What on earth was that lunch bunch doing at a Stones gig? They trawled around the States trailing the band like a bunch of Upper East Side groupies. Wonder what Led Zeppelin thought of all that as they toured the same year and out-grossed the Stones without an endorsement by Truman Capote.

There comes a point, of course, when you say, surely that's enough. But something else is going on at these ageing Stones concerts: an emotional undertow, like an energy current connect-ing their audiences; the unspoken thought that 'this could be the last time, maybe the last time, I don't know'.

It won't be. There'll be another Stones show, there always will be; there'll be another one before the Oasis reunion tour or the Coldplay stage musical. And I'm sure I'll be there, along with the wrinkled army of disciples and devotees, looking once again for whatever it is the Stones' mysterious brew brings them – salvation, affirmation, or just a reason to celebrate in this demented universe. Or perhaps, watching Mick's animated age-defying Jack Flash antics on stage, it's regeneration and renewal.

Not Fade Away, indeed.

Here's to You, Mrs Robinson – Dick

Anne Bancroft

Our most successful writing features men: *The Likely Lads*, *Porridge*, *Auf Wiedersehen, Pet*; then the movies: *The Commitments*, *The Rock*, *Still Crazy*, *The Bank Job*. An interviewer for *Gay News* once asked us very pointed questions about why this was so. Our responses were not the ones he was looking for. We reminded him about Thelma Chambers, Bob Ferris's fiancée and later wife, played brilliantly by Brigit Forsyth, whom Clive James dubbed 'the dreaded Thelma'. And what about Neville's wife Brenda and Oz's wife Marjorie in *Auf Wiedersehen, Pet*? After that we had to own up to a strong male bias.

A few years earlier, keen to prove that we could write for the opposite sex, we conceived a TV series called *Freddie and Max*.

Yes, both those names could have been blokes but they were not. The inspiration came from meeting Elaine Stritch, who lived for a long time in the Savoy Hotel. This inspired us to write a character who did the same: Maxine Chandler, a fading American movie star with three marriages behind her, still glamorous but deeply insecure, capricious and difficult. Freddie Latham was a young Londoner who stumbled into the job of helping her write her memoirs.

We were very pleased when we managed to persuade Anne Bancroft to play Max. The idea of working with 'Mrs Robinson' excited us. We had dinner with Anne and her husband Mel Brooks, meeting two legends for the price of one. We knew a lot of stories about Mel and how wildly funny and unpredictable he could be. None of this was on display that night. He knew we were there to talk with Anne and was happy to let her take the limelight.

They had what might have seemed an unlikely relationship: Anne, the dazzling movie and Broadway star, and Mel, the maverick comic genius; one Catholic, one Jewish. She says she fell instantly in love with him because he looked like her father and acted like her mother. Their secret was quickly obvious to us – they adored each other. In fact one of Anne's main concerns was that the shoot in England would mean they would be separated for several weeks.

She went over the scripts with us in meticulous detail, challenging anything that seemed inconsistent with her character. We were flattered to have 'the text' scrutinised so carefully by a serious artist. When she got to England we introduced her to Charlotte Coleman, who was cast as Freddie. Charlotte was a great talent, later seen in *Four Weddings and a Funeral*. It can't have been easy to go head to head with a star of Anne's stature but she seemed fearless and they instantly hit it off. Tragically, like Richard Beckinsale, she died way too young at the age of thirty-three.

Rehearsals went well until the moment when Anne realised that we planned to record the shows in front of a *live audience*. I never minded this convention with *Porridge* or *The Likely Lads* as it seemed to provide a sounding board for the actors. Not this one. To make things worse, we recorded the shows in Teddington. It might be the birthplace of Noël Coward but to be brutally frank the audiences were not what you might call sophisticated, laughing too much at the wrong things and missing anything remotely subtle. They made Anne nervous, like a skittish racehorse. She was totally professional and soldiered on, facing the music – well actually the audience – every week. She was homesick. She missed Mel. We took her out to dinner. I even managed to take her to the tennis at Wimbledon. It rained all day. She missed Mel.

In hindsight I wish we had sent the audience home and shot the series on single camera. I also wish we had canned the music, which immediately announced 'This is a sitcom'. As a general rule – is this heresy? – I don't really care much for sitcoms with the awful tyranny of 'Where's the laugh on page one?'

I recently watched two of the shows for the first time in a while. Anne looked truly glamorous and her performance was assured and flawless. Charlotte more than held her own. But the press was not especially kind. They somehow got hold of the idea that *Freddie and Max* was the most expensive half-hour comedy ever made in Britain'. Perhaps it was. We weren't the ones who negotiated Miss Bancroft's fee. Naturally they started gunning for it. Once that climate of negativity is established it's hard to escape it. But maybe we had proved to ourselves that we could write for the opposite sex.

We later wrote a movie with a female lead, *Excess Baggage* with Alicia Silverstone. She wasn't only the star, she was the producer with casting approval and she was only eighteen. She had director and writer approval too. This was on the back of her mega-hit *Clueless*. I guess the studio never thought she'd exercise the control they gave her – but her manager did and she was the one calling the shots.

Alicia is a lovely girl and very talented, it's the system that was crazy. It didn't help that the director had never made a feature before and it didn't help when Benicio del Toro was cast and he and Alicia became 'an item'. His one big hit up to then was *The Usual Suspects* – a terrific movie. He's won an Oscar since and made a hit with the *Sicario* movies. Every night they rewrote the next day's scene. We tried to explain what problems this caused, because changing lines affects all the other actors too. So we rewrote their rewrite, trying to incorporate their ideas. But when they went on the set the next morning, they said the first things that came into their heads.

Most of the film was set at night and we were shooting in British Columbia in July when the nights are short, so time was precious. One night a simple shot was lined up outside a motel. All Benicio had to do was drive up, park and get out. When this was explained to him he shook his head and said what became an immortal line:

'My character wouldn't park there.'

We hadn't finished working with the opposite sex. We spent four wonderful years writing for Tracey Ullman – though it's only fair to say that two of the many parts she played were male: Trevor, a gay airline flight attendant, and a horny Hispanic cab driver called Chic.

FAQ # 4

'How Do You Actually Do It?'

Dick & Ian

Dick: People are always curious about 'the process'. How we do it. It's not very complicated, is it?

Ian: Basically it hasn't changed much since we wrote that first sketch together in a pub, with a ballpoint on a legal pad. You did the writing, not me, because my handwriting is illegible. That's basically how we've written ever since, except that a computer has replaced the ballpoint.

Dick: Probably our least favourite time is when we're wrestling with the outline of a story. Sometimes we find we've painted ourselves into a corner and realise we don't have a satisfactory 'third act'. Sometimes, to use another analogy, it hits us that we haven't played our cards in the right order. Spike Milligan obviously felt much the same way because he said the words he wanted on his tombstone were: 'AT LAST – A PLOT!'

Ian: Even when we've come up with a great plot the story only comes alive when we've found the characters. They become our family and we take as much care naming them as parents do with a new child. Peter Sellers told us he had to find 'the voice'. It's the same with us. We start to talk like them. It was very disconcerting for our wives when we were writing a film about black rappers.

Dick: We still prefer facing each other across a desk rather than being in separate places, Skyping or sending e-mails. It works for some people. Elton John and Bernie Taupin have never written a song in the same room together since they met in the late sixties.

Ian: These days 'the room' is in your house and I come round every morning. We don't go straight into it, we discuss what we did the previous night and the Premier League.

Dick: Billy Wilder said before he started work with Izzy Diamond they had a fixed routine in their Hollywood office. They would make coffee, sharpen pencils, discuss the latest movies, read the Trades, make some more coffee. And then Billy would look out the window and wait until he'd seen two cars with Indiana licence plates.

Ian: We've had offices but the truth is, we can work anywhere. Studio back lots, rented villas, hotel rooms, motel rooms, airport lounges, cottages, country houses and on one memorable occasion, pulled up on the hard shoulder of the A1 near Doncaster.

Dick: And when we do our lecture tours on Cunard cruise ships we write on the ocean waves too. They give us a tiny cabin with no porthole but it's conveniently near the lifeboats in case of emergency.

Ian: If we did end up in the lifeboat we'd keep on working there too. Although it's a bizarre thought to imagine asking a Somali pirate for a pot of decaf.

Dick: We need to bounce things off each other, face to face, don't we? Read the lines and hopefully make each other laugh. After all, we're our first audience. A tape recorder sounded a good idea once. I think we even bought a couple over the years. But the batteries ran out, or we forgot to switch them on. And the thought of wading through all the discarded drivel in search of a forgotten gem was too daunting and time consuming.

Ian: Have you switched this one on?

Dick: Oh shit, I hope so.

Saving James Bond – Dick

Sean Connery

Tom Stoppard once told Ian that he had been asked to revise his screenplay for a third time and couldn't imagine why. Ian replied:

'That's usually the one where they want to make the lead an American.'

An article in the British press some years ago reported caustically that instead of doing original work we were now reduced to being 'script doctors' rewriting other people. The truth is that film writing is all about rewriting. Sometimes other people rewrite you; sometimes the boot is on the other foot. Whenever we were asked to do a rewrite – nowhere near as often as we would have liked – it always provoked an adrenalin rush. Somewhere on a sound stage carpenters were hammering nails, costumes were being designed, actors being cast but the script needed work. When we turned up on the set we were greeted like plumbers visiting a house where the basement is flooded – they're very pleased to see you. Maybe you can solve their problems, which were not of your making. This was the case when we worked on our second Bond film.

There is an interesting background to this project. Ian Fleming had a neighbour in Jamaica called Kevin McClory. While walking on the beach one day – well it may have been somewhere else, I'm making this bit up – he apparently gave Fleming the core idea for the book that became *Thunderball*. Fleming offered to pay him. McClory said he didn't want money, he'd settle for the film rights.

Some years later, when Harry Saltzman and Cubby Broccoli set out to turn the book into the fourth James Bond movie, he pointed out this fact. How his lawyers must have salivated. We can only guess about the amount of money that changed hands but whatever it was, the deal included giving him a producer credit and *the remake rights*. They probably tossed that item into the mix without a second thought. After all, who would ever make a James Bond movie twice?

Mr McClory waited eighteen years before he made his move – and his movie. His ace in the hole was persuading Sean Connery to be in it. An oblique reference to his decision to return to the role is in the title: *Never Say Never Again*.

The first Bond film we worked on was *Moonraker*. We feverishly wrote several scenes set in Brazil and were then informed that this was no longer the location because of budget. Not a syllable of ours is in the finished movie but we enjoyed a memorable expenses-paid trip to Paris. It was an experience we were keen to repeat.

Four years later we were at Elstree Studios where the outdoor set of a German building site had been erected for *Auf Wiedersehen, Pet*. Irvin Kershner was still in post-production on *The Empire Strikes Back*. He mentioned to Ian that he was about to direct a Bond film. My partner gave it a decent interval, about eight seconds, before he asked if he needed a rewrite. He said he did, we got excited and then never heard from him.

We went back to Hollywood and started work on a TV pilot. I still remember it as one of the most disagreeable assignments of our entire career. Desperate to do almost anything else, we asked our agent to check whether they were still looking for a rewrite on the Bond film. A positive answer came back instantly. I can still see the appalled expression on the TV producer's face when we told him that we had to fly to Nice. Right away. Behind his back his very friendly secretary, who hated his project as much as we did, was signalling: 'Go, go!'

The film had already been shooting for three weeks so the first thing we did was sit down and view what was already in the can. We made bets with each other about scenes that wouldn't end up in the final cut. Poor Kim Basinger had absolutely nothing to work with. Klaus Maria Brandauer resorted to all the tricks actors use when they don't trust the text: long pauses, facial twitches, brushing imaginary dust from a lapel and lighting a cigarette half-way through a speech. By contrast I saw at once what a very good screen actor Sean was. In takes where he was merely reacting to other people's dialogue, he was always alive and alert.

We found ourselves in the middle of a very political situation. Sean was not happy because he'd been calling for a rewrite for weeks and hadn't got one. He kept calling the production 'a Mickey Mouse outfit'. The producer was terrified of him and left the room whenever he appeared. The director was caught in the middle. We were in a neutral corner so when things got sticky we left the room to book dinner and waited for the survivors to turn up.

On most nights we found ourselves dining with Sean. He opened up to us almost as if we were wearing those pretty blue berets of a UN Peacekeeping Force. He also embraced us as fellow Brits, even though we had not had the sense to be born in Scotland. He was a firm believer in getting a script right before starting to shoot. He had suffered a bad experience on the film *Cuba*, where he was promised that problems in the script were being dealt with. He found out on the first day of the shoot that this had not happened. He promised himself 'never again', yet here he was in the same situation, hence his constant eruptions. We did our best to reassure him we were the plumbers who could unclog the system.

The situation was far from straightforward. The settlement with Saltzman and Broccoli stipulated that nothing in the film could echo the style and hallmark of their previous Bond movies. A clause was inserted saying the director could 'only shoot the book as written'. So one screenplay had been delivered that was almost a scene-by-scene copy of the book. It was, of course, hopeless. Francis Ford Coppola, brother to the producer's wife, Talia Shire, had allegedly written another version, though we never saw it. Every new scene had to be okayed by the producer, the director and the star. This much was fairly normal but it then had to be scrutinised by the insurers, in constant terror of provoking a lawsuit.

We noticed in the current shooting script that the setting changed abruptly to the Bahamas twenty minutes in. This puzzled us and we asked Kersh the reason why. He stroked his rabbinical beard.

'I haven't the least idea. But you'd better find one; the second unit is already shooting there.'

We delivered our pages and finished the week's work we'd been contracted for. At Nice airport, going home, I asked Kersh if he was happy with the pre-credit sequence. As written it was a jousting tournament between a black knight and a white knight – a fake out where you think you're in Ye Olden Days, then find out it's a theme park in the present day.

I made my pitch. It seemed to me that the whole edge with this film was that the audience knew that Sean Connery was the 'real' James Bond. But all they would see for five minutes would be two stunt men in armour beating the crap out of each other until eventually the victor took off his tin helmet and we saw who it was. Kersh stroked his goatee still more.

The upshot was that when we got to London there was a frantic call in the middle of the night – could we stay with the production and go to the next location? Ian was at Tramp and didn't learn this until Audie Charles woke him up in the guest room the following morning.

'Ian, get up, you have to go to the Bahamas!'

She never quite forgave him for grumbling about the inconvenience as he staggered to the bathroom, comparing it with her own prospect of getting three daughters off to school on a frosty morning.

It was a British Airways flight and we were in first class. The chief steward recognised us as we took our seats.

'I know who you two are. I'll bring you a bottle of decent wine once we've taken off.'

He was very camp and added enigmatically:

'If we ever do.'

'What do you mean?!'

'I've said too much.'

No, he hadn't said enough. When pressed he confided that this particular captain had never flown the Atlantic before – he'd always been on European routes. When we took off without incident he caught our eye, flapped his wrist, Bruce Forsyth-style and said:

'Didn't he do well!'

We sat back in relief. After a few minutes we heard the captain's reassuring voice on the PA:

'This is Captain Andrews. We've reached our cruising altitude of

thirty-two thousand feet and are en route across the Mediterranean . . . I mean the Atlantic . . .'

We caught the steward's eye again. He was almost wetting himself. Later he kept his promise and brought us a very good bottle of wine.

In the Bahamas we wrote a new pre-credit sequence, heavily featuring Sean. The crew's morale had been low because inevitably they had picked up on the internal discord. Kersh showed them a rough cut of the new sequence with only the sound of a ticking stopwatch over it. They applauded. Check out the final version and you will see one of the worst post-production decisions in the history of cinema: the sense of tension the sequence had is utterly sabotaged by a totally forgettable song.

Altogether we stayed with the film for about three months, even writing lines over the backs of people's heads in post-production. We had many more dinners with Sean discussing rewrites. We were usually the first to arrive, and order the wine – rather good wine, we saw no reason to be frugal. We even specified that Bond insisted on a bottle of Chateau Cheval Blanc '61 for a dinner scene. The prop master came up to us with a worried frown. He could only find a bottle of the '62. We sighed and said it would have to do. Sean insisted on giving us the bottle after they had shot the scene and we drank it at the Caprice. It was the best bottle of Cheval Blanc I ever had. Also the only one.

Make no mistake, when Sean entered a restaurant no one was in doubt that they were in the presence of a movie star. Heads turned, especially the female ones. The only other star who had a similar effect in my experience was Sidney Poitier.

When the film finally wrapped we felt we had done enough to deserve a screen credit but lost the arbitration. Sean supported our request, though the Writers Guild of America is not prone to having their decisions swayed by actors, however luminary. Good things came of this experience nevertheless, though not till more than a decade later. Jerry Bruckheimer was trying to persuade Sean to do *The Rock* but he wasn't happy with his dialogue especially as his character was supposed to be a Brit. He mentioned our names. We'd already written a movie for Jerry. It didn't get made, but he liked what we'd written so we were hired.

Our brief was to leave the action sequences alone. This suited us just fine. Nothing is more boring than writing a car chase. In the end it comes down to a second unit director and some very good stunt drivers. We heard that in screenplays for Jackie Chan when it came to the fights, writers were told to put simply: 'Jackie kicks ass'.

Sean's character, John Mason, was a Brit who had been locked up without trial for some thirty years on American soil, including a spell in Alcatraz. He escaped before being recaptured. Now a disgruntled army brigadier, played by Ed Harris, had taken hostages and was threatening to destroy San Francisco. Mason clearly knew 'the Rock' inside out so his expertise was needed. We gave him a line where he explains his background to Nicolas Cage when they're holed up together near the end of Act Two:

'I was special services. Military intelligence. They taught me to be a killer. In retrospect I'd sooner have been a poet or a farmer. Which I consider infinitely more honourable professions.'

Whatever we wrote persuaded Sean to sign on and the film was green-lit. We were even invited to rehearsals and found ourselves suggesting line changes to Sean, Ed Harris, Nicholas Cage and director Michael Bay. A month later Ian and I were back in prison. Alcatraz was now a tourist attraction but it provided a grim and forbidding reminder of what it used to be. The film was a massive success. We didn't get a credit on this one either but The Business knew about our contribution and our stock rose.

A few more years passed before Sean came into our orbit again. No, that can't be right. He's a star, so he's the one with the orbit and we came into it. It happened when a chance came up to write a movie about the Lockerbie disaster when Pan Am Flight 103 was blown up over the Scottish town in December 1988. The event had a particular resonance for me because I had flown back to LA with my wife and daughter on the very same plane, *Clipper Maid of the Seas*, two flights before the tragedy happened. It was a subject we wanted to treat with the utmost respect for the feelings of the relatives of the victims.

The Chief Constable of Britain's smallest police force found himself in the middle of a massive investigation. We approached Sean and he agreed that he was the logical person to play the role. With him on board it wasn't difficult to make a deal. We did extensive research, more than on any project we had ever worked on. Opinions were deeply divided over the perpetrators. They still are. It became clear to us that the subject was, to many authorities in Britain and America, a no-go area.

Sean liked our first draft. All of a sudden, his enthusiasm dried up. It is hard to escape the feeling, though we have no proof at all, that someone had a quiet word and said that as Scotland's most prominent citizen it would be better if he didn't lend his name – and his fame – to such a controversial subject. Our film never got made.

Sean was every inch a movie star and every inch a Scot. I have a theory that the Scots are not good at saying 'sorry'. He was loyal to those he thought were doing their jobs and unforgiving when they weren't. I pity whoever had to negotiate his fees. He never forgot his working-class roots and what it was like to be poor. I can't for a moment claim that he was my friend. I'm certainly glad that he didn't see me as an enemy.

He had a very Scottish sense of humour. While we were in the Bahamas I pointed out to him that in the same day Bond has sex in the morning, has a brush with death while scuba diving and sex again with a different woman in the evening. That had to prove something. He answered dourly:

'Aye, it proves it's a movie.'

Footnote from Ian:

When it was over Irvin Kershner ended up with acres of footage in an editing suite in Elstree Studios in North London. Going slightly crazy, by his own admission, we went up and offered advice and suggestions. I stayed a few extra days with Kersh wading through endless underwater sequences of which we must have trimmed half.

On a smoke break I eavesdropped on a telephone conversation coming through the open window of a studio office. An American voice, quite strident and angry, was commanding someone back, I assumed, in Hollywood:

'We need Keaton, we have to nail down Keaton!'

The film they were discussing was *The Little Drummer Girl*, from the novel by our hero, John Le Carré. I knew an English actress who was desperate for the part and I remember thinking that she wasn't going to hear about the decision from me. Diane Keaton did make the film.

In the editing suite adjacent to ours Barbra Streisand was cutting her film *Yentl*.

She knew Kersh and dropped by. Sensing we were both exhausted she gave us a bottle of red wine. Nice gesture, a classy lady. At lunch I walked across the lot to eat with the *Auf Wiedersehen, Pet* cast who were filming the interiors of their famous hut, having already shot exteriors on location in Hamburg. I told the lads that I'd just met Barbra Streisand and she'd given me a bottle of wine.

Silence, then Jimmy Nail, in best Oz mode, simply said:

'Fuck off.'

The others seemed to agree with Jimmy and that was the end of it.

Now Do You Love Me? – Ian

Dave Stewart

Dave Stewart's entry in Wikipedia, including links and discography, is eleven pages long, reflecting an incredible and varied life in music, film and photography. It informs that he was born in 1952 in Sunderland in the North East corner of England, and then lists a litany of accomplishments, the most notable of which is his time with Annie Lennox in the seminal band Eurythmics. It's all very interesting and normal. But nothing about Dave is quite normal, although consistently interesting. When you enter Dave's orbit everything is off-centre, eccentric and bizarre.

The first time I met him, for example, he was wearing a long yellow overcoat. Perhaps there were other yellow overcoats for men but I'd never seen one, especially in the San Fernando Valley in California where the temperatures are usually in the high nineties. He was at the time married to singer Siobhan Fahey, who was in her band Shakespears Sister, having previously enjoyed enormous global success as one of Bananarama. They had two young boys, Sam and Django, who would both go on to become professional musicians themselves.

I had actually met Siobhan a few years earlier for a meeting to discuss an idea for a scripted television series featuring the three girls with producer and best pal Tarquin Gotch. They weren't quite sure what it was about but they had a good title – *Banana-drama*. We met in a small London hotel in the afternoon, a time of day when people usually order Earl Grey tea with cucumber sandwiches. The girls ordered a bottle of vodka, a bucket of ice and five glasses. Which is why I remember absolutely nothing about what was said, what was suggested or how we decided to 'further the project'. Nor did Tarquin, and he's the kind of person who takes meticulous notes.

When I arrived back at the flat my wife and I were staying in she took one look at my incoherent and dishevelled state and said:

'I thought you were going to a meeting.'

When I see Siohban these days it's at a Kundalini yoga class. Times change.

When Dave was a lad, Sunderland was a shipbuilding town, bustling, busy and proud. It was a time of fifties conformity and greyness but the teenage population was about to explode and rebel, and even riot as they did when Bill Haley and His Comets played their first rock 'n' roll tour on our shores. Tommy Steele would become our first home grown pop star, Joan Collins and Diana Dors were the most lusted after starlets and Britain went to war over the Suez Canal.

Dave is a natural storyteller, many of which are told in song. The other stories are straight from Dave's world, bizarre, weird, fascinating. My personal favourite was almost not included in his autobiography, *Sweet Dreams are Made of This*, until I forcibly reminded him.

In the Stewart household the record played most often was *South Pacific* and the first song the six-year-old Dave learned to perform was 'There is Nothing Like a Dame'. Perhaps that was the reason the girl next door became so enamoured with him, even though she was two years his senior. The first expression of her devotion was when she left an ostrich egg on his doorstep. To this day he has never worked out where she acquired an ostrich egg in Sunderland. When that failed she hatched another scheme to capture his heart.

She lived above her parents' pie shop and their back garden

was stained with the blood and entrails of animal carcasses. She took Dave there one day promising that she had something to show him. Dave, like any small boy, hoped it might be her breasts. It wasn't, it was a firecracker stuck in a cow's eye. She lit it and put her hand in his. The firework exploded, covering Dave's face with blood and goo.

'Now do you love me?' she asked him.

Giving up the dream of becoming a professional footballer and still wanting to see girls' breasts, Dave acquired his first guitar and channelled all his emotions and energy into music. When his parents split up his Eko acoustic was an enormous solace in his late-night bedroom hours. He was too young to see music performed in clubs or theatres and the first acts he saw were in church halls and youth clubs. When he did play with bands he was always the youngest, and indeed during those teen years he was almost the youngest person in the room, wherever that room was. He always felt it was around this time that he left the normal world, but that was okay because he had never felt he was part of a normal world in the first place.

Small boys dream of running away: to the circus, to the navy, to the foreign legion perhaps. When Dave 'ran away' he stowed himself in the back of a van of a local band and wasn't discovered until a hundred and fifty miles later in Scunthorpe.

Someone rang his dad and somehow, as it was the summer hols, Dave persuaded him to let him stay and 'learn stuff'. Dave has been in a band, produced a band, managed a band or simply been around a band ever since.

When I met him in 1990 he had just recently split profession-ally with Annie Lennox. This was the night of the yellow overcoat. The occasion, I remember, was a screening of a film. Dave found it silly and I agreed. Actually, he admitted, he thought it was quite stupid. My sentiments, too. We'd got off to a good start. He told me he wasn't in his Encino house very often so I should feel free to use his tennis court. I told him Dick and I had been playing on it for a year. We've been friends ever since.

He was about to get divorced. I was surprised to learn he'd been married once before, even before his relationship with Annie. It was back in Sunderland and he and Pamela were still teenagers. After the registry office ceremony Dave, Pam and their young guests dropped acid and lay in a field in a circle with their heads together. (Dick and I later replicated the scene in our screenplay, *Across the Universe*.) Feeling panicked Dave and his child bride couldn't find their way back home as all the estate houses looked identical. They knocked on a door at random. A couple opened it to find these stoned waifs, the girl wearing a daisy chain and a velvet cloak.

'Excuse me,' Dave said. 'But my wife and I took LSD and we need to go to a hospital.'

'Doesn't that cause permanent brain damage?' the nice housewife asked.

Dave admitted it could. She thought for a moment then said:

'You'd better come in and I'll make a nice pot of tea.'

When he married the delectable Anoushka, third and final of the Stewart wives, the ceremony was in the much more glamorous environs of Antibes in the South of France. But no less bizarre. A canopied throne in the ocean, garlands of flowers and beads, with the rites performed by Deepak Chopra followed by a jam with Dave, Elton, Bono, Edge, Jagger and Liam Gallagher.

I have never met a person more creatively prolific than Dave. Perhaps he has too many ideas and with his antic mind, projects fall by the wayside. On the other hand that is par for the course in an industry where the fate of the creators lies in the hands of suits with chequebooks. It can start with a phone call and that soft North Eastern accent saying: 'Hey, I've had this idea.' It could be for a song, a television series, a stage musical, an animated movie or a feature, a video shoot, an app or an art installation.

Or perhaps something more straightforward like a proposal for creating a new business paradigm for the distribution of artists' royalties. Yes, Dave gets business as much as he gets art and he understood the possibilities of the web before any of us.

Dave has one rule: whatever he proposes, it has to be fun. And interesting. And slightly weird. It was 'interesting', for example, that after the high-octane touring years with Annie – the stadiums, five-star hotels, limousines and fan frenzy – Dave toured France with a small band, travelling in a bus to the prettiest towns, setting up the gear and performing to whoever showed up. And later, food, wine and song with the locals. It was interesting that he borrowed Microsoft co-founder Paul Allen's yacht to record an album cruising down the Amazon. Typically he got restless and decided to go ashore into the snake-infested jungle and shoot a short film with a girl with very large breasts called Rhona.

It was interesting, and brilliant, that when Dave and other musos were asked to help Nelson Mandela's campaign against AIDS ('It's no longer a disease, it's a human rights issue'), he came up with the idea of using the great man's prison number – 46664 – as a dial-in with a prefix so listeners could hear Mandela's words, artists' songs and at the same time donate to the cause.

It was less interesting, but certainly weird, that Dave also opened a sex shop in Covent Garden.

When Dave, Dick and I were working on a reggae musical he decided that the tracks we'd put down in London weren't 'dirty enough'. So in the interests of fun we all decamped to Jamaica and a funky studio in the hills above Montego Bay. For a long time nothing much happened except anecdotes, gossip, tuning and smoking very large spliffs. The legendary Jimmy Cliff dropped by, a god in Jamaica. More chat, more smoke. Being from the movie culture of 'time is money', Dick and I became a little impatient. Dave noticed, took us aside, told us to chill and reminded us:

'We're on Jamaica time here.'

Dick and I flew on to the Dominican Republic where the fourth *Auf Wiedersehen, Pet* series was shooting. As happy as we were to be reunited with the lads we both knew then, and ever since, that musicians have much more fun. And if the phone rings and I hear that soft, Northern voice – 'Hey' – the pulse quickens.

There is nothing Dave doesn't assiduously record, on film or tape. A hypochondriac, he has even filmed his hospital visits, including being stretchered into the operating theatre. So it was inevitable that Dave should make a feature film. And to keep it 'fun' he would not cast actresses in the leads but the three girls from the group All Saints. Dick and I wrote the screenplay based, of course, on an idea of Dave's and it was called *Honest*.

And honestly it wasn't all that great but by no means as bad as the British critics made it out to be. I think their reviews said more about themselves than Dave as a director. He had crossed an unpardonable line, from pop to film. He had stepped out of his box into one in which he didn't belong. But Dave has resisted being compartmentalised all his life and feeds on reinvention.

Once upon a time there was a band that may have the record for the shortest career in rock 'n' roll history. They drove to their first gig in a borrowed butcher's van. The smell of congealed blood was so nauseating they stopped at a chemist's and bought a large bottle of very cheap perfume. They doused the van with it then drank the rest. As a result they were out of their heads when they went on stage and ended up fighting each other and duly broke up. They were called the Berserk Crocodiles.

Only Dave could have told me that story.

A Passage to India – Dick

Belinda Wright

For a long time Ian and I were quite proud of our track record: about one in three of our screenplays got made. In the capricious world of the film business that's a pretty good average. It's gone down a bit since. I think of many of the 'rejects' philosophically; it's usually obvious in hindsight why they didn't make it. There are some exceptions that we look back on with regret. I really wish *Trail of the Tiger* had made it to the screen.

Belinda Wright – or 'Blue' as everyone calls her – has pale skin, light-brown hair and blue eyes. Her ancestry and accent are English but in every other respect she is Indian. She was born there and apart from a brief spell at school in England has lived there most of her life. She was fourteen when she decided she wanted to work with wildlife. She became a photographer, then a successful documentary filmmaker. Around 1990 she discovered that poaching was rampant in India. The skins of over two hundred wild cats were discovered in Kolkata. Tigers were especially threatened and she decided to do something about it. She founded the Wildlife Protection Society of India. This wasn't a job where she sat behind a desk, making calls and raising funds. Blue went undercover, sometimes posing as a buyer to expose poachers and put them away. She received death threats.

We heard about her through Ian's wife, Doris, and thought her story would make a terrific movie and maybe do something to help the cause she cared about so passionately. We had a good relationship with Jerry Bruckheimer ever since we did our rewrite on *The Rock*. So we took Jerry to lunch and pitched the idea. He bought it right away. One of the cardinal rules of pitching is not to linger once you're got a 'yes', but we hadn't even seen the menus yet. We probably filled the time talking about the business – Jerry doesn't talk about much else – and walked out feeling elated.

He still had to run it by Disney, with whom he had his deal, but he was making millions for them and they were unlikely to turn him down. So we had another meeting and this time Jerry was pitching alongside us. It went well until the very last moment when Jerry summed up how great the movie would be: exotic, exciting, putting wildlife on the big screen as never before. And then he added:

'And it's a great love story.'

We stared at each other. No it wasn't. That had never been a factor. But now that Jerry had mentioned it, Disney would expect us to deliver.

There was another complication: Peter Guber, a rival producer, was also bidding for Blue's story and she was wavering. I volunteered to go and see her in Delhi on my way to see my daughter Sian, now living in New Zealand. If you get the atlas out you'll see that this involved a considerable detour involving my one and only flight on Concorde. (The studios had money for travel in those days.) I had a very brief meeting with Blue in a motel near the airport. She agreed not to sign with anyone until she had visited Hollywood and met everyone involved.

This happened a few weeks later. I'm sure Jerry thought he'd be dealing with someone wide-eyed and unworldly, a bit like Dorothy when she first arrived in Oz. He took her on a sound stage where he was shooting *Armageddon* with Bruce Willis. I asked him how Bruce was behaving. 'Just great,' said Jerry, who never bad-mouths anybody. I asked the same question of an assistant two minutes later and got a different reply: 'He's a fucking nightmare.'

Blue took it all in without comment. She was used to dealing with Indian bureaucrats, sleazy poachers and corrupt policemen. Hollywood was child's play. She knew the kind of movies Jerry made and wasn't at all sure that her story fitted the mould. (She was absolutely right, it didn't.) On the other hand, Peter Guber was cut from very much the same cloth. His main edge seemed to be that the logo for Mandalay Pictures was a tiger. We took Blue to dinner a few times and tried to reassure her about the approach we wanted to take – without mentioning the love story – and eventually she agreed to go with us and Jerry.

So in January 1998, Ian and I arrived in Delhi to spend time with Blue, see how she operated and what she was up against. In no time at all I realised that she was more relentlessly driven than anyone I'd ever met. She introduced us to one of her network of informers, a brave man with no English. An earlier generation of our countrymen had hanged his grandfather, but his father had never mourned him, believing he had died a noble death for a just cause. This man felt the same would be true if he died for wildlife, which had a special place in the culture and core beliefs of his religion.

Blue took us to the courts. Like a scene from Kafka, rows of attorneys sat under wooden awnings in the open air with their framed credentials and their Remington typewriters, filling out forms in triplicate for poor souls desperately seeking justice. This ugly forties building, she told us, is where she battled to convict the villains of her world.

Next day we took a train to Sawai Madhopur. One of her oldest friends and allies met us. He was very dark with white hair and a white moustache, which she said he bleached every day. She confided in us later that he'd been in love with her for years. After lunch we were summoned for a trip to Ranthambore National Park. It's an extraordinary place, full of ancient ruins: everything that Disneyland recreates in an ersatz fashion in The Jungle

Cruise. We saw monkeys, deer, wild boar and alligators in the lake. A change came over Blue. She stood up on the seat of the jeep, the wind in her face, scenting the air, scanning the forest, back in her habitat.

A problem with a wounded tigress needed delicate negotiation. The park director did not want 'foreigners' in this part of the park, which is not open to the public. Blue must have persuaded him to change his mind because the next morning we set off before dawn in a jeep, huddled under blankets. No one had ever told me India could be this cold. Shortly after 8 a.m. we turned off the road into a clearing and there in front of us was a tiger!

The jeep stopped and we held our breath, speaking in David Attenborough whispers. Blue immediately said there were three tigers. I didn't see the others at first; they were waiting while this one ate her kill, an unfortunate deer. We groped for our cameras. One of the other tigers loped out of the grass and walked slowly forwards. Casually, she decided to lie down beside us, about fifteen feet away, unbelievably beautiful, both in profile and when she turned her magnificent head towards us. Blue said later she was one of the cubs, the equivalent of a teenager and decidedly cheeky. She walked off again soon afterwards, curiosity satisfied. Mama was eating, and we heard the cracking of bones.

Another tiger appeared, a fully grown male, making four in all. Blue was very excited. She gestured for the jeep to inch forward a little to get a better view. Blue keenly observed the mother to gauge the extent of her injury – a broken toe, probably from a trap. She limped, but the cubs were a little older than reported. If Blue could keep the mother under observation for a while, maybe help her with food occasionally, she thought the prognosis was good. In about four months the cubs should be able to start hunting for themselves. Otherwise they die, or end up in zoos. With tigers there are no reported cases of aunts and uncles taking over the family.

After about an hour they got up and we followed them slowly to the nearest water hole. The only nervous moment was when a tiger head suddenly appeared over the top of a slope – an indelible moment. A good place from which to leap onto the jeep, I thought, and Blue was saying,

'Don't be silly, don't be silly!'

She admitted later that the mother – with cubs, eating, and wounded – was the only one who made her edgy. Then the encounter was over and we went back to our base, elated. Blue rated it as one of her top five sightings ever, which made us feel very lucky indeed.

A side note here: when Ian and I are ad-libbing dialogue for a script he very often gets the names mixed up. He'll say 'Bob' when he means 'Terry', 'Oz' when he means 'Dennis', for example. Sometimes it's the first name that comes into his head. I used to point this out but he found it irritating. 'You know who I mean,' he grumbled. Usually I did, so I don't mention it any more unless I'm genuinely confused. When we returned from our trip into the forest he couldn't wait to share what we'd witnessed with the other guests in the lodge.

'Can you believe it – we saw four lions!'

The experience convinced us that we might possibly make a difference with this movie to help tigers survive in the wild. We debated how to handle the love angle without having it unbalance the story. How could we avoid the 'I think you love those tigers more than me' scene? I thought we should be like *Out of Africa* and the male lead should have the same weight as Robert Redford. Our original approach had been to stick to the truth, which was that Blue had a former husband who came back into her life. Ian suggested that we left him out and invented an adventurer who floated in and out of the movie, maybe turning up at a bad moment when she's undercover.

Blue made it clear that she didn't give a damn how we portrayed her private life. She was not someone who was at all interested in self-promotion. As far as she was concerned there was only one reason why she had agreed to make the movie: to raise consciousness about the problem of poaching and to save tigers.

The next day we set off to a town called Tonk. The car was an Ambassador, the Indian version of the Morris Oxford, straight out of the fifties, with a bench seat across the front. The driver had complete faith that if he maintained a steady speed the camel driver, cow, pig or truck coming towards us would in time move out of the way. They did. Several times I caught Ian or Blue, like me, doing some silent backseat driving: 'Don't overtake, oh I suppose you can, yes you were right after all.' But after Tonk (bit of a non-event, Tonk), on a busier road we saw evidence of at least three major crashes. Later Ian wrote a limerick:

There was a young fellow from Tonk
With a very unusual conk
It was twisted and thin
But never so slim
As his chances of getting a bonk.

We flew back to Delhi from Jaipur and had two days there before setting off into deepest India. Blue insisted that we took the train, a seventeen-hour ride in 'Second Class AC' (Air Conditioning) to give us a feel of India. She gave us tips: bring your own pillow, your own sandwiches and your own water. It was better than I had feared. I finally got off to sleep and had a dream: about being on a train. It arrived on schedule at 7.30 in the morning. We went to a moderately nasty hotel for breakfast then made a detour to a hospital in Jabalpur.

In one of the tribal villages Blue had noticed a young girl whom no one was ever allowed to see. She found out eventually that she had a cleft palate. After three years she talked the grandparents into letting her have an operation, though she never let them know she was paying for it. Luckily she found a surgeon locally who knew how to do the procedure because they would never have gone to Delhi. The little girl was here recuperating so Blue felt we had to go and see her.

I'm ashamed to say I had deep misgivings about visiting a Third World hospital but felt I had to bottle this out or I would lose whatever respect Blue might have for me. There were pigs in the grounds. We took a long walk up carbolic-smelling ramps to the top floor, overlooking a courtyard with bees' nests under the windows. We entered a large open ward, the children sitting on their beds, almost all with relatives looking after them. The little girl had never learned to speak. She was tiny, about seven, though no one seemed sure. She had other operations to come but at least Blue had given her the chance of a life. She gave her a teddy bear. The little mite had never seen a toy so we had to show her what to do with it. As we walked out she was hugging it.

The next leg of the journey was a long drive over very poor roads in a Tata Sumo, a rugged but brutish beast. This time the driver was very horn-happy and made us all wince with one near miss. Ian expressed surprise that there were any dogs left in India on the grounds that they were all so bloody ugly he was amazed they fancied one another. Finally, twenty-six hours after leaving Delhi, we were almost there, only to discover the river was too high for the car to ford. We had to take our bags across in a dugout canoe, me clutching the laptop.

We finally arrived at Blue's house in Kanha, one she had built herself, a key location for our movie. In front of it was a lake, on the far side a herd of chital. She clearly adored being there.

An elephant lumbered into view, looking for snacks on the veranda. Blue introduced us to Tara, who is a celebrity in her own right, the subject of Mark Shand's book *Travels on My Elephant*.

Blue had somehow inherited her and was convinced that she thought of herself as human.

Before we turned in for the night she warned us to close our windows because a leopard had recently been seen in the vicinity. I settled in under a mosquito net, very aware that I was a long way from home. Blue told us she walked into her bathroom one day and found a monkey sitting on the loo with his feet in a bucket of water. She instinctively said 'Oh, sorry!' and walked out.

Tara took us for a ride to begin the day the following morning, clomping through the forest, Ian and I back to back on the howdah, Belinda facing her tail. We only saw a few monkeys before an improvised picnic of Marmite and marmalade sandwiches on rocks looking out on forest all around us.

For such huge animals elephants move amazingly quietly. I was standing around later when a breeze fanned my face. I turned to discover it was made by an elephant's ear. Tara was suddenly behind me, huge as a house. Elephants have a reassuring air of reliability, though Blue said they can be unpredictable when they're in season, *musth* for the males. One had recently torn some poor guy limb from limb and even gentle Tara once killed somebody. It happened while her *mahout* was in jail for some minor offence. He was the only person who would have been able to control her. In the States there would have been lawsuits; nothing like that here, along with crash helmets and seat belts. The only seat belt I saw on this trip was in Blue's car. It didn't work.

We had a second elephant ride and found a tiger sleeping in the grass. I dropped my camera and groaned at my klutziness. The *mahout* gave a few guttural commands, the elephant backed up and picked up my Nikon in its trunk. The tiger ignored us completely, apparently indifferent to human beings peering down at him from a pachyderm.

We visited a Baiga village after dark. The Baigas and Gonds are the equivalent of the Australian aboriginals. They were in India long before anyone else, so naturally every other Indian looks down on them. There was no electricity, the only light came from kerosene burners. Families huddled round a wood fire on the earth floor, livestock in one compound, people the other. They'd just lost a goat to a leopard. Ian and I ad-libbed a routine on the importance to the Baiga tribe of Frank Cooper's Oxford Marmalade, which is smeared on maidens at certain times of year then licked off by the elders. Perhaps it was the heat.

Blue was the focus of attention everywhere we went. She was their champion, even though she had put numbers of them away for poaching. She took us to the local school. The children were neatly dressed in uniforms but the schoolroom was completely devoid of desks or chairs. We wanted to provide pens, pencils, crayons, maps and posters. She warned us that it wasn't easy to send them to this remote spot.

We admired her enormously. She was tireless and utterly committed, able to talk to anybody in a handful of languages though, as we witnessed, she had no time at all for people asking stupid questions at cocktail parties. She had some sympathy for the grass roots poachers. Some of them saw tigers as a menace to their own livestock. Others were only trying to make some money to feed their families. But the people behind them were ruthless and dangerous and totally prepared to kill her.

Tiger skins were only half of the problem. The Chinese believe that their bones are an aphrodisiac. These went to China through Tibet, exchanged for the fine wool of the chiru, a Tibetan antelope, to be made into *shahtoosh*. The chiru is often mowed down with machine guns and is another endangered species. We thought this was an irony that belonged in the screenplay and wrote in a Tibetan sequence.

It was under fire right away, perhaps for budgetary reasons. That wasn't the worst of it. Someone from Disney said they had expected a story a bit more like *Born Free*. This, we argued, was a much tougher, more contemporary story. The love angle was only part of the problem. I think we made it reasonably credible by the fourth or fifth draft but Blue's first instinct had been right: this was never going to be a Jerry Bruckheimer movie. We kicked casting ideas around – Nicole Kidman, Charlize Theron – talked to directors, even took it to an Indian producer but no one signed on.

We have followed Blue's progress over the years. Her organisation has expanded and the battle against poaching continues. In Ranthambore part of the process is enlisting the help of the local villagers. The number of tigers has increased but the demand from China is getting worse – they seem particularly fond of Tiger Penis Soup. A tiger can be killed for just over a dollar for the cost of poison, or nine dollars for a steel trap. Profits are sometimes funnelled into the arms trade.

Blue, if you read this, please accept our apologies for failing to hack our way through the Hollywood jungle. We're willing to take up our pens again at any time to help you in your fight. Nicole, Charlize, call us any time. Has anyone got about sixty million dollars?

So Bill, Do You Sing? – Ian

Bill Nighy

That was one of the first questions director Brian Gibson asked Bill Nighy when they discussed him playing a part in our film *Still Crazy*. We would have used Bill anyway, and pre-recorded someone else's voice, but it would make life much simpler and the film more authentic if our actor provided his own vocals. So it was with our collective relief when Bill answered:

'*Every day in the shower.*'

The role was that of fading rock frontman Ray Simms, lead singer with seventies outfit Strange Fruit – or, as their adoring fans refer to them, the Fruits. The band had broken up twenty years earlier, an acrimonious and bitter event, with the members heading their separate ways to lick their wounds, plan solo enterprises and spend most of their royalties on lawyers contesting who wrote what and when. And when the movie starts Ray, with the vulnerable fragility of a Rock God, is facing mortality with thinning hair, insecurity and irrelevance.

The premise of the film was simple: a Fruits reunion tour mooted by former keyboard player Tony Costello, whose fortunes had varied since the break-up. For a while he ran a record label. Only one of his acts, a punk band called Concrete Boil, had charted and that was only briefly at 93. He squired a Guinness heiress and when her family paid him to go away he ploughed the windfall into supplying condom vending machines to the bars and discos of Ibiza. The problem was the condoms he'd bulk bought did not fit the make of his machines. Reeling from this fiscal fiasco, Tony tries to persuade the rest of the Fruits to re-form.

'Lot of veteran outfits coining it these days, surfing the nostalgia wave.'

That's what he tells Ray when he unexpectedly drops by on the day that he is making a speech at his daughter's wedding. His ex-wife is present along with his current one, the much younger, Swedish, Astrid. Ray has all the trappings of success but his country mansion with its fifteenth-century moat is heavily mortgaged. And his solo work has never taken off in spite of Astrid's contribution – writing lyrics and playing tinker bells. He's also worried about the reaction of other band members. He confides to Tony:

'There was always heavy karma between Les and me.'

Tony reassures him:

'He says you're a wanker but he always thought you had a great set of pipes.'

Bill Nighy's conflicted facial expression as he processes this information is one of the film's highlight moments.

It's unlikely that bass player Les will resist the reunion given that he's now a roofer with a wife and two kids in a gloomy Midlands town. Drummer Beano Baggot is evading the Inland Revenue and living in his mother's garden shed, and lead guitar Brian is believed to have died. We were pleased that Les and Beano were played by two *Auf Wiedersehen, Pet* veterans, Jimmy Nail and Timothy Spall. None of the surviving band members views the old days with much affection, still nursing memories of jealousy, anger and betrayal. On the other hand, what was that about veteran bands coining it?

Still Crazy was not imagined as a feature movie but as a six-part television series. And that idea came from a conversation I had with Alan Price, keyboard player with the Animals, who had enjoyed enormous success and critical acclaim, right up there with the Beatles, the Stones and the rest of the British invasion who conquered America in the mid-sixties. Like the Fruits, which our conversation would inspire, they too had broken up acrimoniously. But several years later they reformed and toured again.

When I bumped into Alan it was a few months into their comeback tour and I asked him how it was going.

'How's it going?' he rasped in his distinctive Geordie voice. 'It only took our first get-together in the dressing room of the first gig to remind us why we'd split up in the first place.'

That one remark fired my imagination, and Dick's too. We had enormous fun inventing the characters, their back-stories, their fears and foibles, passions and pet peeves. We avidly watched a marvellous BBC series called *Rock Family Trees* and read countless record reviews trying to decide the perfect sound for our Fruits. We also wrote imaginary critiques of the Fruits' gigs and liked inventing the titles of their albums, our personal favourite being the Grammy-shortlisted *Tequila Mockingbird*. I showed the first draft of the pilot script to Bob Geldof, who found our band a hapless bunch of total tossers. I hoped he meant that as a compliment.

Dick and I travelled to Edinburgh to have a meeting with a senior television exec. He didn't show up but his assistant told us he wasn't interested. I would like to name that guilty man but I've forgotten it. We were left dismayed and dejected until Amanda

Marmot took us to lunch in London and said she wanted to de-
velop our idea as a movie. And we did just that and she secured a
deal at Columbia Pictures.

Dick and I had toyed with the idea of using a real-life rocker
to play Ray, someone with authentic lead singer looks, lungs and
locks. In Los Angeles we met David Coverdale, who'd been front
man with Deep Purple and Whitesnake and looked, with his
Robert Plant hair and sonorous voice, the perfect prototype. He
offered us an expensive claret but with plastic cups, a perfect rock
'n' roll gesture. In fairness to David he was everything we imagined
but when we showed his screen test to Tracey Ullman, with whom
we were working at the time, she advised that we'd be safer with a
real actor – the exact sentiments of director Brian Gibson.

I don't remember how many actors were on our shortlist but
Bill, I'm sure, was at the top. He had not starred in a movie although one of his first acting roles was in a film called *The Bitch*
(1979) and featured Bill as 'Flower Delivery Boy' (uncredited); his
television and theatre credits were impeccable. Early in his career
he had worked at the National Theatre in David Hare's *Pravda*,
alongside Anthony Hopkins. Later, in *Map of the World*, he met
his first wife, Diana Quick, with whom Dick and I had worked on
the musical *Billy*. In the years preceding *Still Crazy* he had been in
Tom Stoppard's *Arcadia*, Hare's *Skylight* and the cop drama *Blue/
Orange*. Dick, Brian, Amanda and I were huge fans.

In many interviews Bill is so often described as ' immaculately
attired and impeccably mannered'. Or 'impeccably attired and
immaculately mannered'. I'm sure he showed up to meet Brian
Gibson wearing, as he almost always does, a tailor-made navy-
blue suit and a sky-blue shirt. Sometimes he embellishes with a
dark-blue tie or a silk scarf and in 2015 he made *GQ* magazine's
Best Dressed Top Fifty list. Bill doesn't wear casual clothes and
despises 'leisure wear'. Asked by a journalist why he didn't do
Shakespeare he answered:

'I can't operate in tights.'

Apart from being considered 'the thinking woman's crumpet', he has well and truly paid his dues and fought personal demons, once admitting to a journalist that he'd been a sober alcoholic since 1992. So when he walks onto a stage or a film set he always brings with him an enormous wealth of self-knowledge.

Bill could not only sing rock, he is an avid rock music fan, the serious sort who has a record collection and goes to live shows and can quote lyrics and remember obscure music trivia. And gets incredibly excited because Van Morrison personally asked him to go to a show in Belfast. And who else could name the line-up of Doctor Feelgood? He claims that he ran away from home at the age of fifteen on the strength of the first Bob Dylan album, throwing a suitcase out of a window when he heard that Highway sound.

He loved Ray Simms and made him so much more than a cadaverous poseur desperate for past glories as he lies on his four-poster bed watching endless Grand Prix races. He invested Ray with enormous pathos and vulnerability and conveyed so well the issues that plague him as a recovering addict, as well as capturing his pathetic attempts to cope with the challenges of an ordinary day. Used to being cosseted by Astrid, Ray is panicked at the thought of travelling alone. What if he needs to buy something, like an airline ticket? Astrid tells him to simply give his credit card number.

'I don't know my credit card number.' Astrid patiently explains, as she might to an infant.

'It-is-on-your-credit-card, Ray.'

There was much in the script I owed to my great pal Jeff Lynne, the genius behind ELO who later produced Tom Petty and George Harrison, among many others, and was a fully paid-up member of the Traveling Wilburys. When I first met him, in a Japanese restaurant in Hollywood where you had to leave your shoes outside the door, we discovered we were almost neighbours;

we then spent literally years of evenings together, mostly at my house, where we told jokes, spun yarns, recalled anecdotes and often ended the nights with Jeff and my son Michael trading licks on guitars – licks, of course, that Jeff taught him. My wife wondered how it was possible to consume so much red wine and still function.

Dick and I knew George Harrison but Jeff introduced us to the rest of the Wilburys and we directed one of their videos. We derived enormous childish pleasure from telling Bob Dylan: 'Action!'

There were hints of Ray in Jeff in that both are consumed by music and delegate other people to micro-manage the rest of their lives. When I went to the South of France with Jeff I was delayed a few hours, by which time he had rented the largest and most expensive Mercedes on the Riviera. Not exactly made for narrow Provençal roads and navigating the Route Napoléon. I took it back next day and swapped it for a plucky little Peugeot. At least he knew how to use a credit card.

There was a line of Jeff's I really wanted in the film but couldn't find a place for. When I asked him what on earth he'd been doing in the years between leaving ELO and making a solo album in LA he replied, in that droll, funny Brummie way of his:

'I was down the pub with my best mate Phil.'

Jeff and I wrote songs for the Fruits along with Chris Difford, Mick Jones, Guy Pratt and Gary Kemp. We had a shadow band of real musicians who composed the songs and arrangements and also dispensed advice. Gary Kemp taught Ray how to move on a stage. Given the subject of the film I asked Gary if his old outfit, Spandau Ballet, might ever get together again.

'Not a snowball's chance in hell,' he barked. 'The bloody singer's suing me as we speak.'

A few years later Spandau reformed and toured again. I guess 'surfing the nostalgia wave' was too good to turn down.

The Shadows, as I thought of them, loved the Fruits as much as Dick and I did. They took enormous trouble honing songs to the style they now imagined our fictitious band should perform. One night they recorded a track. They listened to playback and considered the results. After a few moments bassist Guy Pratt shook his head.

'It doesn't work, fellas. It's just not Fruits.'

The film is flawlessly cast, the band portrayed by Tim Spall, Jimmy Nail, Stephen Rea and Hans Matheson. Billy Connolly plays the long-suffering roadie, Juliet Aubrey the manager and Helena Bergstrom is Astrid. Dick and I hold it in enormous regard and affection, one of our personal faves. When it was released in 1998 many critics found *Still Crazy* a kinder, gentler version of *This is Spinal Tap*, perhaps because middle-aged rockers are so often targets of satire. The reviews were mostly excellent and it was nominated for Best Picture (Music or Comedy) at the Hollywood Golden Globes. We knew we weren't going to win the moment we were shown to our table at the Beverly Hills Hilton, which hosts the Globes every year. It was far too far from the stage to accept an award; by the time we reached it the network would have certainly cut to a commercial.

We'd like to claim that Ray Simms launched Bill Nighy's second act and his prolific and varied movie career. That, however, is nearly always ascribed to his character Billy Mack, another ageing rocker, in Richard Curtis's 2003 film *Love Actually*. Certainly many more people saw the latter. We worked again with Bill on the returning series *Auf Wiedersehen, Pet* when he still appeared impeccable and immaculate, even when filming in a Navajo reservation in Arizona. And he was one of the voices in our only produced animated feature *Flushed Away*. We wait with bated breath for the chance to work with him again.

The Billy Mack/Ray Simms debate still rankles. A few years ago we met Richard Curtis to discuss doing something for Comic

Relief. Over drinks we unburdened ourselves, that 'Billy' was a thinly disguised version of our creation, Ray.

'I absolutely did not rip you off, chaps,' he protested. 'It was homage.'

Footnote from Dick:

Bill is a serious actor who thinks deeply about his craft. He's also very funny. We had lunch with him not long ago and he launched into a riff about how many actors, when cast in a Chekhov play, instantly take on the mindset of what they assume to be 'Chekhovian', full of gloom, despair, introspection and frustration. They are no longer fun to have dinner with.

'It's the same with Pinter. They think: "I'm in a Pinter play, full of hidden meaning." Why can't they just say the words and get on with it? Instead, every line is read with dark significance, as if there's a weasel under the sideboard.'

According to George – Dick

George McIndoe

In 1971 a robbery took place at Lloyds Bank in Baker Street, round the corner from Madame Tussauds. A radio ham picked up thieves talking to their lookout on the roof of a building across the street. He was cold and tired and wanted his dinner. A crackling reply told him they were almost in the vault. He replied:

'Money may be your god but it's not mine – I'm off home.'

This made all the papers and Ian and I weren't the only people who thought it was very funny. About twenty years later we were approached to write a movie about this event. We were introduced to a fellow Brit called George McIndoe. He told us he knew the main villains because before the robbery he used to hang out with them in a pub called The Globe in Marylebone Road. He gave us a lot of details about how it was done. The thieves rented a shop two doors along from the bank and over a period of several days they tunnelled beneath a fast food restaurant into the vault containing the safety deposit boxes. A woman was involved because one of the voices the radio ham recorded was unmistakably female. When the police were informed that a robbery was taking place they checked all the banks in the area, including the one where it was happening, but never went down into its vault.

George told us that unknown to the villains, MI5 were behind the robbery. The spooks didn't really care what they got away with as long as they handed over compromising photographs of a member of the royal family. These were kept there as insurance from prosecution in a safety deposit box belonging to a man calling himself Michael X. He had previously worked for Peter Rachman, the notorious slum landlord in Notting Hill, as his front man and enforcer. He moved easily within the counter-culture with friends like John Lennon, Yoko Ono and Vanessa Redgrave. There was more: a woman called Norma Levy ran a brothel in St John's Wood. She had squirrelled away blackmail material of her prominent customers in another box including more than one member of the House of Lords.

This was mouth-watering material. Even George didn't know who the mystery female was so we made her the connection between the spooks and the villains. We called her Martine Love and decided to make her extremely attractive. Well, why not? . . .

George also told us something about the two leaders of the gang. One of them was a used car dealer, the other a street photographer. We called them Terry Leather and Kevin Swain. They didn't sound like hard-core criminals and we wanted the audience to be rooting for them, following the old screenwriting maxim: *'Introduce us to people we like, get them in trouble, then get them out of it.'*

When we looked at the time frame it hit us that *Villain*, the film we had written starring Richard Burton, had been shooting while this robbery was taking place. So we came up with an opening where Terry and Kevin were casing the Burtons' yacht when it was moored on their turf in Wapping. Their plan was to kidnap Elizabeth Taylor's dogs and hold them for ransom. One of their mates called Dave Shilling joined them and apologised for being late.

Here is their dialogue:

Kevin: We haven't seen Elizabeth Taylor yet.
Dave: You won't. She's with Richard at the Dorchester.
Kevin: (snidely) Oh, we're on first name terms, are we?

Dave: Yeah well I'm on this film he's making. Funnily enough he plays an East End villain.

Terry: What are you, technical advisor?

Dave: No I'm his stand-in.

Kevin: What's that exactly?

Dave: I 'stand in' for Richard when they're lighting the shot.

Terry: Can't he do that?

Dave: No, he's in his dressing room. Resting.

Terry: If you stand around for him all the time, why's he need a rest?

Dave: 'Cos he's a wanker. They all are.

Later, when they turn up to do the actual dognapping, a derelict on the wharf informs them that the yacht has sailed to Mustique.

We took the project first to Miramax but Harvey Weinstein was never in the same time zone as us so we eventually pitched from a hotel room in London with Ian on the extension in the bathroom. It was perhaps the easiest pitch we ever did. Harvey bought it and we went to work.

We wrote several drafts and talked to more than a few directors. One of them was our friend Jonathan Lynn, co-writer of the incomparable *Yes, Minister*. Jonathan has a brilliant, incisive mind and was wary about some of the facts we had taken on board as gospel. He would listen and then say:

'Yes . . . that's the way it happened – according to George . . .'

Miramax didn't make the movie. Nine years went by. It was George who called us to break the long silence. The movie was on again – according to George. We were initially sceptical but he was right on the money. Lionsgate was financing it and Roger Donaldson was set to direct. Jason Statham was cast as Terry and Saffron Burrows as Martine. *Baker Street*, the title we had always used, was ditched in favour of *The Bank Job*.

Before the film started shooting I had a chance to meet one of our heroes, David Cornwell, better known as John Le Carré. Ian and I read everything he writes the moment it is published and it is a sore point that to date we have never been asked to adapt any of his novels for the screen. I was due to take a holiday near where he lives and used our friend Audie Charles to get in touch and invite him to dinner. He politely declined but asked me to lunch instead.

It was a perfect August day as I drove with wife and daughter to the very end of England. My tenuous excuse was that I wanted to check some facts with him on the film we were writing about the Lockerbie disaster. Once that was done I thought I might as well ask him about the Baker Street bank robbery. After all at the time it happened he was still within the intelligence community. Was it really credible that MI5 would use some 'innocent' villains to obtain photographs from a bank vault? He didn't buy this.

'In my experience, if we wanted to open a certain safety deposit box we would have called the bank manager, told him when we were popping round and asked him to put the kettle on.'

He thought it far more feasible that the people who set up the villains to do the job were some bent coppers – and there were quite a few to choose from at the time. Armed with this inside information, Ian and I were keen to do another draft but by then production wheels were turning and it was too late to make changes.

Roger did a fantastic job and *The Bank Job* is a compelling movie. Sadly, the dognapping sequence didn't survive, which we found sad because it amused us to be referencing our previous work. We have screened the film many times when we do lecture tours on Cunard voyages and the cinema is always packed, with people sitting in the aisles. There is never any shortage of questions afterwards as many of the passengers are our age and remember the original robbery. On one occasion a man with flushed cheeks rose to his feet and gave us both barrels. He felt it was disgraceful that we had irresponsibly tarnished the reputation of a member of the royal family. The majority of the audience groaned in disapproval – not of us, but of him.

In the version of the film released in Britain we only hinted at the identity of the person in the photographs. I don't need to be coy about it any more as Wikipedia makes it quite clear that it was Princess Margaret. What is indisputably true is that the Baker Street bank robbery disappeared from the headlines of British newspapers after a few days, which implies that a 'D' Notice had been imposed on the press. It's a matter of public record that Michael X was later hanged for murder in Trinidad. We also learned that a file on him is 'sealed' until 2043. Somehow I can't believe that he was dealing in nuclear secrets.

We weren't around very much during the shooting, which is a shame because we heard that George brought either 'Terry' or 'Kevin' to the set one day and it would have been an interesting encounter. They lived somewhere in the South of France and had yachts.

According to George.

Being Paid to Hang About – Ian

Michael Caine

Michael Caine credits his break into global stardom on two things: one, the people casting the role were American and, two, the auditions were held in the longest bar in London, at the Prince of Wales Theatre.

The film was *Zulu*, a retelling of the British Army's valiant stand at Rorke's Drift in South Africa in 1879, an event that still has the distinction of the most Victoria Crosses being awarded in a single conflict. Michael went up to read for the cockney sergeant. He was told the role had already been given to James Booth, a contemporary of his with the same London working-class pedigree. (He would show up years later as the cockney villain in the second series of *Auf Wiedersehen, Pet*. But that's another time.)

The producer and director apologised to Michael. They had been unable to get hold of him as there were no mobile phones then and Michael couldn't afford to have a landline in his flat. And so he set off down London's longest bar but just before he reached the door there was a shout:

'Can you come back, Michael?'

A normal-sized bar and he would have been out of there and drowning his sorrows in a Piccadilly pub. But it wasn't, and he rejoined the men from Hollywood and changed his life.

'Can you do a posh accent?' they asked.

He told them he'd been in various repertory companies most of his professional life up to that time. He claimed he could do any accent. And so he read for the officer and was cast in his first starring film role. As Michael recalled in our documentary, *My Generation*:

'If those two men hadn't been Americans, they would never have cast a cockney boy as an officer. Never in a million years. That's how strong the class system was in England in those days.'

It was true. Britain was endemically class prejudiced until the mid-sixties. Michael wanted only to be a steady working actor and never imagined in his wildest dreams that that would include being a movie star. He hoped for work in the West End, or television parts, something of a step up from the years of provincial rep.

He was always at the cinema when he was a kid in the Elephant and Castle area on London's South Bank but he thought the British actors were the sons of lords and duchesses because of their plummy upper-crust accents. He and his mates couldn't understand a word exchanged between Trevor Howard and Celia Johnson in *Brief Encounter*. All the heroes were posh, and in British war films the heroes were the officers. They performed valiant deeds with incredible bravery, and when they went on leave there was always a pretty, pliant young woman who talked like Celia Johnson, and he would drive her to country pubs in his two-seater sports car. The 'other ranks' dug latrines, drove lorries, mended Spitfires or stoked boilers. In real life, Michael had been a soldier with active service in Korea with the Royal Fusiliers. He reckons he won a couple of parts in war films so he could act as an unpaid technical advisor.

Elocution lessons were compulsory at the leading drama schools of the day, meant to iron out the flat vowels of the northern students. Later, when the class barriers were starting to erode, Malcolm McDowell told us about reading for Lindsay Anderson, the theatre director. When he'd done Lindsay told him:

'Very good; now do it again in the voice you had in the school yard.'

Malcolm said it was a liberating moment in his career, and all the other young actors down from the provinces.

Michael never did lose the accent, in life and in all his subsequent films, unless it was for a foreign voice. In an interview a few years ago he said that he kept his cockney accent in order to let other working-class boys know that if he made it, they could too.

The irony is that Michael became a movie star by playing a posh officer. But he solidified his newly won stardom with the cockney *Alfie* and became part of an astonishing transformation in British film, and indeed British cultural life. So Michael, a lad from Bermondsey whose dad worked as a porter at Billingsgate Fish Market, became a movie star and a leading player in the new classless affluence and, especially, the London scene of the Swinging Sixties. In truth Michael was a generation older than the pop stars and designers, photographers and artists who were breaking through the class barriers. He admitted as much on an American talk show, telling his interviewer he felt like a grandfather at the age of thirty-three. Perhaps that's what gave him a sense of proportion. He was not an overnight sensation; he had paid his dues in the trenches of his very precarious profession. Michael would outlast, and outlive, most of the Swinging Sixties' beautiful people. He transcended the decade and all subsequent ones including the present.

I first met Michael in a West End club; late night, drinks, disco music, cigarette smoke shrouding the room like a London fog. He had just completed filming *Get Carter*, Mike Hodge's noirish, gritty gangster film set in the North East of England. My patch. When he learned that he laughed:

'You know, I always make a big thing about my working-class roots, in interviews and bios and such. Well, now I've been up to your neck of the woods, I realise I'm middle class!'

In 1983 we sent him a script we'd written with Bill Persky called *Water* and financed by George Harrison's company HandMade Films. The plot was about an impoverished Caribbean island whose fortunes are changed when a company drilling for oil hits Perrier instead. Michael was in LA and he and Shakira went one Saturday to a party in the Beverly Hills home of composer Leslie Bricusse and his wife Evie. I was also asked and went with the knowledge that Michael might well have read the script by now. Or he could say he hadn't had time, or make some excuse about another offer blah blah, the kind of turndowns you try, as writers in Hollywood, to brace yourself against. I walked into the main room and saw Michael immediately, through a sliding glass door that separated the pool area from the house. He saw me, and gave me two thumbs up.

These moments are rare, folks, and need to be savoured. A major star says yes and a green light on your project replaces the amber. I didn't stay at the party, glamorous though it was with Hollywood 'A' Listers of the day, the Poitiers, Joan Collins, Rod Stewart, Dudley Moore and others. I went straight to Dick's house and he, Nancy and I drank champagne and cooked sausages.

As always, it took a few months to nail down the money to make the movie. We had a great trip scouting locations in the Caribbean and finally settled on the chilled-out island of St Lucia. Doris and

I had finally married a few days earlier before we arrived there to start shooting. We'd had some turbulent times and there would be more to come, including addiction and rehab but common sense and true love prevailed, bolstered by the presence of our son Michael, who has always been a symbol of sanity and pride in our lives.

The locals viewed the film crew with a mixture of amusement and suspicion. Some dreadlocked Rastas had a juice bar on the port. They were charming and flirtatious with our wives but less so to the rest of us. Then one of our actors performed a stroke of genius. On a trip back to the States he brought back a blender, which immediately tripled the Rastas' profits. From then on they treated us like their homeys. When Dick got a nasty attack of the squitters they mixed him a cure that contained guava and God knows what else that had him back on his feet in a day.

Water was not only written by us, it was produced by me and directed by Dick so there is no one else to blame for its less than spectacular impact, certainly not Michael who, as usual, invested his character with charm, wit and wisdom. Impeccably prepared as usual, he was first on the set in the morning, always there when a scene was ready to be shot, line perfect, helpful, patient.

Young actors sought his company and counsel and it was willingly imparted, even to veterans. One day Valerie Perrine, who had won an Oscar for her role in *Lenny* a few years previously, was appalled to find out that Michael had been called to the set all day but had never shot a scene. Wasn't he furious? No he wasn't and he explained why:

'They don't pay us all that money for the moments when we do the actual filming. That's the fun bit, it's why we became actors in the first place. They pay us to hang about.'

Valerie told us later that it changed her whole approach to acting in movies.

We had memorable dinners on a moonlit terrace in St Lucia with Michael and co-star Billy Connolly. Dick and I are fairly humorous people who know our way round a joke or a story, but with those two trading anecdotes as fast as a pair of Chinese ping-pong players, it was best to shut up and listen. Michael is the best storyteller, namedropper and raconteur in the business. And he always chooses the wine and picks up the bill.

In his countless films he has portrayed soldiers, diplomats, spies, butlers, murderers, zoologists, actors, architects, homo-sexuals and bisexuals, transvestites, professors, racists and our stoned Caribbean Governor. Some films were great commercial successes, some were critically acclaimed, and some were best forgotten. They ranged from the sublime to, frankly, the ridicu-lous. He reacts to the latter with pragmatism and self-deprecating humour. On *Jaws: The Revenge*, he remarked:

'I have never seen the film, but by all accounts it was terrible. However, I've seen the house that it built, and it's terrific.'

With Olivier and Nicholson he is one of only three men to have been nominated for an Oscar in five consecutive decades.

'He very much acts himself, doesn't he?'

I've heard that remark many times ascribed to Michael and other actors. In his case I think it's a tremendous compliment. It means he's made brilliant, subtle, nuanced performances look effortless.

It was a joy to work with Michael again on *My Generation*, which was inspired by his desire to tell the story of Britain in the sixties through the prism of his own experience. It reminded us all over again of his professionalism and what a pleasure it is to be in his company. We'd heard a lot of his stories before but Michael tells them so well that they're worth repeating. When he talks about the first time he met Hollywood greats like Cary Grant, Humphrey Bogart, Grace or Gene Kelly, he still conveys the ex-citement of an East-End lad who can't believe his luck. In his early years of stardom he admitted that he was always expecting a tap on the shoulder and some bloke telling him:

'You've had a good run, now back to the factory.'

In his memoir, published when he was sixty, Michael admits to something that surprised me: that what fuelled his life was ambition and anger, despair and determination, the everyday driving force of the poor who wished to find a ladder out of the well of hopelessness. I don't think it's meant to be as peevishly pissed-off as it sounds. I think it's an acknowledgement of his past, and the pride in, and affection for, his working-class roots and the background that shaped and informed so much of his life. No, Michael, you are in no danger of being considered middle-class. When he received his knighthood he chose to be Sir Maurice Micklewhite, his real name, and the one his father would have recognised.

Peter Sellers once said Michael was a mine of useless information, based on his penchant for coming out with obscure facts that he seems to have culled from the pages of *The Guinness Book of Records*. And the fact was always followed by the words that have become a catch phrase for Michael's legion of impersonators:

'Now not many people know that.'

I have a personal favourite fact. Please, please try and imagine Michael's voice and delivery. Or Steve Coogan or Rob Brydon will do just as well.

'Did you know that it takes only five and a half seconds for a man in a tweed suit to fall from the top of Big Ben to the ground?'

Now work that into your next dinner party conversation.

Footnote from Dick:

I'd like to add something about that gathering at Michael and Shakira's house in Beverly Hills, not to shed more light on Michael but as a tribute to the wit of my partner.

The guests subjected every new arrival to intense scrutiny,

anxious not to miss a glimpse of a celebrity. Halfway through the party, Jonas Salk showed up. Nobody paid him any attention. This offended my wife.

'What's wrong with all these people? There's a man whose work has saved millions of lives and he's invisible – they're only interested in movie stars!'

Ian shrugged.

'You know what they say in Hollywood – you're only as big as your last vaccine.'

A Knight to Remember – Dick

Billy Connolly

Ian and I discovered a play called *Bullshot* by the Low Moan Spectacular Group, who had a success with their first off-Broadway show called *El Grande de Coca-Cola*. As the name suggests *Bullshot* is a parody of the Bulldog Drummond genre. The lantern-jawed hero was fervent in his view that British was best and all other races were to be treated with the utmost suspicion, especially if they happened to be German. He was unapologetically heterosexual, 'straight as a tent pole'. Women existed to be cosseted and kept out of danger. We thought it was funny and showed it to Denis O'Brien at HandMade Films. It made him laugh too and suddenly we had a deal. We collaborated with the authors, Alan Shearman and Ron House, adapted it for the screen and I was assigned to direct.

Most of the men who had served with Bullshot in the Great War had ended up maimed or impaired in some way. Billy Connolly was cast as 'Hawkeye' McGillycuddy, Bullshot's 'look-out' man, who happened to be blind. It was only a brief appearance but he was very funny, playing the part with gusto, thrashing the air around him with his white stick.

I'm very fond of the film. It may be too broad for some tastes but it is exactly what it set out to be and on a limited budget we put a lot on the screen, including aerial dog-fights, stunts on a train and Bullshot winning a race at Henley single-handed because the rest of his eight-man crew were down with flu. George Harrison liked it, which was just as well as HandMade was financed with his money. He and Denis subsequently had a spectacular falling-out complete with lawsuits. One of our regular tennis games came to an end as a result: Jeff Lynne, out of loyalty to his friend George, felt he could no longer be on the same court as Denis.

All that came much later. While I was shooting the film my relationship with Denis was perfectly affable but I've heard that many other directors locked horns with him and had stand-up rows, particularly over casting. He read our script for *Water*, written with Bill Persky, and called us to say he wanted to make it. In the previous chapter Ian described the wonderful moment when Michael Caine agreed to play the lead. Even before Michael signed on, Denis was insisting on casting Billy, convinced that he was the funniest man in the world. It was hard to disagree. I have seen Billy live on stage at least four or five times. When I first saw him perform he told *jokes*. Sometimes he abandoned them halfway through then 'remembered' them sometime later and finally got to the punchline. I remember one joke in particular, the one he was warned not to tell on *Parkinson* because it was too rude. Naturally he couldn't resist the temptation. It was about a man in a Glasgow tenement who told a friend that he'd murdered his wife. He showed him where he'd buried her in the courtyard. The man was astonished to see her bum protruding above the concrete and wanted to know the reason.

'*Aw, I needed somewhere to park my bike.*'

Of course it got an enormous laugh. A few years later I saw him again and at the end of ninety minutes it hit me that he hadn't told a single 'joke' all evening. It's an astonishing talent to be able to stand alone on stage for a whole evening and entertain a massive number of people by just talking, only occasionally resorting to playing a banjo. Later on I met the man who booked his dates in Australia and he told me how Billy prepared for a gig: he would hang out at the post office and talk to people to find out what was either enthusing or infuriating them. This provided him with the fuel for his act, which is really an extended monologue, tailor-made for wherever he happened to be playing.

Billy used to be a welder in Glasgow so it would be a massive understatement to describe his upbringing as 'tough'. The social conscience he developed in the shipyards was never far from the surface. In her biography *Billy*, his wife Pamela Stephenson says that even while you're laughing at what he is saying you can 'unconsciously sense his underlying rage'. Happily he found an outlet for it in comedy rather than blowing things up.

The only problem with casting him in *Water* was that Denis wanted him to play the rebel leader fighting Britain for the island's independence. Billy's skin, through no fault of his own, was the wrong colour. We tried to compromise by renaming the character Delgado Fitzhugh, a sort of Hispanic-Caledonian hybrid, but the essential problem never went away, which tends to be the way with problems.

We were on location in St Lucia when Billy arrived. He'd had quite a lot to drink on the plane. A whole bunch of us, including Michael, Valerie Perrine, Brenda Vaccaro and Dennis Dugan, had dinner together and drove back on a twisting mountain road to our hotel. Pamela wrote about what happened on the way back when Billy went slightly crazy and scared the crap out of all of us. Michael behaved like a true leading man and talked him down. I waited the next day for Billy to refer to the incident, expecting some sort of apology. None came. He didn't drink for the rest of the shoot in the Caribbean but Pamela makes it very clear in her book that he was wrestling with his demons for the rest of that year. He gave it up on 30 December and has been sober ever since.

In hindsight this may have contributed to the fact that he and I never had a meaningful discussion on how he planned to play Delgado: none of those conversations that actors are famous for where they want to know if their character loved his mother and hated his father. Is he mean to animals? Did he used to wet his bed? Perhaps Billy had the same misgivings that I had, but we never got around to debating it. He was incredibly funny – at dinner, in the make-up room, on location. I remember him making the crew laugh while we were setting up a shot and Michael muttering:

'Billy, Billy, don't leave it in the locker-room, Billy . . .'

He became a really accomplished actor, winning well-earned praise for playing John Brown with Judi Dench in *Mrs Brown* and movies such as *Brave*, *The Hobbit*, *The Last Samurai* and *Quartet*. He made one in Australia called *The Man Who Sued God*, which we were later asked to rewrite for Will Smith. We worked with him again when he was perfect as a cynical seen-it-all roadie in *Still Crazy* and in our favourite sketch for *Tracey Takes On* as a drunken poet lecturing on a female American campus, a Glaswegian Dylan Thomas.

He invited us and our wives to celebrate his sixtieth birthday at what, without a shadow of a doubt, was the best party we ever attended. It took place over three days at his baronial manse in Scotland. He's fond of saying on talk shows that it has pointy turrets with tiny windows – the sort that trapped virgins look out of and cry for help from a passing prince. It's also supposed to be haunted by 'a headless dog' but we never saw him and naturally never heard him bark.

The men were required to wear kilts – a first for both of us. We sent in our measurements in advance. I was told that the name 'Clement' was a distant 'sept' of the 'Lamont' clan, so that was the tartan I was assigned. Somehow they couldn't find any Scottish connection to 'La Frenais', so they gave him something generic. When we arrived we tried everything on, including the hairy socks. I rather enjoyed the air-conditioning that a kilt provides.

Nancy's complaint was that all the men looked better than the women. We had several glasses of champagne on the lawn to the sound of pipers. It would be an understatement to call the event 'star-studded'. At one point I turned to her and said I'd just seen someone I *didn't* recognise. Top of the list was Prince Charles, who arrived with Camilla. There were too many guests to fit everyone inside the house to meet the royal party, but Ian smuggled us in. He's very canny at being in the right place at the right time, a skill he acquired getting into the backstage inner sanctum of rock stars.

Early in our marriage we went to Peru and adopted a baby girl, a very happy decision for all of us. We named her Annie after Nancy's mother. In her early teens she went to school with one of Billy's daughters so she was staying with her in the house. Even so it was a surprise to enter the reception room and find Annie standing at the Prince's side, nodding sagely at everything he said like a personal equerry. How had she wangled that? Doris was less subtle. She touched Charles's sporran – surely forbidden in royal etiquette – and asked him if that was where he kept his stash.

I heard later that the Prince of Wales was a fairly frequent visitor. He was there on one occasion when a friend who knew Billy from childhood challenged his lifestyle. How could a former welder feel comfortable living in such splendour? Billy was unapologetic.

'Come the revolution, everyone will be living in a castle!'

Charles shook his head ruefully.

'I won't.'

Billy's big dinner was for about two hundred and fifty in a large tent comprised of assorted plaids in case we'd forgotten we were in Scotland. Pamela had arranged everything. Billy's main contribution was to have everyone change tables after each course to mix us all up. During the meal the official 'address to the haggis' was made by Jimmy Reid, the former trade union firebrand. He liberally quoted Robbie Burns and Robin Williams responded, presumably on behalf of the haggis.

Robin is worth a chapter on his own, except that I can't say I really knew him. We had met in Bangkok when he was shooting *Good Morning, Vietnam*, but only briefly. This weekend gave me more than one glimpse of his genius. He responded to Jimmy Reid's address by doing about ten minutes of mock Robbie Burns in the same cadences. Words that might have taken us a week to write poured effortlessly out of him. They were almost certainly impromptu. When a baby cried nearby he picked up on it without breaking stride and said something like:

'And e'en the mewling of the weeist bairn shed tears for heroes yet unborn.'

Robin was not someone who was always 'on'. He could be serious. He could be quiet. The next day the guests were in little groups on the lawn and I wandered over to one that included Robin, Terry Gilliam, Jackie Stewart and John Hurt. A chance remark triggered Robin into an imagined conversation between Marlon Brando and his neighbour, Jack Nicholson, complaining that Brando's attack dog had eaten one of his girlfriend's lapdogs. I only remember fragments:

'You've gone too far this time, Marlon.'

'Man, I've had a lot on my plate recently.'

'Well, can you at least wait until your dog shits out the bones so we can give the little fucker a decent burial?'

John Hurt casually mentioned a film he'd done with Marlon in

Hong Kong. They thought a bank was financing the picture until it turned out to be a man who owned a parking lot. Robin then did ten minutes as the Chinese parking lot proprietor.

'I happy to pay Marlon a million dollar, he big star. But I doan know John Hurt, who he? I doan pay him shit, I doan even park his car!'

Without doubt the three funniest men I ever met were Robin, Peter Cook and, of course, Billy. In an incredibly short time he made an astounding leap from playing the Traverse Theatre in Edinburgh to major arenas like the Sydney Opera House. He took America by storm, the first British comic ever to do so, opening the door for others like Eddie Izzard, Ricky Gervais and Russell Brand.

He never lost touch with his inner child, which is probably why he told so many fart jokes – and why not? It hit me when I became a parent that the very first thing we find funny is a fart, particularly if it happens in the bath. And I still love his definition of 'perfect pitch':

'The ability to hurl an accordion into a dumpster.'

The last time I saw him perform he was already suffering from the onset of Parkinson's disease. It was sad to see him physically hampered because Billy always used his body language brilliantly on stage with movements that were almost balletic. Typically, he talked about how he was dealing with this new situation head-on, explaining one of its symptoms by incorporating *Whole Lotta Shakin' Goin' On*.

People who make us laugh hold a special place in our hearts. I can't think of Tommy Cooper, Tony Hancock or Eric Morecambe without smiling. Billy is in that category and I love him. That he was given a knighthood pleased almost everyone in Britain. If there's a pecking order in our list of national treasures, he's right up there with Sir David Attenborough. Sir Billy's funnier though.

With a Little Help From Our Friends – Ian

Across the Universe

The first two pop stars I met in quick succession were Rolling Stone Brian Jones and Tony Hicks of the Hollies. And then the ultimate, a Beatle, which in 1966 was as famous as it's possible to be. This was courtesy of photographer and ultra-cool hipster Robert Freeman who had just hired me to write a script and had taken pictures of the Fabs several times. He had a meeting scheduled with Ringo and asked if I would like to come along. All the way to Weybridge, in what we used to call the Stockbroker Belt, I sat in a state of anticipation, awe and disbelief. Who would I phone and tell first – my partner Dick? The girl I was trying to impress? Or my mother?

We were shown into the kitchen of the large modern villa and offered tea by a housekeeper. We met the man himself in a room filled with audio equipment, vinyl and framed posters. He played us a track they had finished only the night before. It was 'Hello, Goodbye' which, in all honesty, summed up the entire conversation I had with the world's most famous drummer.

The Beatles lived in a rarefied world and none of us ever expected any connection or contact with them. The nearest Dick ever got to them in those early days was standing in the wings of the Finsbury Park Empire watching their Christmas show. Rolf Harris was the opening act.

It was the late seventies when I met Ringo again and and we've been close pals ever since. By an extraordinary coincidence his wife Barbara had known my wife Doris for years, since they were both models together in Paris. And his first wife Maureen and Doris were very close. Ringo, or Rich as he's known to friends and family, and now elevated to Sir Richard, spent many post-Beatle years drinking too much cognac, taking too many drugs and eating sausages and baked beans, if he ate at all. Now he is one of the fittest men I know who lives on a diet of mostly plain pasta and broccoli, except at Thanksgiving when he allows himself two slices of turkey.

His conversation is always filled with wit and honesty. He has great affection and gratitude for the legacy of the band and he recently finished his eighteenth solo album, one of his best ever. Ignoring his place in the age of streaming he tours every year with his All-Starr band and loves every minute of the 'on the road' experience.

I met George the same day Dick did, when we were filming *Bullshot* and he visited the set in Henley-on-Thames with his wife Olivia. I became good friends with them both, and son Dhani. He was a very special person and certainly his spirituality and lifelong love of India and the Krishnas informed his character and the way he viewed the world.

When the Traveling Wilburys recorded their second album, they rented an old Spanish mansion on a hilltop in Beverly Hills. It offered them great privacy and acoustics and they often re-corded in different rooms with the drums set up in the library. It also had a tennis court, which Dick and I frequently used. One day George, having a smoke break outside the house, beckoned me over.

'Come with me,' he said and led me inside and across the chan-deliered hall to large double doors. He pushed them open slightly.

'Look!'

'What is it?' I asked him, and peered into the next room.

'It's Bob Dylan,' he told me like an excited schoolboy.

I was amazed, never believing that a Beatle could be that impressed with anyone or anything.

Just for the record I never met John Lennon and to this day have never even been in the same room as Sir Paul, although if I was I would have the same air of excited expectancy as the younger me when I was driven to Ringo's house in Weybridge.

That's how I feel about the Beatles, as I'm sure everyone of my generation felt. They revitalised and transformed pop music and their records were the sound track of our youth, as they would be for generations to come.

Ten years ago an LA-based producer, Matt Gross, asked Dick and me to lunch.

We'd never met but he loved our music-driven films *The Commitments* and *Still Crazy*. He told us he had negotiated a deal to acquire the rights for the Beatles' music – the publishing not the recording masters – for a reasonable amount of money and he wanted to make a film musical and us to write it. We agreed to meet again when we came up with something. For three weeks we didn't have the remotest idea and had nothing to show for it but a blank page on a computer screen under the title 'Beatles Project'. He called: could we have another lunch at which we could tell him the story? Driven by guilt we shaped a plot in two days that, quite substantially, would be the basis for what would become *Across the Universe*.

Pitching the film to studios was difficult and discouraging. The mention of the magic word 'Beatles' was a portal to arranging meetings but we were met with puzzled faces when we explained it was, yes, a musical.

'You mean,' exclaimed one startled executive, 'people, like, open their mouths and sing?'

Other execs told us they liked the story but could we lose the songs.

And then, magically, we had a deal with Joe Roth's Revolution

Studios and within weeks we were flown to New York to meet Julie Taymor, creator of *The Lion King*, who had expressed a desire to make a Beatles-inspired movie. Incredibly the film was made the same year, an almost unprecedented experience for us: concept to principal photography in a few months.

We set our story in the sixties because that was the decade in which Beatles music impacted the world, and believed the film should be set in Britain as well as America. The story involved a young man from Liverpool jumping a merchant ship in New Jersey so that he could trace his father, a former GI stationed in Britain who was ignorant of the fact that he'd fathered a son. And he met a college grad and her family and fell in love, as young people do in movies.

We wanted the story to be told by the songs, so that wherever possible the words of Lennon-McCartney would replace those of Clement-La Frenais. So we were not choosing our favourite songs, only those that furthered the narrative. In a three-day session at Dick's house we refined the list with Julie and listened to scores of cover versions, one of which, a female version of 'I Wanna Hold Your Hand' gave her the idea of using the song in the film as an expression of lesbian not hetero love. Julie also insisted that the story was much more than an 'All You Need Is Love' adolescent romance but should reflect the turbulence of the political and cultural zeitgeist of America in 1968.

And so the Washington Peace March, and its violent confrontation, was told in 'Helter Skelter', and the New York anti-war protests by 'Dear Prudence'. Four songs reflected the Vietnam War: an Army Recruitment Center in 'I Want You'; a veterans' rehab hospital for 'Happiness Is a Warm Gun'; 'Strawberry Fields Forever' underscored actual conflict and 'Let It Be' a military funeral. These songs and all the others Julie realised in brilliant and imaginative ways that Dick and I could never have conceived, unless, for sixties' old times' sake, we had dropped several tabs of acid.

Like all the best directors she researched prodigiously, explored creative options more intently and worked longer hours than anyone else.

We love what Julie did with this film. We loved watching her work with her young cast in the first days of rehearsal on the East Coast and were constantly amazed by the way she visually re-imagined the songs to fit the story and her choice of guest cameos: Bono, Joe Cocker, Eddie Izzard, Selma Hayek. We were encouraged by the reaction of the Beatles camp, following screenings for Ringo, Paul, Olivia and Yoko. We were excited by the euphoric response the film received at the Toronto Film Festival and dared think of Oscars, Golden Globes and global acclaim. But none of this happened.

After the screening for Ringo I asked him how he liked the film.

'It's great,' he said. 'But maybe it's a bit long.'

He was right, but that wasn't unusual in an early cut and subsequent edits would only improve and tighten. But Julie didn't want to trim the film as much as the studio requested. There's something admirable about a feisty woman taking on the might of a major film studio, Sony in this case, and we still respect her for her creative convictions. But it may well have been one of the reasons why the film was not given a wide release or an awards-season marketing push and it received virtually no publicity or support overseas, which is why many of you reading this have not seen *Across the Universe* or even heard of it. For us, proud and excited to have been involved, it was devastating.

Even more frustrating, it appealed enormously to younger people. We learned that high school girls had weekly *Across the Universe* viewings, usually at the cinemas in their local malls but later at Friday night video and pizza parties. And so many people have told us over the years:

'I just saw *Across the Universe* on television. It's great. How come I missed it?'

It was gratifying that in the summer of 2018 the film was rereleased in the States in 450 cinemas.

So the years pass and Beatles music is as enduring and admired and loved as ever. And younger generations experience the movie on Blu-ray or cable or download it onto laptops or, God forbid, wristwatches. And they don't know about director's cuts and studio conflicts and creative differences; they just see Julie Taymor's version and vision of what Dick and I consider to be a wonderful film – astonishing and bold, audacious and emotional.

And yes, people do open their mouths and sing. It's a musical, folks.

Postscripts – Ian & Dick

There's a cupboard in our office. Open the door and you will see stationery, DVDs, coloured covers and dozens of screenplays. Many of them have never been produced, testimony, if you like, to disappointment, frustration, failure or just bad luck. Between the crisp, white covers there are situations that will never be seen, characters that will never come to life, and, most painful, words that will never be spoken. Some of them are thirty years old, some were written in the last twenty-four months.

There's a script called *Final Call*, about the Lockerbie air disaster, our first venture into international terrorism, and next to it a thriller about a Nazi plan to assassinate FDR. Another thriller was supposed to star Pierce Brosnan and the one that's almost out of reach on the top shelf was written for Mel Gibson and Jodie Foster. *Amulet* was written for Will Smith's children and *The Man Who Sued God* for their dad. There's one about a famous heist and another about a VAT scam; a script about the Kinks, another on Keith Moon, legendary drummer of the Who, and one about the making of *The Monkees*.

Within easy reach you can spot a script on motorcycle racing and another on curling; a retelling of the *Bounty* Mutiny and a reinvention of the Sherwood Forest saga, told from the point of view of the Sheriff, a decent cop who predated CSI Nottingham and exposed Robin Hood as a cad and a coward. *Playing Joe* is a romantic thriller set in Brazil and *Airtight* chronicles a prison break in Florida. There's a story about maids who service the rich and famous and two animated scripts: one about cane toads in

Australia, the other about a *Holy Cow* in India. A story about the theft of the Elgin Marbles is wedged between *The Doolittle Raid* and *The Jungle Book*.

We invested hours, months, years on these scripts; they are our friends, we believed in them when we wrote them and we still do; and some of them are in, what they say in Hollywood, 'active development'. It would help, in the current creative climate, if our projects were based on Marvel super heroes or video games, but they don't come our way.

We have never been sure what's worse – the script that is produced and doesn't work, or the favourite one that still languishes on that cupboard shelf. The first case exposes us more, of course, to critics and 'the business' and has a more adverse effect on future work for which we might have been considered.

But we have a weird kind of loyalty to the fictional friends we created and feel we've let them down when they are not realised on the screen, large or small, and are consigned to gathering dust on wooden shelves. We revisit them occasionally, mostly to plunder good material and relocate it in current assignments. We don't regret any of them, which is why they haven't been thrown out in the recycling bin.

In this business a lot of people over sixty feel marginalised, convinced their opportunities are diminishing. Are we sometimes the victims of ageism? We must be from time to time. After all there's nowhere to hide these days, your age is in plain sight on the internet and the bloody papers never fail to flag our birthdays. Of course it's mostly below the surface. We'll never know how many young Turks have looked at our résumé, checked the year of our birth and decided to 'move on'.

The Chinese are not so circumspect. We recently wrote a screenplay about the Doolittle Raid, when FDR was determined to avenge Pearl Harbor and ordered a raid on the Japanese mainland. The finance came from China. Early on the producer showed us a note he'd received that said bluntly:

'These writers are very old. Can we get younger ones?'

And we'd always thought the Chinese were supposed to revere their elders. We stayed on the job and wrote a very good screenplay. It's still in the 'pending' file. At least the subject matter won't date.

We always agreed that the word 'retire' gave us shudders, even when we were seventeen. Perhaps if you have hated your job all your life it must be a relief to pack it in, play bowls and prune your roses. We are lucky enough to like what we do. Matisse never stopped painting. Bruno Walter didn't stop conducting. George Abbott was over a hundred when he was sitting in the stalls of a theatre watching a revival of *Damn Yankees*, for which he'd co-written the book some fifty or so years earlier. We'd like to be doing that ten years from now at a revival of *Billy*, pointing out to the director where he's missed a laugh that Michael Crawford always used to get.

And who knows, next time the phone rings – the business line – we may hear that interest in one of our scripts has suddenly been revived; the producer found the money, from a bank in Zurich or a cartel in Mexico, we don't need to know. Or perhaps two major stars love it. We'd settle for Chris Pratt and Gal Gadot. Or an Oscar-winning director insists it's his next project.

We're proud of our durability. We imagine a researcher working on the latest edition of *Who's Who*. His boss asks him if he could spare a moment. He shrugs apologetically.

'Too busy, guv. I'm updating Clement and La Frenais. Again.'

Index